# FULL STEAM AHEAD

## Ohio River Mainstem Navigation System: General Plan and Profile

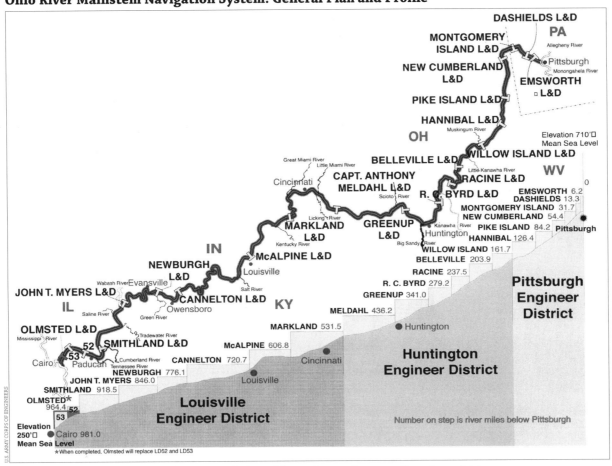

*The Ohio River in 2011, showing placement of locks and dams, along with major tributaries and cities*

# FULL STEAM AHEAD

## REFLECTIONS
### on the IMPACT of the FIRST STEAMBOAT on the OHIO RIVER

### 1811-2011

EDITED by RITA KOHN

Published with the generous support of the Rivers Institute at Hanover College

Indiana Historical Society Press | Indianapolis 2011

Printed in the United States of America

This book is a publication of the
Indiana Historical Society Press
Eugene and Marilyn Glick Indiana History Center
450 West Ohio Street
Indianapolis, Indiana 46202-3269 USA
www.indianahistory.org
*Telephone orders* 1-800-447-1830
*Fax orders* 1-317-234-0562
*Online orders* @ http://shop.indianahistory.org

Artwork credit for front cover: Gary R. Lucy, *The* New Orleans *Steaming Upstream by Moonlight, 1811.*
Courtesy of the Gary R. Lucy Gallery, Inc., Washington, Missouri, http://www.garylucy.com/.

The paper in this publication meets the minimum requirements of American National
Standard for Information Sciences—Permanence of Paper for Printed Library Materials,
ANSI Z39. 48–1984

Library of Congress Cataloging-in-Publication Data

Full steam ahead : reflections on the impact of the first steamboat on the Ohio River, 1811-2011 / edited by Rita Kohn.
    p. cm.
ISBN 978-0-87195-293-6 (alk. paper)
1. River steamers—Ohio River—History. 2. Steamboats—Ohio River—History. 3. Ohio River Valley—History. 4. New Orleans
(Steamboat)—History. 5. Ohio River—Navigation—History. I. Kohn, Rita T. II. Hanover College. Rivers Institute.
F518.F85 2011
977—dc23
                        2011024036

To the memory of Captain Fred Way Jr.,
who devoted a lifetime to collecting and preserving materials
related to the history of steamboating and its progression
to modern towboating and who was instrumental in founding
The Sons & Daughters of Pioneer Rivermen.

# Contents

# Foreword

Hanover College sits on a bluff overlooking the Ohio River Valley. It is the only place along the river where you can actually see three bends in the river at one time. For the 182 years of the college's existence, the Ohio River has played a significant role in the life of the Hanover College community. Every day we are reminded of the symbiotic relationship between the college and the river.

From the very beginning the story of Hanover College has been entwined with activities on the river. When the college was first founded there were no roads to the small campus, so students arrived by boat and climbed the bluff to reach their destination. The following is one account of this process from Edward Gilpin, class of 1870: "I have seen the [boats] throw out the gang plank and land passengers in two feet of mud, and there was no freight or passenger transportation. New students had to carry their grip-sacks up the hill, but they had to work their trunks up by trigonometry or any other method. Sometimes a Good Samaritan would haul one up for a dollar."

Because of this heritage, it is most appropriate for Hanover College to be closely associated with this publication. The Rivers Institute at Hanover is responsible for keeping this heritage alive and for bringing attention to the impact the river has had on towns and communities spread along its banks.

The students and faculty of the college have watched steamboats, commercial vessels, and pleasure boats cruise past its campus for its entire history. The steamboat was in existence for a mere sixteen years before the founding of the college in 1827. Boatmen used Old Classic Hall, the first college structure on the bluff, as a navigation landmark as they came upriver. Classic Hall burned down in 1941 and was relocated to another spot on the campus. Later, the boats on the river became a source of entertainment. From the early 1940s until the 1960s, students took rides on steamboats for entertainment. At one time the entire student body could fit on one boat for an excursion. The boat used for this cruise was the current *Belle of Louisville*, which operated under two different names in the past—the *Idlewild* and the *Avalon*.

Today, Hanover owns riverfront property that stretches from the top of the bluff down to the water's edge. Visitors are stunned by the vista from the bluff as well as the view from the banks of the river. Future plans are to make this a viewing site for environmental studies.

This book of essays traces a story of change, chronicling the continuing effect of Nicholas Roosevelt's historic river trip on America and its people. Roosevelt's steamboat, the *New Orleans*, was the first to travel down the Ohio and Mississippi rivers to

New Orleans. For those of us who live on the Ohio, the impact is there for us to see every day.

Sue DeWine
President, Hanover College

*Dr. Sue DeWine became the fifteenth president of Hanover College in 2007. Previously, she was provost of Marietta College in Ohio and a professor of organizational communication and research and consulting from 1985 to 2000 at Ohio University, where she was also director of the School of Interpersonal Communication. She has served as a consultant to Fortune 500 companies, government, and educational institutions on subjects such as communication and conflict, for strategic planning, and to facilitate off-site team-building meetings. DeWine has written more than sixty communication-oriented books and professional articles and more than one hundred convention papers and programs.*

**SELECTED BIBLIOGRAPHY**

Ebenezer Gilpin Papers, MSS 122, Joseph Wood Evans Memorial Special
    Collections and Archives Center, Duggan Library, Hanover College.

# Preface

With the appearance of the first steamboat on the western waters of America in 1811, travelers no longer were dependent on shoe leather, four-legged beasts, the winds, or downstream currents to move from one location to another. Through the interplay of many nineteenth-century entrepreneurial luminaries on the stage of American history, the application of steam power to a floating vessel was introduced, tried, proven, and perfected. The steamboat became the principal technological agent that transformed the Ohio–Mississippi basin from a raw frontier society to economic and social maturity.

Shortly after the realigned Rivers Institute at Hanover College was announced in 2008, it became apparent that this was the appropriate entity to take a lead role in celebrating the bicentennial of the first successful trip by steamboat on the Ohio River in 1811. Contact was made with Dr. Larry DeBuhr, the executive director, who agreed to play an organizational role, supported by a group of historians, social scientists, economists, river-related industrialists, practitioners, and Ohio River enthusiasts who would help organize events, activities, and programs in communities along the Ohio. The Steamboat Bicentennial Committee (SBC) laid out a framework of projects and events that could be implemented by river interests along the 981-mile route. DeBuhr and the committee chair, Chuck Parrish, with the assistance of committee members, conducted regional meetings from Pittsburgh, Pennsylvania, to Cairo, Illinois, during

which the mission and intent of the celebration was outlined and promoted. Enthusiasm and creative ideas burgeoned at each location.

The major purpose of this bicentennial celebration is to take a message to the nation about the importance of the trip of the *New Orleans* from Pittsburgh to New Orleans in 1811–12. Captain Nicholas Roosevelt, his wife, Lydia, and their small child were aboard, along with the necessary crew members. Unlike previous modes of river transport, this little steamboat proved its worth by showing a skeptical public that it could move upstream under its own power against the unpredictable currents of the Ohio River. Most impressive was its successful achievement in navigating over the treacherous Falls at Louisville, causing Lydia to express "feelings of profound gratitude to the Almighty."

In the aftermath of this successful journey came many sweeping changes in America's experience during the Industrial Revolution. Indeed, the triumph has been hailed as a "harbinger of revolution." While this event transformed transportation in America, it also brought about changes in the nation's culture, economy, political strategies, and thoughts about river improvements.

The 1811 venture of the *New Orleans* was accompanied by the Great Comet streaking across the sky and by the greatest earthquake ever recorded in America. Certainly, those who witnessed this steam-belching, fire-spitting "work of the devil" must have been struck with a sense of shock and wonderment.

In an 1815 communication to the *Cincinnati Gazette*, a writer boasted, "The invention of the steamboat was intended for us [in the West]. The puny rivers of the East are only as creeks or convenient waters on which experiments may be made for our advantage."

In 1828 John James Audubon reflected on his first trip down the Ohio two decades earlier. He recalled the grandeur and beauty along the riverbank, the "unspoiled and lofty summits of the forest," adding that now, "this grand portion of our Union is covered with villages, farms, and towns, and steamboats are gliding to and fro over the whole length of the majestic river, forcing commerce to take root and prosper at every spot." It is worth noting that this river wanderer called attention to the role of the steamboat in transforming the Ohio River region.

Shortly after the trip of the *New Orleans*, structural and operational modifications to steamboats were achieved that ultimately made possible the packet boats, the wondrous "floating palaces," and the first towboats. Steamboats played a role in American life into the twenty-first century with the grand excursion boats that plied the Ohio, Mississippi, and other rivers until 2008. That role has been portrayed through the years in literature, music, drama, and public discourse.

The Rivers Institute at Hanover is to be commended for its able and forward-looking leadership in bringing about a celebration for and emphasizing the educational value of steamboats. Noteworthy is the institute's willingness to fund in large part the publication of *Full Steam Ahead* as a collection of essays on relevant subjects related to steamboat history, the Ohio River system, and conditions on the contemporary river. Each writer has diligently researched and written on topics that will be enlightening to anyone interested in steamboats and their evolution into today's powerful diesel towboats. In addition, exhibits of art and photographs, displays of steamboat artifacts, musical performances, speakers' programs, and a commemorative trip on the venerable *Belle of Louisville* are part of the bicentennial celebration.

One research challenge of the SBC is the documentation of extant structures and buildings along the shores of the Ohio River that might have been seen by the Roosevelts and the crew as they made their historic voyage. As of this writing, several such places have been identified. This information and much more can be found on the web site, http://rivers.hanover.edu/steamboat2011/.

The SBC has provided direction and focus during the past few years of planning and promotion. Many organizations, agencies, institutions, and individuals have come on board to play a part in the numerous commemorative activities from Pittsburgh to Cairo. We consider all these "river rats" our capable and devoted friends, and we offer our deepest thanks to each one. To all we say, "Keep up steam and be on watch for what lies around the next bend."

Charles E. Parrish
Chair, Steamboat Bicentennial Committee, 2010

*Charles E. "Chuck" Parrish is former historian of the Louisville District, Army Corps of Engineers. He has authored numerous articles on navigation development of the Ohio River and has advised many other authors on work pertaining to local and regional history in the Ohio Valley. With Leland Johnson he coauthored* Kentucky River Development: The Commonwealth's Waterway *and* Triumph at the Falls: The Louisville and Portland Canal. *He has been a presenter on navigation history aboard numerous Ohio River excursion boats. He retired from the corps in 2004 after thirty years of service.*

# Acknowledgments

"River rat" is the highest accolade to be bestowed on those whose lives connect with the waterways coursing throughout our nation. The contributors to this volume are "Ohio River rats." They are recognized nationally and internationally for their expertise in fields related to the river that has become known as the United States' first interstate transportation byway. They share their passion, their insights, and their analysis of the present and their hopes for the future while being firmly grounded in the Ohio's storied past. As editor, it has been my good fortune to bring forward with them this unique array of essays to mark the bicentennial of the daring voyage of the *New Orleans*. I am grateful for their thoughtful caring throughout the process of shaping an idea into a book.

For initiating the impetus "to do something" to mark 2011, Charles Parrish earns full fathoms of gratitude. Parrish is the Ohio River's historian and the consummate cheerleader for our commitment to connecting its past with present and future. As chair of the 1811–2011 commemoration committee his imprint is in the bones of *Full Steam Ahead*, whose pages he has meticulously read from first draft to final manuscript. The best is what he asked for and gave.

Dr. Larry E. DeBuhr is the executive director of the Rivers Institute at Hanover College (RIH) where he directs an interdisciplinary program on promoting understanding of the natural and cultural history of river environments. He brings with him a breadth of dedication to our natural world and the field of public education, having held positions at the Chicago Botanic Garden, the Missouri Botanical Garden in Saint Louis, Missouri, and the University of Missouri at Kansas City. DeBuhr's early financial embracement of the book epitomizes his exemplary leadership.

Douglas Denné gave unstintingly of his time and sleuthing to provide the most up-to-date documentation of the holdings and newest acquisitions in the Agnes Brown Duggan Library at Hanover College.

Elsa Conboy of the RIH good-naturedly and expertly oversaw the orderly and accurate progression of manuscripts as they flowed in and out with additions, deletions, and emendations. She moved past the snags and other dangers to bring us error free to publication submission.

Robert Reid, emeritus vice president for academic affairs and professor of history at the University of Southern Indiana helped shape the arc of the book, read the manuscript in its earliest draft, and provided critical guidance.

Wilma Moore at the Indiana Historical Society (IHS), R. David Edmunds at the University of Texas at Dallas, and Joe Trotter, at Carnegie Mellon University, assisted in developing breadth of content and context.

At the IHS Press, editors Teresa Baer and Kathy Breen masterfully oversaw publication with the skillful assistance of contract editor Rachel Popma, editorial assistant Karen Wood, and intern Kevin L. Combs. The good humor and expertise of the IHS Press is greatly appreciated.

Equally, Erin Kelley, the IHS's director of adult and community programs, has been a source of collegiality in the development of the traveling steamboat exhibit; John Herbst, president and CEO of the IHS, has been a supportive partner for the 2011 commemoration; and Ray Boomhower, senior editor of the IHS Press, has lent his expertise to ensure the readability of the exhibit text for the general public.

Throughout the work on this project, family and friends have been supportive in too many ways to recount. I especially thank Andrew Hein for his insightful suggestions to make the best possible book.

To everyone named and unnamed here, who has assisted in any way, thanks for being (or becoming) a "river rat" and for giving your full measure of caring to the making of *Full Steam Ahead*.

Rita Kohn
Editor, *Full Steam Ahead*

*Rita Kohn served as coordinator of the National Endowment for the Humanities–Six States Humanities Councils' award-winning book and exhibition* Always A River: The Ohio River and the American Experience *(1986–1992). She is editor for the University Press of Kentucky Ohio River Series, and her books have been published by Indiana University Press, Scarecrow, McFarland, Garland, and Children's presses, among others. Her plays have been produced nationwide. Kohn conceived, cowrote, and coproduced the WFYI-public television Emmy-award-winning documentary* Long Journey Home: The Delaware Indians of Indiana. *She has served on the faculties of Illinois State University, Butler University, and Indiana University–Purdue University at Indianapolis. Her byline appears nationally, and she is senior writer for NUVO Newsweekly.*

# Introduction

RITA KOHN

The year 2011 marks the bicentennial of the voyage of the *New Orleans*, the first steamboat to travel down *and up* the Ohio River. This daring 1811 event, undertaken in the midst of a swirl of attendant human and natural happenings, immediately affected our young nation's commercial and settlement patterns. Collectively, we have been dealing with and adjusting to the repercussions ever since.

This book is part of the larger project spearheaded by the Rivers Institute at Hanover College to bring attention to the excitement surrounding the voyage of the *New Orleans* and to its impact particularly upon the Ohio River Valley and generally upon the resultant way of life of residents across the United States. In concert with *Steamboat a Comin': The Legacy of the* New Orleans, the traveling steamboat exhibit created by the Indiana Historical Society, and with programs offered by communities along the Ohio, *Full Steam Ahead* is intended to provide citizens with "opportunities to explore the ways this voyage impacted the economy, technology, culture and folklife of the Midwest and the U.S."

The goal of the 2011 project is to stimulate widespread engagement with people, ideas, events, and ever-present challenges along the Ohio River and to invite public dialogue and participation with concurrent historic celebrations over the next decade. Individuals intimately connected with the diverse elements of life along the Ohio River, who have been engaged in a variety of Ohio River Valley occupations, offer their personal perspectives on the aftermath of this very personal voyage undertaken by Captain Nicholas Roosevelt and his family and the financiers, builders, and crew of the *New Orleans*.

A special-purpose volume, *Full Steam Ahead* is not intended as a definitive treatise for scholars. Rather, it taps into our core humanity and offers a mix of analytical, descriptive, historical, and narrative approaches for the general reader by an eclectic group for whom writing may not be a first line of expression. While some hold doctoral degrees, most are representative of people whose voices are not usually heard but whose names and contributions are recognized and valued by those who live and labor in the Ohio River Valley. Because their lives are tied to the river, they offer personal connections to and perspectives on an event of two hundred years ago. Their ways of expressing themselves differ, from blunt to chatty to factual. They were invited to serve on the steering committee to get the 2011 project under way and to bring their constituencies into the mix—to cause excitement now as Nicholas Roosevelt did in 1811.

Ohio River historian Leland R. Johnson brings us on board Roosevelt's newly designed vessel in "Harbinger of Revolution." Naval architect Captain Alan L. Bates shares his knowledge of and experiences with building and navigating steamboats in "Structural Evolution of the Western Rivers Steamboat." Steamboat historian Jack E. Custer takes us into the generation following the steamboat with an overview of the range of steam-powered vessels in "A Synoptic History of Towboating and Its Origins." Social historian Rick Bell follows in the scholarship of urban historian Richard C. Wade with an analysis of why one town flourishes and another fails in "The Era of Town Building Below the Falls." Cultural historian Thomas C. Buchanan analyzes the effects of the steamboat on nineteenth-century African American and American Indian populations in "'Omen of Evil': Steamboats and the Colonization of the Ohio River Valley." Joe William Trotter Jr., historian of the African American experience, examines "The Steamboat and Black Urban Life in the Ohio Valley."

Sandra M. Custer taps into her family's steamboat piloting heritage for a brief overview of "Steamboat Music." Gerald W. Sutphin digs into his years of service with the Army Corps of Engineers (ACE) for a detailed description of changes wrought for steam-powered boats in "The Steamboat *New Orleans* and Its Impact on Navigation on Ohio River Tributaries." Robert Willis likewise utilizes his ACE tenure to examine the Ohio River's place within the world's rivers for "The Ohio River: A World-Class Inland Waterway." Kenneth A. Wheeler shares his entrepreneurial expertise for the forward-looking "Afterword: The River Today and Tomorrow." CEO Linda Harris and education coordinator Kadie Engstrom of the *Belle of Louisville* highlight the seventy-five-year-old boat in "*Belle of Louisville:* Sole Survivor of the Pioneering *New Orleans.*" The text closes with an annotated bibliography, describing the treasure trove of materials at Hanover, titled "The Rivers Institute at Hanover College: A List of Materials on River People, Steamboats, and the Ohio–Mississippi River System in the Agnes Brown Duggan Library," compiled by archivist Douglas Denné and librarian Katherine McCardwell.

For writers and editors, creating an anthology, such as *Full Steam Ahead: Reflections on the Impact of the First Steamboat on the Ohio River, 1811–2011,* is a journey to be shared over years with people we may never meet in person. Nevertheless, together we endeavor to communicate in the pages something that touches and connects and thus transmits our passion for the topic and our joy in making it public.

# 1

## Harbinger of Revolution

LELAND R. JOHNSON

Who would have thought a steamboat trip could spark a revolution? Yet, the epic voyage of the *New Orleans*, first steamboat to descend the Ohio and Mississippi rivers to New Orleans, changed American civilization as well as the lives of its passengers and crew. Departing Pittsburgh in October 1811, this new kind of boat received gala welcomes at nearly every port, and its passage was marked by the Great Comet of 1811 streaking across the sky and by the greatest earthquake ever recorded in the continental United States. That year, the largest slave revolt in the nation's history failed violently at New Orleans, and Tecumseh's tribal confederation suffered defeat at Tippecanoe. Aboard the *New Orleans*, the passengers and crew saw their craft under supposed threats of tribal attack and fire. They experienced romance, weddings, and births on deck; weathered disbelief and discouragement; forged new destinies; and participated unknowingly in the demise of tribal civilization and the rise of technical culture. America was never the same after the first inland river steamboat chugged its way to glory.

This first steamboat on western waters, harbinger of the Industrial Revolution that changed America, was owned by Robert Fulton and Robert Livingston and was constructed by Nicholas Roosevelt, whose pregnant wife and daughter joined him as the first steamboat passengers on inland rivers. From the voyage of the *New Orleans* in 1811 until the docking of the *Delta Queen* in 2008, steamboats carried passengers along the Ohio and connecting rivers day and night. Steamboats stimulated manufacturing and economic development along the inland rivers, moving the nation's freight until supplanted by railroads, trucks, and towboats. To fuel the *New Orleans*, some of the first coal mines in the Ohio Valley opened, presaging the boating of coal along the rivers to generate power for homes and industry. Pressing the frontier steadily west, steamboats carried Native Americans to new homes and converted agricultural villages into boat construction centers, manufacturing emporiums, and, ultimately, cities, altering the social fabric of both Native American and Euro-African settlers alike. This account of the *New Orleans* adventure presses full steam ahead to its influence on the lives of all Americans.

The *New Orleans* was neither the first steam engine nor the first steamboat in America. Experimental steamboats were

*1911 Centennial Replica of the* New Orleans *passing Marietta, Ohio*

tested in America as early as 1786, and in 1807 Robert Fulton had operated a steamboat profitably on the Hudson River. The first steam engine had come to America even earlier, in 1753. Thomas Newcomen of Great Britain in 1712 had devised the first industrial steam engine for use in pumping water. These were ponderous, inefficient single-stroke machines, but dozens were installed to draw water from mines in Britain and across Europe. When a flood filled the Soho copper mine near Passaic, New Jersey, its owner ordered a Newcomen steam engine from Britain in 1753 and installed it to pump out the mine. Benjamin Franklin went to see its operation; and John Adams and Thomas Jefferson studied it as the finest technology of the age, offering them a glimpse into America's future.

The brute Newcomen engines used too much fuel, and James Watt at Scotland's Glasgow University investigated smaller and improved steam engines. Reviewing the energy burned by these machines, Watt devised the "horsepower" and "watt" standards still used to measure energy efficiency. He designed more efficient dual-stroke steam engines and entered into a partnership with Matthew Boulton for their manufacture. Boulton saw the potential of these smaller steam engines to replace wind and water mills for manufacturing; and it was Boulton who coined our word "factory."

Many inventors in Europe and America sought to apply steam power to boat propulsion, supplanting the sail and manual labor then powering boats across oceans and along rivers. Among these inventors were James Rumsey of Kentucky, John Stevens of New York, and John Fitch of Connecticut. Fitch demonstrated a small steamboat on the Delaware River for delegates to the Philadelphia Constitutional Convention of 1787 and made efforts to establish steam ferries. Among witnesses to Fitch's early steam projects was young Nicholas Roosevelt

of New York, scion of the Dutch family that later produced two presidents of the United States.

Enthralled by revolutionary steamboat technology, Roosevelt joined with Fulton and Livingston in efforts to design and build commercially profitable steamboats. Roosevelt purchased the Soho copper mine in New Jersey, where the first steam engine in America still pumped water from the mine, and near the mine he constructed a metal-machining plant to build steam engines. With Livingston, Roosevelt participated in experimental steamboat design testing in 1797, which failed because of propulsion problems. Roosevelt insisted steamboats should use his propulsion method with paddle wheels on both sides of a boat, but his time was limited by other projects. He took a contract with the navy to supply copper plates for protecting wooden hulls of warships, and he accepted a contract from Benjamin Henry Latrobe to manufacture steam engines and copper boilers for Philadelphia's water supply system. (Steam engines earlier were adapted for pumping water supplies at London and Paris.)

Latrobe had come to the United States in 1796 from Great Britain, where he had studied architecture and engineering under John Smeaton, designer of steam engines used as pumps for London's water supply. In the United States, Latrobe won contracts in Philadelphia for his designs of buildings in Greek and Gothic Revival styles that eventually earned him acclaim as the "father of architecture" in America. He also received contracts for designing public water supply systems at New Orleans and Philadelphia, and for these contracts he made steam-engine manufacturer Roosevelt his business associate.

After he was elected president in 1801, Jefferson appointed Latrobe as architect of the nation's capital, and Latrobe began designs for the U.S. Capitol and other buildings in the District of Columbia. Jefferson canceled the navy's orders for new warships, however, thus suspending Roosevelt's contract for manufacturing copper sheathing. Thereafter, Roosevelt resumed his participation in the Fulton and Livingston steamboat experiments, which proved successful in 1807 when the first steamboat splashed along the Hudson River, using Roosevelt's side-wheel propulsion system.

Roosevelt became enamored with Latrobe's daughter, Lydia, and she returned the affection. Her father strongly opposed this match because Roosevelt was twenty-four years older than Lydia, but the lovers persisted and at last gained his consent. The couple had a gala wedding on Capitol Hill in Washington, D.C., in November 1808, with society's luminaries attending, including Dolley Madison. President James Madison was too ill to attend.

After developing his successful steamboat in 1807 on the Hudson River, Fulton expected to profit most from building steamboats on the western waters, including the Ohio and Mississippi rivers. He declared that his steamboats would "give a cheap and quick conveyance to the merchandize on the Mississippi, Missouri, and other great rivers, which are now laying open their treasures to the enterprise of our countrymen." Obtaining patents on their steamboat design, Fulton and Livingston sought to profit by acquiring exclusive rights granted by state governments to steam navigation on the Hudson River and also in Louisiana on the Mississippi River. To test the western waters, they dispatched their partner Roosevelt to survey the Ohio and Mississippi rivers, while also searching out coal deposits that could be mined to fuel their steamboats.

Taking Lydia, pregnant with their first child, with him, Roosevelt traveled to Pittsburgh in the spring of 1809. Having constructed a flatboat with comfortable accommodations, he traveled down the Ohio and Mississippi rivers, measuring river channels and depths and exploring the banks for coal. Coal mines were then operating at Pittsburgh, but Roosevelt found few deposits downstream along the Ohio and Mississippi, the notable exception being near modern Cannelton, Indiana. Here, he purchased property and ordered coal mined and moved to the riverside for use when he and his partners sent steamboats down the rivers. When Nicholas and Lydia reached New Orleans, they returned east by ship to New York, where Lydia gave birth to their first child, a daughter named Rosetta. Roosevelt reported to Fulton and Livingston that the rivers from Pittsburgh to New Orleans had great commercial potential and recommended they should proceed to build steamboats for commerce. Roosevelt had learned the Falls of the Ohio at Louisville often could not be crossed by boats, so he expected to divide the western river steamboat commerce into two sections, one operating steamboats from Pittsburgh to the Falls at Louisville and the other from Louisville to New Orleans.

With approval and funding from his partners, Roosevelt and his family returned to Pittsburgh in 1810 to build a substantial steamboat, which Roosevelt would steam downriver and put into service at New Orleans. Roosevelt brought with him shipbuilders and steam engineers from New York and began building the steamboat designed by Fulton on the bank of the Monongahela River a short distance above its juncture with the Allegheny River that formed the Ohio River. He named the boat the *New Orleans* after the city that would become its home port.

Built by shipwrights from the East, at 148 feet long, 20 feet abeam (wide), and 7 feet draft (depth of water necessary for boat to float), the *New Orleans* was substantially larger than the flatboats and keelboats then conducting the Ohio River's commerce. It also contained comfortable cabins below the deck for its crew with space sufficient for up to sixty passengers. Its engine parts and copper boiler apparently came overland to Pittsburgh from Roosevelt's Soho mine and mills in New Jersey. Engineers William Robinson and Nicholas D. Baker assembled them aboard the boat to become a steam engine based on Watt and Boulton's design. Historians have debated whether the boat had a stern-wheel paddle—like the *Delta Queen* and other modern steamboats—or two side-wheel paddles, but it probably was a side-wheel, if only because Roosevelt himself patented that propulsion system. Two passengers aboard at its launch in 1811 described the great boat: "She was built after the fashion of a ship, with port-holes in the side—long bowsprit [spar projecting from boat's stem]—painted a sky blue. Her cabin was in the hold." Like Fulton's other steamboats, the *New Orleans* had two masts with sails, serving as backup in case the steam engine malfunctioned. Marine engineers later dropped sailing masts from river steamboat designs because sails were seldom useful on narrow river channels, but masts were retained on ocean steamships for nearly a century, allowing ships to continue voyages when their engines failed.

At Pittsburgh old boatmen who had laboriously poled and pulled keelboats up the Mississippi and Ohio rivers laughed at this first steamboat, telling Roosevelt his project was hopeless. No engine could ever prevail against the western rivers' powerful currents. Determined, Roosevelt pressed ahead.

When the *New Orleans* was completed and launched, Roosevelt took it on a test run down the Monongahela to the Ohio, then turned up the Allegheny River to test its power against river currents. On this first test run, Roosevelt learned he had interesting competition. The inventive Connecticut Yankee Daniel French had arrived on the Monongahela after challenging Fulton's Hudson River monopoly. While the Fulton steamboats, including the *New Orleans*, used the low-pressure Watt-and-Boulton engines, French used a high-pressure engine. In 1809 he patented a horizontal, noncondensing, directly connected engine for boats and mills. His efficient engine had greater power and lighter weight than Watt and Boulton's.

French began building his steam engines, and his experiments found support at Pittsburgh, notably from George Shiras, wealthy owner of Pittsburgh's brewery. Shiras owned a thirty-foot fishing boat, and he paid French to install a small high-pressure steam engine aboard it to turn a stern-wheel paddle behind. Thus, when Roosevelt first tested his *New Orleans*, Shiras had his small boat ready to race. Shiras and his boat fell behind as the two steamers cruised down the Monongahela. At the Pittsburgh Point, Roosevelt turned the *New Orleans* up the Allegheny to learn its upstream capabilities. He found he could achieve a speed of three miles per hour against the current. But on the upstream course, the little Shiras boat closed the gap. When the boats arrived at the first rapids on the Allegheny, the *New Orleans* stalled against the strong current, while the little Shiras boat shot ahead, up and over the rapids. This presaged events to come, because a company soon formed at Brownsville, Pennsylvania, on the Monongahela River to build small steamboats with French's efficient engines, offering major competition to Fulton, who had planned to dominate inland river steamboating.

While Roosevelt was busy testing his new steamboat, Lydia, eight months pregnant, was being warned by Pittsburgh dowagers not to accompany her husband on his foolish and dangerous venture to New Orleans. Her friends told Lydia it was folly, if not madness, to attempt the trip while pregnant. She ignored the warnings and insisted on accompanying her husband on the voyage. Nicholas ensconced her and Rosetta aboard the *New Orleans* in a cabin especially designed for their comfort. The boat had two cabins, the largest toward the bow (front) for men. The ladies' cabin was in the stern (back) with four berths for Lydia, Rosetta, and two maids.

Historians have not found crew lists for the first steamboat trip down the Ohio and Mississippi, but Roosevelt took along his steamboat engineer Nicholas Baker and employed Andrew Jack as the boat's pilot. Baker had worked for Fulton and Roosevelt in New Jersey before moving to Pittsburgh to help build the *New Orleans*. Little is known of the pilot except that he had earlier experience steering keelboats along the Ohio and Mississippi rivers, where he had become intimately familiar with the rivers' channels and navigation markers. Jack and his family lived on Jack Run, a small Ohio River tributary three miles below Pittsburgh Point. Also aboard the boat were six deckhands, a cabin boy, and a cook. The Roosevelts also brought along a pet, an immense Newfoundland dog named Tiger.

An account of the trip written by Lydia's brother, Henry Latrobe, describes the boat's departure:

On Sunday last, the Steam-Boat lately built at Pittsburgh passed this place on her way to N. Orleans—The citizens of this place were much disappointed in not having an opportunity of viewing her, only as she passed—she made no stop here. From the rapidity with which she passed this place it is supposed she went at the rate of 12 or 14 miles an hour.

*News of the* New Orleans *from Cincinnati's* Western Spy, *November 2, 1811*

The people of Pittsburg[h] turned out in mass and lined the banks of the Monongahela to witness the departure of the steamboat, and shout after shout rent the air, and handkerchiefs were waved, and hats thrown up by way of "God speed" to the voyagers as the anchor was raised, and heading up stream for a short distance a wide circuit brought the "New Orleans" on her proper course, and steam and current aiding, she disappeared behind the first headlands on the right bank of the Ohio.

At first the boat's passengers and crew were apprehensive, but the steamboat maneuvered swiftly past bend after bend in the river, making about ten miles per hour. The regular chugging of its engine, the ample supply of steam, and the uniformity of its speed inspired confidence. Pilot Jack was delighted by the ease of steering the boat at such a high speed—it was traveling faster than any boat ever seen on the river. News of the steamboat's passage came across the long river bends to riverside towns such as Beaver, Pennsylvania, and Steubenville, Ohio. Recognizing how momentous this voyage was in comparison with the unpowered craft then transporting river commerce, people of these villages crowded the riverbanks to see the novel boat and cheer as it passed. The Roosevelts and the jolly crew assembled on the boat's deck, waving and returning the cheers. At Wheeling, Virginia, Roosevelt made the first stop to mail letters back east and to display the boat's design. Charging twenty-five cents for people to satisfy their curiosity, Roosevelt welcomed a large crowd aboard, and people roamed the boat, examining its engine, the sailing masts fore and aft, the eight-foot-long bowsprit, and the paddle wheels. With his pockets filled with change, Roosevelt ordered departure, and the crew cast off again toward the west.

As the *New Orleans* approached Marietta, Ohio, Judge Paul Fearing timed the boat over a three-mile stretch of river. He pronounced it an elegant boat, speeding faster than anything ever before seen, at an estimated twelve to fourteen miles per hour. A booming cannon alerted Marietta to the boat's approach, and an enthusiastic crowd collected to see it land briefly. Farther downriver, it stopped at Point Pleasant at the mouth of the Kanawha River for an hour to take on wood. Roosevelt again collected twenty-five cents from visitors who came aboard to fund his purchase of several cords of firewood fuel. Anxious to get on to Louisville, Roosevelt did not land at Cincinnati, but residents forewarned of its passage gathered along the riverbank to sate their curiosity. He anchored the steamboat off the bank to take on another boatload of fuel, then steamed away. The Cincinnati newspaper reported the steamboat left there at five in the afternoon of October 27, running rapidly with the tide at ten to twelve miles per hour.

A few miles downstream, people in Madison, Indiana, had received no warning that a steamboat was approaching. At that time, General William Henry Harrison and his army were marching north to confront the Indian confederation organized by Tecumseh and his brother, the Prophet. When fishermen upstream of Madison heard the noisy steamboat, they thought they were hearing guns firing. They ran in fear to the town to warn that an Indian force might be coming downriver.

The *New Orleans* did not stop at Madison or elsewhere until about one in the morning of October 28. The steamer rounded to at Louisville's wharf, releasing steam in a shrill blast that awakened sleepers in homes near the wharf. Later reports declared the roaring steam and the sparks flying from the boat's smokestack excited fears that the Great Comet of 1811, then arcing overhead, had fallen into the river. At dawn Roosevelt

welcomed visitors, and they continued flocking aboard throughout that day and the next. Visiting stopped on October 30, however, as Lydia's labor began. Attended by her maids and a midwife from Louisville, Lydia, lying in her cabin with dim light through the portholes, presented Nicholas with his first son. They proudly named him Henry Latrobe Roosevelt after Lydia's father. When the news reached her father, he sent his congratulations to Lydia:

> The birth of your little boy, has given me sincere pleasure. To the sanguine and buoyant temper of his father, and the golden hopes with which it spangles his most dreary prospect, I hope he will add the sober sense and command of himself that his most beloved mother possesses. . . . He who was born in a Steamboat, must surely have a singular course in life. I hope it will be a happy one. Your little Girl shares I am sure your happiness.

At meetings with Louisville's river men and civic leaders, Roosevelt received the same faint praise he had heard at towns upstream. They complimented him on his successful trip thus far down the Ohio and extended their profuse wishes for a safe trip on to New Orleans. However, they never expected to see him again, believing that no boat could overcome the powerful currents in an upriver trip. All along his route, Roosevelt sought to recruit investors in the Fulton steamboat company, so he planned a surprise for the critics, inviting them to a gala dinner aboard the boat in the large forward cabin. After the feast was under way, his guests heard the engine rumble and felt the boat begin to move. Their first fear was the boat had broken from its mooring and was drifting down into the Falls, the whitewater rapids that could destroy the steamboat and take their lives. The guests rushed topside to the deck and soon saw the boat was not drifting downstream, but instead steaming upstream and picking up speed as it went. Roosevelt took his surprised guests on an upriver excursion, then returned the delighted passengers safely to the wharf.

Roosevelt learned the ship-like hull of the *New Orleans* at seven-foot draft set too far down in the water for safe passage over the Falls. October on average was the driest month of the year in the Ohio Valley; winter rains and resulting river rises typically began in late November. The licensed Falls pilots would not attempt to steer his steamer down the Falls until river flow had increased sufficiently for its hull to clear jagged rocks in the chute channel near the Indiana bank. An attempt a few years earlier to take sailing ships with deep-draft hulls like that of the *New Orleans* over the Falls before the depth was sufficient had wrecked two ships, an extremely costly financial disaster. A third ship that held back to await a larger rise was forced to remain at Louisville for an entire year, its cargo rotting, before depths became adequate.

To use the Falls delay profitably, Roosevelt ran excursion trips upriver a few miles and back for a dollar a ticket. He also celebrated Rosetta's second birthday on November 11. Public interest in the steamboat waned, however, when news came of Harrison's battle at Tippecanoe on November 7. Harrison's forces were driving back Tecumseh's warriors, although the chief himself was still in the south, seeking allies among the Creek and Chickasaw tribes.

After a month passed at Louisville without a deepening river rise, Roosevelt returned his boat to Cincinnati on November 27, demonstrating the revolutionary upstream capability of his craft. This confounded Cincinnati's river men, who, after the boat had passed in October, had declared they would never see it again. Hundreds of people bought dollar tickets for the honor of riding the first steamboat short distances upriver from the

Queen City and back. After a week at Cincinnati, the river began to rise, and Roosevelt steamed back to Louisville to cross the Falls of the Ohio.

Louisville had no canal bypassing the Falls until 1830, so Roosevelt hired one of the experienced pilots licensed to steer boats safely through the chutes over the Falls. When the river rose and offered a scant five-inch clearance between the steamboat's hull and the sharp rocks, Roosevelt and the pilots determined to chance the crossing, rather than miss the rise and perhaps be delayed for months. Nicholas preferred that his family stay ashore during the crossing, but Lydia insisted on sharing her husband's challenge. Standing near the stern, she witnessed the fearful crossing and later described it to her brother:

All hands were on deck. . . . The two pilots, for an extra one had been engaged for the passage through the rapids, took their places in the bow. The anchor was weighed. To get into the Indiana channel, which was the best, a wide circuit had to be made bringing her head up stream, completing which, the New Orleans began the descent. Steerage way depended upon her speed exceeding that of the current. The faster she could be made to go, the easier would it be to guide her. All the steam the boiler would bear was put upon her. The safety valve shrieked. The wheels revolved faster than they had ever done before; and the vessel, speaking figuratively, fairly flew away from the crowds collected to witness her departure from Louisville. Instinctively, each one on board now grasped the nearest object, and with bated breath awaited the result. Black ledges of rock appeared only to disappear as the New Orleans flashed by them. The waters whirled and eddied, and threw their spray upon the deck, as a more rapid descent caused the vessel to pitch forward to what at times seemed inevitable destruction. Not a word was spoken. The pilots directed the men at the helm by motions of their hands. . . . The tension on the nervous system was too great to be long sustained. Fortunately, the passage was soon made; and, with feelings of profound gratitude to the Almighty, at the successful issue of the adventure . . . the New Orleans rounded to in safety below the Falls.

Roosevelt landed the *New Orleans* at the French village of Shippingport to take aboard his children and the maids who had portaged around the Falls in a carriage. They lingered at Shippingport several days while loading supplies for the downriver trip. From his previous survey, Roosevelt knew few river towns furnished supplies below Shippingport until the boat reached Natchez, Mississippi.

According to Lydia, it was at Shippingport in mid-December that the boat felt the first of a stunning series of earthquakes estimated to be the strongest ever recorded in the continental United States. The first shock felt as if the boat had suddenly grounded, its hawsers (large ropes for securing the boat) to the shore trembling like plucked strings. The passengers became nauseous. As the *New Orleans* steamed to the south, the earthquake shocks continued by the thousands, but river water cushioned the boat, and the noisy steam engine and beating paddle wheels obscured the vibrations.

Below Shippingport the boat passed through wilderness broken only by occasional villages. The earthquake had disrupted regular mail services. The Roosevelts, therefore, passed out of contact with Fulton and their friends in the East. Each afternoon the steamer rounded to and tied to the bank while the crew went ashore to cut firewood. Sometimes villagers came aboard and related stories of the land trembling beneath their feet. When the boat landed at Roosevelt's coal mines near Cannelton, Indiana, the crew found that the local residents had left

some coal piled at the riverside as Roosevelt had instructed but had taken much coal as well. The coal would prove convenient for the crew, and they loaded all the boat could store before proceeding toward the Mississippi River.

When the *New Orleans* passed the mouth of the Tennessee River, it entered Indian Territory. Land along the riverbank in western Kentucky and Tennessee was claimed by the Chickasaw tribe, and the passengers often met warriors in canoes, who dubbed the steamer a Penelore, or "fire canoe." Although the Battle of Tippecanoe a month earlier had suppressed the tribes, fighting north of the Ohio would continue through the War of 1812. The British would appoint Tecumseh a general, and he would lead the warriors until his death at the Battle of Thames

STEAM-BOAT.
*Louisville, November 15.*

Arrived at this place on the 28th ult. Mr. Roosevelt's steam-boat NEW-ORLEANS—we are informed she is intended as a packet boat between Natchez and New-Orleans; her burthen is 405 tons, and can accommodate from 60 to 80 cabin and steerage passengers, in a style not inferior to any packet in the union. She arrived at this place in 64 hours sailing from Pittsburg. Frequent experiments of her performance have been made against the current, since her arrival; in the presence of a number of respectable gentlemen, who have ascertained with certainty she runs thirteen miles in two hours and a half.

*News from Louisville in the* Cincinnati Western Spy, *November 23, 1811*

in 1813. Meanwhile, General Andrew Jackson's army would punish the Creek tribe (Redsticks), Tecumseh's allies in Alabama and Mississippi.

Amidst the warfare, concern arose aboard the *New Orleans* when a large canoe packed with Chickasaw warriors gave chase. However, the action may not have been as dangerous as it seemed. The Chickasaw tribe had been peaceful allies of the American legion in earlier years, and the tribe had declined Tecumseh's offer in 1811 to join his fight. Perhaps the warriors were satisfying their curiosity about the novel machine or testing its speed. In any event, the steamboat's unflagging pace outdistanced the warriors' paddles. The Chickasaw would continue to control western Kentucky and Tennessee until 1818 when General Jackson offered the tribe payments to cede their property.

A greater threat to the *New Orleans* arose shortly after the canoe race. The Roosevelts and the crew were asleep when shouting roused them. Thinking the warriors had returned, Nicholas sprang up and grabbed his sword—the sole weapon aboard—and, climbing to the deck, saw the boat was afire. The crew formed a bucket brigade, frantically splashing water to extinguish the flames and save the boat. The cabin boy had left firewood too near the stove before going to bed, and the hot stove ignited the wood, spreading flames to the cabin woodwork. The passengers were fortunate the cabin boy awoke to sound the alarm; great disasters subsequently destroyed other wooden steamboats when fires forced passengers to leap into the river or burn.

As their boat left the Ohio River and entered the Mississippi, effects of the early earthquake shocks became apparent. Maps of the channel no longer served as a guide, nor were Roosevelt's memories of his 1809 trip very useful. The quakes had surged the river in new vectors, caving in its banks, collapsing trees, and sinking islands. One of the most uncomfortable incidents of the voyage was Pilot Jack's confusion at the great changes in the channel. Where he expected to find a deep channel, he found standing tree stumps, forcing him to search for alternate passages. Tall trees that had served as visual navigation markers had disappeared, and the shapes of islands had changed. The river had cut across its former bends through the forested land, forming cutoffs and shortening the channel. Through unknown and dangerous new channels the *New Orleans* steamed down the Mississippi amid the chaos of devastated towns, desolate farmland, and floating snags (trees and branches).

The pilot and crew followed the downriver course as best they could, stopping frequently because the steam engine had consumed all the coal. They chopped driftwood as fuel, sometimes meeting dazed settlers on the bank, all with horrifying tales of the earthquake. The river had engulfed the town of New Madrid, Missouri; the earth had opened in chasms, swallowing buildings and their inhabitants. Some stricken refugees begged to be taken on board the *New Orleans*, but the food provisions were insufficient to feed many passengers, and no more supplies could be had until the boat reached Natchez.

The steamboat was forced to leave the refugees ashore, sobering both passengers and crew and silencing their former euphoria. Even the Roosevelt's dog, Tiger, prowled the deck, disturbed and growling. Their apprehension made sleep at night problematic, and they became haggard. Lydia later complained she "lived in a constant fright, unable to sleep or sew, or read." She had good reason for concern. One night when the crew tied the boat to trees on an island, Lydia's sleep was disturbed by gurgling noises and jars and other objects striking and grating down along the hull. At dawn the crew and passengers saw that the entire island had disappeared; their mooring hawser stretched down beneath the surface. Cutting the hawser, they drifted on their way, searching for a channel and hailing flatboats they passed, but flatboat captains had no more clue where to steer than Pilot Jack. Lydia described their passage to Natchez as replete with "anxiety and terror." Passing Fort Pickering (at present-day Memphis, Tennessee), they saw the fort tumbled by the quake. Soon thereafter, they passed out of the central earthquake zone. This passage proved timely because great earthquake shocks continued, the largest coming in February 1812, when the Mississippi flowed upstream for a time and water filled a sunken area in Tennessee later named Reelfoot Lake.

A few days after Christmas 1811, a great crowd assembled on the bluff at Natchez to welcome the first steamboat on the river. The crowd was disappointed when the *New Orleans* did not initially land. Its steam pressure was insufficient to round to against the current until the crew added fresh fuel and stopped the engine so the pressure would rise, then lifted the valve for the engine to again thrash the paddle wheels to regain headway and land at Natchez. Here a wedding celebration occurred when Captain Nicholas Baker married one of Lydia's maids. After celebrating, Roosevelt took on freight for the final run to New Orleans, a cargo including bales of cotton, the first of millions of bales to make the same trip to market.

Near the end of December, the *New Orleans* left Natchez and continued its voyage, an uneventful leg of the trip on a comparatively wide and deep channel. The Roosevelts' arrival at the Crescent City on January 10, 1812, was greeted by civic celebrations led by Governor William Claiborne of Louisiana and Edward Livingston, son of Robert Livingston. Henry Latrobe, Lydia's brother, soon arrived at New Orleans to deliver letters from home and to become manager of the waterworks his father would build at New Orleans. In opening America's waterways to trade, transport, and travel, the *New Orleans* had blazed a path down the Ohio and Mississippi rivers for countless other steamers to follow.

Soon after landing at New Orleans, Roosevelt learned he had lost favor in New York. News reports had described the *New Orleans* as "Roosevelt's steamboat," neglecting to mention his partners Fulton and Livingston. His reports on the voyage after departing Louisville had miscarried due to the earthquakes, leaving Fulton and Livingston in the dark for months. Moreover, his partners were upset by the high costs of building the *New Orleans*, blaming this on Roosevelt's other ventures. He had, for example, purchased distilleries and factories in Pittsburgh. The federal government also sought to attach Roosevelt's assets on account of money advanced on his navy contract to furnish copper sheathing for warships, which was not delivered.

Nevertheless, under his agreement with Fulton and Livingston, Roosevelt was entitled to a third of the *New Orleans* earnings, and it proved immensely profitable. Soon after arriving, Captain Baker initiated the steamboat's regular run between New Orleans and Natchez, and it was crowded to capacity on every trip. Indeed, the trips proved so rewarding that when a snag punctured the *New Orleans*'s hull in 1814, Fulton's company moved its engine and machinery onto a new hull, also named the *New Orleans*, and continued the Natchez trade.

Seeing that Roosevelt and Fulton could not reach an amicable settlement, Lydia's father, Benjamin Latrobe, met personally with Fulton to negotiate. Knowing Roosevelt's assets might be legally seized by the federal government, Latrobe persuaded Fulton to assign Roosevelt's profit share to his daughter Lydia and her children. When Fulton agreed, Lydia became independently wealthy, receiving thousands of dollars every year. The Roosevelts returned to New York, and Nicholas resumed his entrepreneurial ventures, including steamboat enterprises, but not as a partner of Fulton and Livingston.

A few months after the *New Orleans*'s first voyage, the United States declared war on Great Britain. The British navy soon controlled the high seas, blockading American commerce and landing troops at will along the coast. For the war's duration, Congress ceased construction of the Capitol building, ending Benjamin Latrobe's service as architect. Latrobe had sent his son Henry to New Orleans to build the city's waterworks, but shipping steam engines for the waterworks by sea risked loss to the British blockade. Recognizing engines could be fabricated at Pittsburgh and shipped safe from the British fleet downriver to New Orleans, Latrobe discussed the plan with Fulton. In 1812 Fulton had dispatched his engineer, Charles Stoudinger, to Pittsburgh to build the steamboats *Vesuvius* and *Aetna* for service from Louisville to New Orleans. He also asked Latrobe to move to Pittsburgh and build a steamboat, the *Buffalo*, for the Pittsburgh to Louisville trade. Seeing he could work with Fulton and also build steam engines for the New Orleans waterworks, Latrobe accepted and moved to Pittsburgh in 1813, taking along Captain Baker as his chief engineer.

Latrobe and Baker began fabricating steam engines at Pittsburgh in 1813, building one to power woolen mills at Steubenville. With the British fleet blockading the coast, planters and manufacturers could not obtain steam engines from Europe, so Henry Latrobe took many orders for steam engines at New Orleans, mostly to power rolling mills to extract sugar from cane. With no competition from overseas, steam-engine manufacturing quickly multiplied in Pittsburgh, and by the end of the war Pittsburgh ranked with New York and Philadelphia as the nation's steam-engine centers.

In the meantime, Latrobe and Baker also built the *Buffalo* for Fulton to run from Pittsburgh to Louisville. Like the earlier *New Orleans*, *Vesuvius*, and *Aetna*, the *Buffalo* had a Watt and Boulton engine and was designed like deep-draft ships. Latrobe was also building a smaller boat intended to serve as a freight barge towed by the *Buffalo*. However, when the deep-draft *Vesuvius* hit a sandbar and was stranded six months awaiting a river rise to refloat it, Latrobe recognized the *Buffalo*'s draft was too great for efficient service on the Upper Ohio River. He therefore installed a steam engine aboard its smaller freight barge, converting it to a small steamboat named the *Harriet*, after Fulton's wife.

In 1815, at the request of President James Madison, Latrobe left Fulton's company and returned to Washington, D.C. With the end of the War of 1812, he was needed to rebuild the Capitol and other structures burned by British forces in 1814.

Meanwhile, Daniel French and Oliver Evans were also building small steamboats with high-pressure engines to compete with Fulton's boats. These first steamed along the Ohio River, where Fulton had no state-government monopolies. In late 1814 the French steamboat *Enterprise*, under Captain Henry Shreve, loaded at Pittsburgh with military ordnance and took it to New Orleans for the use of General Jackson repelling British assault forces. After the Battle of New Orleans, Fulton sought injunctions against operating the *Enterprise* in Louisiana, a state in which his company had acquired exclusive rights. Thereafter, Captain Shreve returned the boat to Louisville, making the *Enterprise* the first steamboat to make this upstream trip. The trip

*1911 Replica of the* New Orleans

was accomplished in twenty-five days, a feat celebrated in Louisville because manually powered keelboats typically required ninety days for the trip.

During the following decade, court decisions broke Fulton's monopoly in both Louisiana and New York, and steamboat construction thrived thereafter. From Pittsburgh the steamboat construction industry moved downriver to Cincinnati and Louisville. French, for example, relocated his steamboat construction business to Jeffersonville, Indiana, and lived there until 1860, long enough to learn his engines and designs for western river steamboats had outpaced Fulton's. In the end, French's little shallow draft, stern-wheel, high-pressure-engine fishing boat that had raced the *New Orleans* at Pittsburgh in 1811 proved to be the prototype for the western rivers steamboats that revolutionized transport and commerce along the inland rivers.

Although Livingston died in 1813 and Fulton in 1815, Roosevelt survived to witness French's victory. After his *New Orleans* experience, Roosevelt moved from one business venture to another, and Lydia always moved with him. It was said that none of their nine children were born at home, but all at different temporary quarters. In 1831, however, Nicholas and Lydia purchased an estate at Skaneateles, New York, overlooking one of central New York's Finger Lakes, and retired. They enjoyed a placid life until Nicholas died at eighty-seven in 1854. Lydia and son Henry continued living at the estate until her death in 1878 and his in 1884. Henry, born aboard the *New Orleans* in 1811, became, like his Roosevelt grandfather, a hardware merchant and bank director at Skaneateles. He enjoyed fast boats and owned racing boats that won the annual regattas on the Finger Lakes.

Nicholas Roosevelt had boldly defied popular opinion and conservative engineers to design steam-powered boats like the *New Orleans*. When asked at Skaneateles why Fulton had received credit for the original steamboat design, rather than him, Roosevelt quietly replied he had been too busy manufacturing steam engines for Philadelphia and warship plating for the U.S. Navy. However, accompanied by a wife half his age and pregnant with a second child, Roosevelt had tested the *New Orleans* on the treacherous Ohio and Mississippi rivers, overcoming earthquakes and fire to achieve his goals. With this success, he had changed America.

The *New Orleans* became the first of thousands of steamboats that converted the pioneer river commerce from almost all downstream to two-way traffic, opening the Mississippi and Ohio valleys to national and foreign commerce. Steamboat construction centers developed from Pittsburgh through Cincinnati and Louisville to smaller towns such as Evansville, Indiana, and Metropolis, Illinois, along the Ohio River and elsewhere. Uniquely designed western rivers steamboats entered trades on all the larger tributaries of the rivers, spreading the wings of steamboat commerce from Olean, New York, on the Allegheny River west to Fort Benton, Montana, on the far Missouri River.

Steamboat construction centers also fabricated steam engines that powered factories built throughout the Ohio and Mississippi valleys, freeing manufacturing from the geographical limitations of water power and launching the industrial revolution that converted the region from agrarian provincialism to cosmopolitan society. Accompanied by an influx of immigrants from Europe, this new culture drove Native Americans from the region and often transported them west to new reservations by steamboat. Steamboats brought former slaves north, along with banjos, blues, and jazz, and took south music from the pens of songwriters such as Stephen Collins Foster and Will S. Hays. They carried Yankee notions and Yankee guns south and returned with southern crops, music, and culture.

The need of steam engines to consume fuel also changed America. Coal became the fuel of choice. Roosevelt opened coal mines for the *New Orleans*, and coal mines subsequently opened wherever the black veins could be found. Coal was transported along the same route taken by Roosevelt in 1811, fueling sugar mills, cotton gins, and ocean steamships near New Orleans along with the steam-powered factories lining the rivers at every city and town. To transport immense coal tonnage from mines to markets, steamboat designers devised unique and powerful steam towboats that plied the rivers from Pittsburgh to New Orleans, switching from wooden to steel construction in the twentieth century. To support this economic development, the rivers themselves were redesigned to make them less treacherous and more reliable arteries of commerce, not only in the Ohio Valley but throughout North America and overseas where steamboat applications became the key to an urban and prosperous civilization.

The consequences of the *New Orleans*'s 1811 journey have resounded through American history for two centuries. The follow-on construction of steamboats and steam engines affected almost every aspect of national demographics, from mining and manufacturing to music, theater, and even cuisine. The *New Orleans* was the harbinger of seismic changes in American culture. While modern internal combustion engines and electric motors in the twentieth century superseded steam engines as America's manufacturing and motive power sources, it is worth noting that the watts energizing our lights, computers, and appliances

and powering our factories are generated by giant steam engines at the steam-electric and nuclear power plants lining our rivers. Despite advances in hydroelectric, wind, and solar power sources, steam engines like that aboard the *New Orleans* still produce 80 percent of the world's electricity, using high-pressure steam to spin turbines instead of paddle wheels. The voyage of the *New Orleans* changed not only the lives of its passengers and crew; it changed ours.

*Dr. Leland R. Johnson holds degrees from Vanderbilt, Murray State, and Saint Louis universities. For a half century he has conducted research concerning water resources development, river history, military history, and nuclear applications, publishing widely on these subjects and more.*

**SELECTED BIBLIOGRAPHY**

Buchanan, John. *Jackson's Way: Andrew Jackson and the People of the Western Waters.* Hoboken, NJ: John Wiley and Sons, 2001.

Charles Stoudinger Papers, Maryland Historical Society, Baltimore, Maryland.

Dahlinger, Charles W. "The New Orleans, Being a Critical Account of the Beginning of Steamboat Navigation on the Western Rivers of the United States." *Pittsburgh Legal Journal* 59 (October 21, 1911): 570–91.

De la Hunt, Thomas. *Perry County: A History.* Indianapolis: W. K. Stewart, 1916.

Dohan, Mary Helen. *Mr. Roosevelt's Steamboat: The First Steamboat to Travel the Mississippi.* New York: Dodd, Mead, and Co., 1981. [fiction].

Evans, Nelson. "The First Steamboat on the Ohio River." *Ohio Archaeological and Historical Quarterly* 16 (July 1907): 310–15.

Hamlin, Talbot. *Benjamin Henry Latrobe.* New York: Oxford University Press, 1955.

Johnson, Leland, and Charles Parrish. *Triumph at the Falls: The Louisville and Portland Canal.* Louisville: U.S. Army Engineer District, 2007.

Latrobe, Benjamin Henry. *The Journal of Latrobe.* Boston: D. Appleton and Co., 1905.

Latrobe, Charles Joseph. *The Rambler in North America, 1832–1833.* 2nd ed. London, 1836.

Latrobe, J. H. B. *The First Steamboat Voyage on the Western Waters.* Baltimore: John Murphy, 1871.

*Louisville Courier,* July 20, 1851.

*Louisville Courier-Journal,* January 5, 1902.

Maass, Alfred R. "Daniel French and the Western Steamboat Engine." *American Neptune* 56 (Winter 1996): 29–44.

*Natchez* (MS) *Democrat,* February 14, 2001.

*National Intelligencer* (Washington, D.C.), November 2, 1811.

*New York Evening Post*, November 15, 1811.

*Pittsburgh Gazette*, October 18 and October 25, 1811.

Pursell, Carroll W., Jr. *Early Stationary Steam Engines in America: A Study in the Migration of a Technology.* Washington, D.C.: Smithsonian Institution Press, 1969.

Ryder, F. Van Loon. "The 'New Orleans': The First Steamboat on Our Western Waters." *Filson Club History Quarterly* 37 (1963): 29–37.

Stewart, David, and Ray Knox. *The Earthquake America Forgot: Two Thousand Tremblers in Five Months, and It Will Happen Again.* Marble Hill, MO: Gutenberg Richter Publications, 1995.

Sutcliffe, Alice C. *Robert Fulton and The* Clermont. New York: Century, 1909.

Van Horne, John C., and Lee W. Formwalt. *The Correspondence and Miscellaneous Papers of Benjamin H. Latrobe.* 3 vols. New Haven, CT: Yale University Press, 1986.

*Vincennes* (IN) *Western Sun,* November 30, 1811.

William, M. Beauchamp. *Past and Present Syracuse and Onondaga County, New York.* New York: S. J. Clarke Publishers, 1908.

# 2

## Structural Evolution of the Western Rivers Steamboat

CAPTAIN ALAN L. BATES

Mariners are a conservative and hardheaded lot. They do not welcome change and seldom break away from established usage, materials, and methods. This is true at sea, at the builders' shipyards, and on the western rivers (the Mississippi and its tributaries). The unforgiving marine environment in which a small mistake can lead to disaster enforces this conservative outlook. The prevailing attitude was, and remains, that if a practice or material of the past did the job, then it should be continued. New ideas are accepted slowly and with caution. This conservatism made the evolution of the steamboat a slow process, accomplished in small increments largely by anonymous mechanics, until the end of the steamboat era.

Every elementary school pupil is told that Robert Fulton "invented" the steamboat, as if one evening there was no steamboat and the next morning the *North River Steamboat* (later known as the *Clermont*) steamed up the Hudson River to Albany, New York. This bare-bones notion is true to a limited extent, for Fulton *did* discover the elements of a steamboat and combine them into a practical machine. He did not invent the boat. He did not invent the steam engine and, in fact, imported one from

England to power his boat. Paddle wheels had been in use for centuries to drive gristmills.

This adaptation of older elements does not diminish his accomplishment in any way. Many other men before him had tried and failed. Fulton himself built at least one unsuccessful steamboat before he won his laurels. He made a number of basic scientific experiments prior to starting construction and in doing so, determined ratios and measurements of resistance that remain basic in naval architecture. This scientific approach was new in its day and had only a few adherents in America: men such as Benjamin Franklin and Thomas Jefferson.

During the eighteenth and nineteenth centuries the United States was a land of wooden construction. Today we cannot conceive the subtleties of its use, for most of the forests of native woods are gone. Americans of that earlier period were very much aware of the characteristics of the various species of wood. Its use was specialized even to the lowly firewood used for cooking and heating. One wood was used for quick and hot fires, while another would burn slowly to sustain the cabin fire overnight. In construction, men knew that the so-called soft woods, pine and fir, were used where strength was required, while hardwoods such as oak, maple, and birch withstood wear and abrasion. This was empirical lore, gained by observation and use, with little or no scientific examination or testing. Builders and designers were innocent of such concepts as tensile, compressive, and shear strengths. They used the experience gained by themselves and others and added their mite of innovation to them. If a beam or post failed, they would use a bigger one next time or reduce the spacing between frames. Fulton did not break away from these concepts when building his boat.

Fulton was aware of the shortcomings of the Boulton-and-Watt steeple engine that he imported and, as a hedge, he included masts, spars, and sails on his design for the *North River Steamboat*. Further, he knew that the heavy boiler and machinery created severe stresses on the hull. As a result the hull was built like that of an oceangoing wooden cargo ship. Such a ship was framed with closely spaced, heavy timbers and clad with thick planking. On the deep and placid Hudson River this heavy construction caused few problems. Like other mariners, he was inclined to duplicate his successful steamboat when he had the *New Orleans* built at Pittsburgh.

Further, ship-form hulls were characterized by rounded shapes with the keel as an appendage beneath the hull. In naval architecture there is a ratio called the block coefficient that compares the actual immersed volume of the hull with a rectangular block that would contain it. The volume of the block is stated as "one," and when the actual immersed volume is deducted from it, it is expressed as a percentage. For sailing ships in Fulton's day the block coefficient ranged between 0.550 and 0.700. Such a hull floated deeply in the water.

The *New Orleans* soon proved that such heavy hulls were not practicable in the shallow and swift currents of the Ohio and

Mississippi rivers. Thus, upon completion of her epic first voyage, she was placed in regular service between New Orleans and Natchez, Mississippi, where the waters were deepest and the current's velocity somewhat abated. Fulton's next boats, the *Vesuvius*, the *Aetna*, and the *Buffalo*, were also too heavy and drew too much water for the western rivers (here, again, a mariner refused to make any rash changes).

Fulton's successes caught the attention of others in the Mississippi River system, men who had navigated it in light and shallow flatboats and keelboats, among them Daniel French and Henry Shreve. The vessels with which they were familiar had very high block coefficients, in the nature of 0.650 to 0.750. They knew from experience that river vessels had to be light. They experimented with placing engines on the vessels with which they were familiar, and those hulls were made of relatively small scantlings. In 1817 Shreve's *Enterprise*, a combination of steam engines and a keelboat, made the first upstream voyage from New Orleans to Louisville in twenty-five days. The design of this vessel was a radical departure from that of the *New Orleans* and her successors. The progress of steamboat design after that was measured in lightness and its consequent reduction of draft. The hulls were made shallow and broad, to reduce draft to a bare minimum, and the block coefficients reached as high as 0.800 in the fully developed western rivers hull.

The shape of a hull is a determining factor in draft. As the steamboat hull developed, it became wider and longer to utilize as much waterplane area as possible. In addition to changing the shape of hulls, builders used ever-lighter timbers and spaced frames ever farther apart.

The engines, boilers, and most of the freight were carried on the main deck (the top of the hull). Such hulls had little longitudinal beam strength. Indeed, they were nearly as limber as a raft

**Figure 1.**

*Comparative drafts for ship-form and steamboat hulls of equivalent capacity**

**Figure 2.** A comparison of weights for ten lineal feet of hull

| Ship-form hull | | Steamboat hull | |
|---|---|---|---|
| Frames | 29,700 lb. | Frames | 11,884 lb. |
| Keelson | 1,609 lb. | Keelson | 685 lb. |
| Keel | 604 lb. | Keel | 0 lb. |
| Planking | 9,075 lb. | Planking | 7,838 lb.[1] |
| Ceiling | 8,348 lb. | Ceiling | 0 lb. |
| Deck | 5,184 lb. | Deck | 7,178 lb.[2] |
| Totals | 54,560 lb. | Totals | 27,585 lb. |

Note: Weight of minor members such as futtocks, brackets, cocked hats, and clamps are not included in this analysis.

[1]Planking was half as thick. Because the perimeter of the streamboat hull is greatest, the weight of the planking is more than half of the ship-form hull.

[2]Deck was three-fourths as thick. Because the width of the deck is greater, its weight is more than the ship-form hull.

and flexed with the waves of the water and the strokes of the engines. This problem was resolved in the late 1840s with the development of the hog frame. Even in still water, a long, limber hull would droop at the ends and rise at midships, a condition

called hogging. On side-wheel boats this condition was somewhat ameliorated by the centrally located weight of the boilers and machinery, but stern-wheelers had the engines located far aft and were additionally burdened by the paddle wheel, which had no buoyancy at all.

The hog frame consisted of a number of diagonal or vertical posts, called braces, resting on the hull-bottom frame with iron rods, called chains, fixed in the bottom at the ends and carried over the tops of the hog-chain braces. This made a light, strong

**Figure 3.**

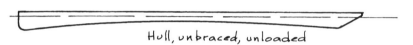

**Figure 4.**

*If long, limber hulls were unbraced, they would bend as indicated in Figure 4.*

truss with the hull itself in compression and with the rods resisting the tensile forces. The complete system pulled the ends of the hull upward and pushed the midships downward, thus resisting the hogging effect.

*All drawings in this essay are by Alan L. Bates, and all photos are in Alan L. Bates's Collection. The illustrations are reprinted by permission from *The Western Rivers Steamboat Cyclopoedium* by Alan L. Bates (Leonia, NJ: Hustle Press, 1968, 1981).

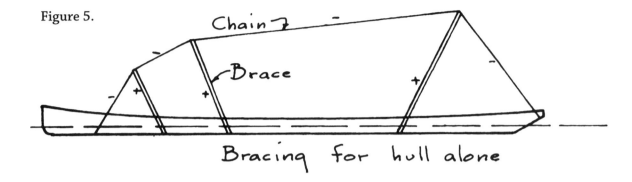

Figure 5.

Chain

Brace

Bracing for hull alone

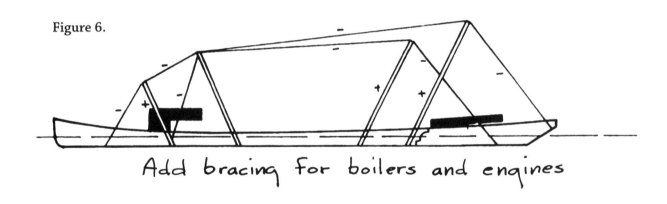

Figure 6.

Add bracing for boilers and engines

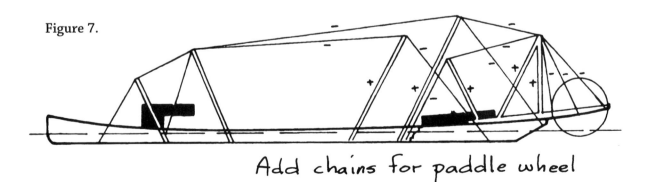

Figure 7.

Add chains for paddle wheel

**Figure 8.**

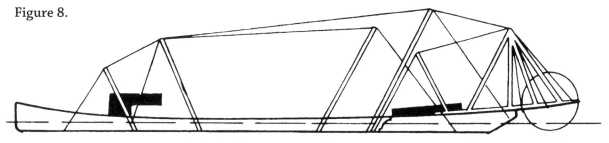

Add braces for paddle wheel and complete hog-chain system.

**Figure 9.**

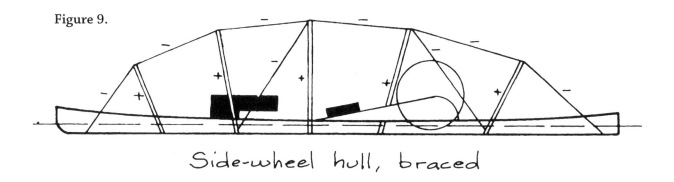

Side-wheel hull, braced

*In Figures 5 through 9, the braces, shown as double lines, were in compression ( + ) and pushed the hull downward. The hog chains, shown in single lines, were in tension ( - ) and lifted the hull upward.*

**Figure 10.**

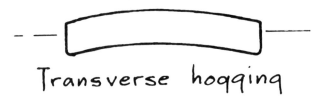

**Figure 11.**

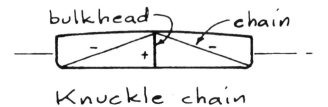

**Figure 12.**

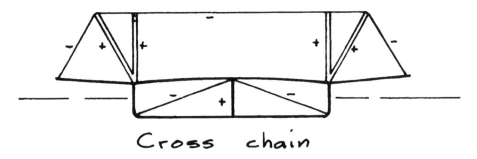

*Boats, especially side-wheelers, could hog laterally. Figures 10 through 12 show how lateral hogging was resisted.*

The passenger accommodations were in a second deck cabin. There were no private staterooms; passengers slept in berths surrounded by curtains. Everything was made as light as possible, and as a result the boat literally heaved and bent in time with the strokes of the engine. Even so, the engines were not powerful enough for rapid movement in the Mississippi.

**Figure 13.**

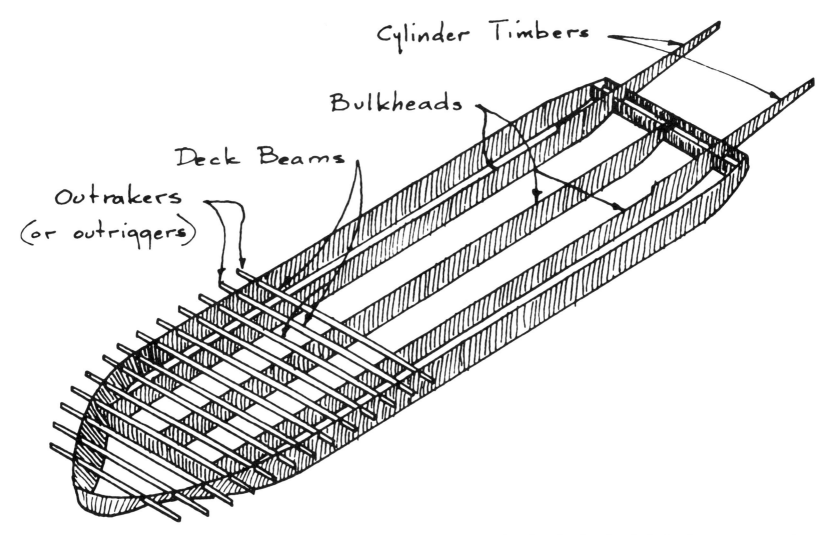

Cylinder Timbers

Bulkheads

Deck Beams

Outrakers
(or outriggers)

*Figures 13 through 18 show how the fully developed superstructure, or cabin, was framed. The superstructure was built of very thin and light wood, for every pound saved there enabled the steamboat to carry another pound of freight.*

Figure 14.

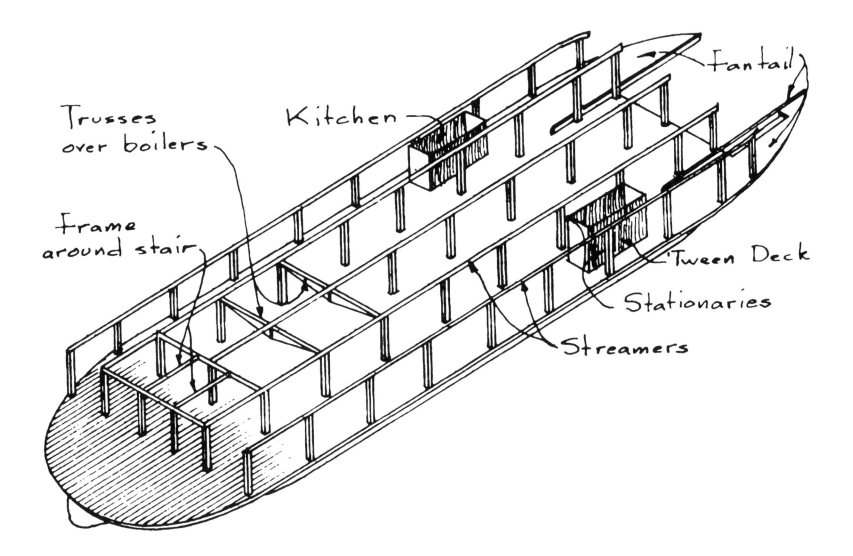

Fantail

Kitchen

Trusses
over boilers

Frame
around stair

'Tween Deck

Stationaries

Streamers

Figure 15.

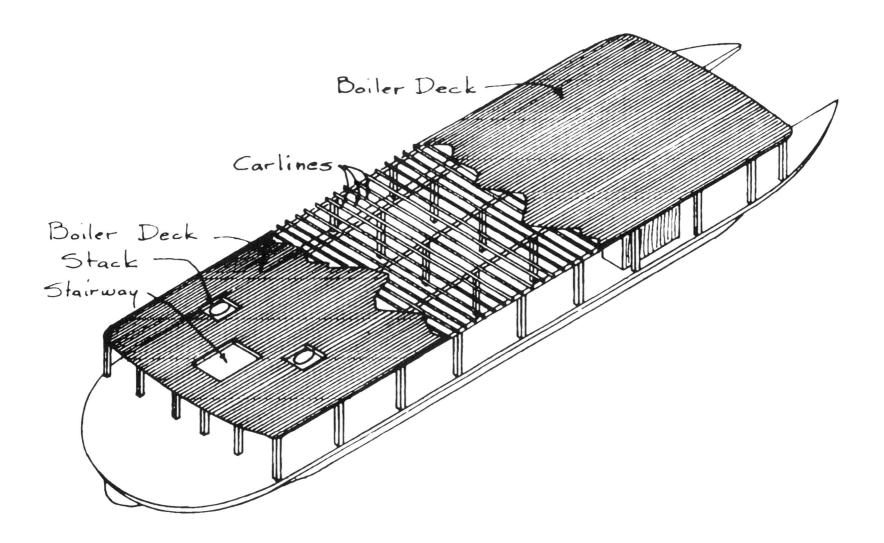

Boiler Deck

Carlines

Boiler Deck
Stack
Stairway

Figure 16.

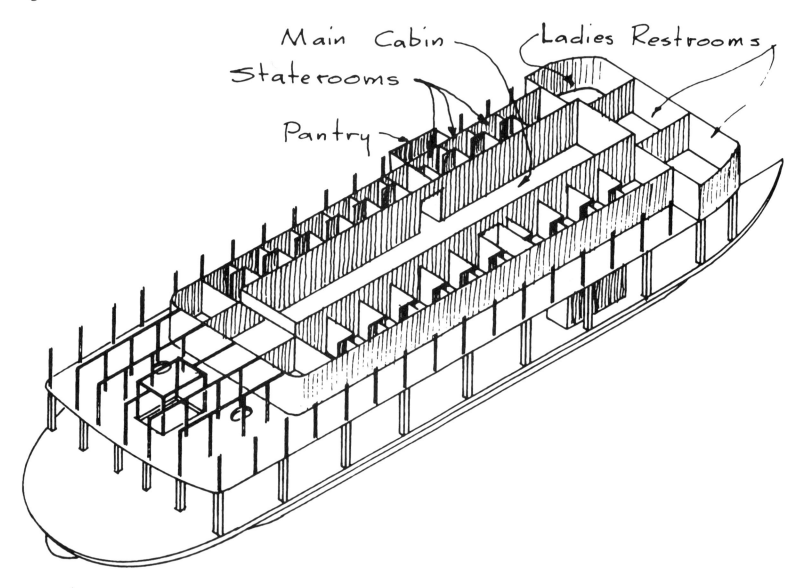

Figure 17.

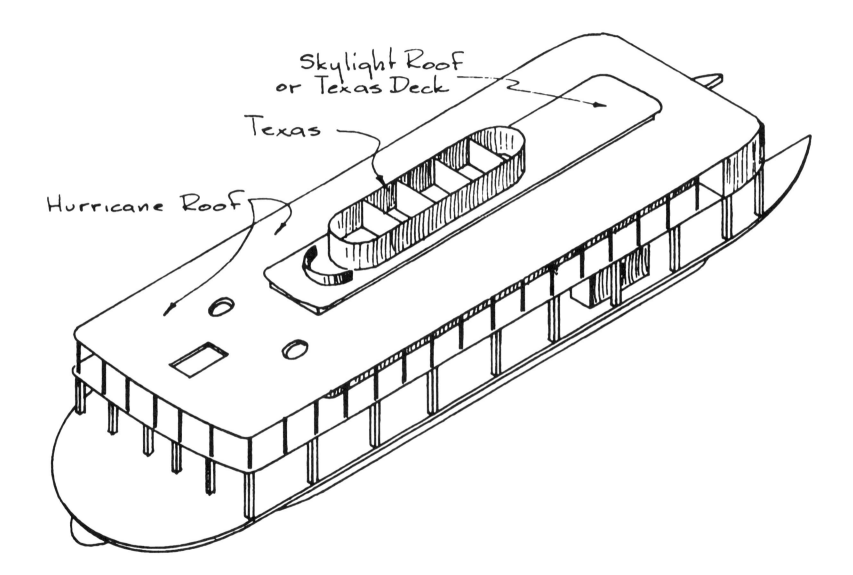

Skylight Roof or Texas Deck

Texas

Hurricane Roof

Figure 18.

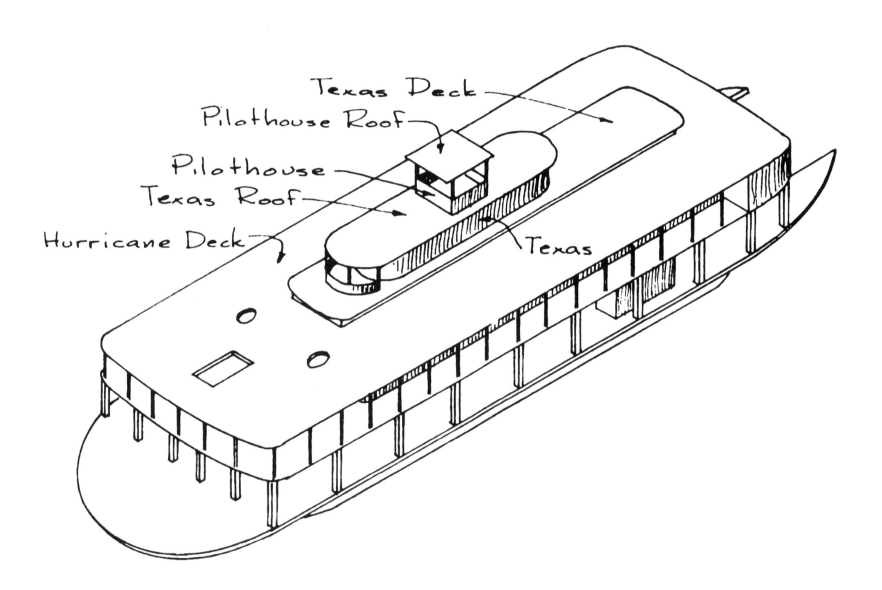

Texas Deck

Pilothouse Roof

Pilothouse

Texas Roof

Hurricane Deck

Texas

**Figure 19.**

**Figure 20.**

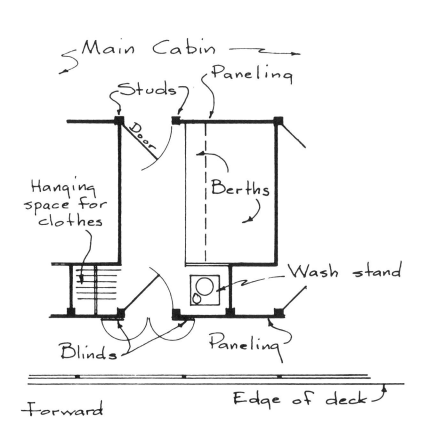

Main Cabin

Paneling

Studs

Door

Berths

Hanging space for clothes

Wash stand

Blinds

Paneling

Edge of deck

Forward

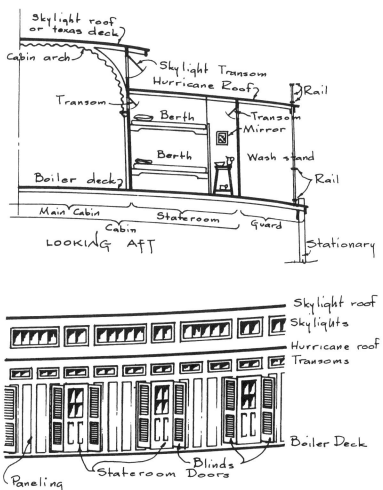

Skylight roof or texas deck

Cabin arch

Skylight Transom
Hurricane Roof

Rail

Transom

Berth

Transom Mirror

Berth

Wash stand

Boiler deck

Rail

Main Cabin

Stateroom

Guard

Cabin

LOOKING AFT

Stationary

Skylight roof
Skylights

Hurricane roof
Transoms

Boiler Deck

Paneling

Stateroom Doors

Blinds

**Figure 21.** River boat structure

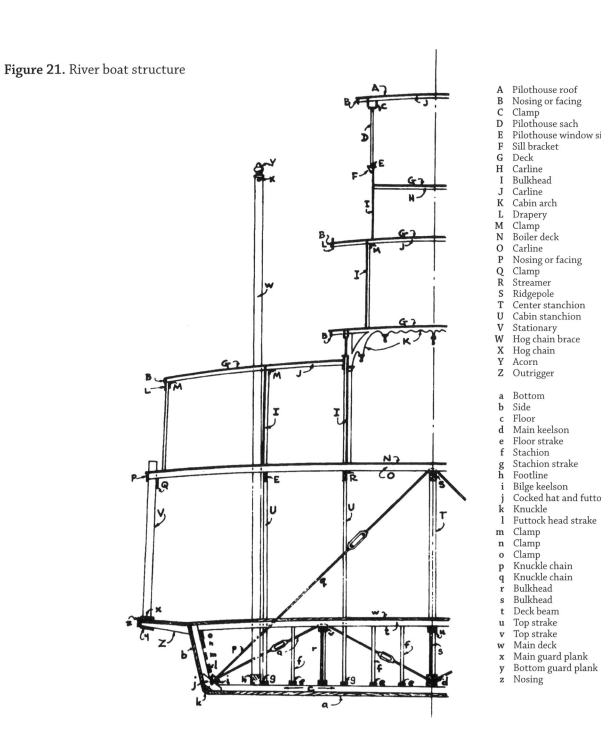

A   Pilothouse roof
B   Nosing or facing
C   Clamp
D   Pilothouse sach
E   Pilothouse window sill
F   Sill bracket
G   Deck
H   Carline
I   Bulkhead
J   Carline
K   Cabin arch
L   Drapery
M   Clamp
N   Boiler deck
O   Carline
P   Nosing or facing
Q   Clamp
R   Streamer
S   Ridgepole
T   Center stanchion
U   Cabin stanchion
V   Stationary
W   Hog chain brace
X   Hog chain
Y   Acorn
Z   Outrigger

a   Bottom
b   Side
c   Floor
d   Main keelson
e   Floor strake
f   Stachion
g   Stachion strake
h   Footline
i   Bilge keelson
j   Cocked hat and futtock
k   Knuckle
l   Futtock head strake
m   Clamp
n   Clamp
o   Clamp
p   Knuckle chain
q   Knuckle chain
r   Bulkhead
s   Bulkhead
t   Deck beam
u   Top strake
v   Top strake
w   Main deck
x   Main guard plank
y   Bottom guard plank
z   Nosing

Figure 19 shows a typical stateroom plan. The cabin studs formed doorjambs and corners, and the spaces between studs were clad with light paneling or with vertical boards. Each stateroom had two doors, one leading into the main cabin, or saloon, and one opening to the deck. There were transoms above the doors and upper berths for light and ventilation. The lower berth was for two persons, and the upper (shown by dashes) was for one. Offsets in the bulkheads between staterooms provided a small closet and a washstand with pitcher, bowl, and chamber pot. A dime-store mirror was hung above the washstand.

Following 1817 progress was swift, and the best steamboats evolved into a marvelous combination of the freight carrier and elegant resort hotel of song and story. Shipyards were established at many points along the rivers, and their ancillary suppliers multiplied. Local foundries made engines. Tinners, roofers, painters, planing mills, and furniture plants were established to serve residents as well as the boats. By 1845 to 1850 the process was complete, and steamboats assumed their now-familiar shapes. Steamboats capable of speeds up to twenty-two miles per hour were built. Passenger staterooms became truly private, and many of the amenities of the day were provided. Ham-hock and collard-greens cooks were replaced by chefs. The boats became relatively safe.

Achieving lightness was not limited to hull construction. There is evidence that Fulton's boiler was borne on a masonry foundation. The Boulton-and-Watt steeple engine was very heavy and complex for its time. The steam pressure was low and depended upon a condenser to provide a vacuum to literally draw the piston. The piston area had to be very large to achieve enough power. Like most pioneering devices the fact that it ran at all was enough; perfection came later, when boiler pressures were raised to increase the efficiency and lightness of the engines. (For pistons of equal area, high-pressure steam produced more power. Conversely, high-pressure engines could be as powerful with a smaller piston area.)

Emphasis must be placed on the utter ignorance of the early builders and operators of steamboats. Boilers were made by smiths, and castings were made by iron-pot founders. There were no testing laboratories to verify the strength and consistency of boiler sheets, pipes, or engine components. There were no safety valves to relieve excessive boiler pressures, nor were there accurate gauges to measure those pressures. For many years boiler explosions were regarded as "acts of God." Nobody knew the effects of silt in boilers, and many believed some sort of "electric fluid" caused boilers to explode like thunder. Hundreds of steamboat crew members and passengers gave up their lives to this ignorance as high-pressure steam confined in boilers of unknown strength led to disastrous explosions with large life and property loss.

By the 1830s the public and state and federal governments began to protest the carnage. Slowly, engineers and philosophers began to analyze what happened in those catastrophes. The importance of simple cleanliness began to be recognized. In 1838 Congress passed a steamboat inspection law. It was a poor thing, one that expected owners and steamboat engineers to regulate themselves. The never-ending quest for speed and greed was not overcome. In 1853 a new Steamboat Inspection Service was formed. The inspectors had the power to examine candidates for licenses and to prosecute offenders as well as to inspect and demand corrections and repairs to the steamboats. This law was not accepted meekly. In fact, one prominent steamboat captain complained, "What's the use of being a steamboat captain if you can't tell everybody to 'go to Hell'?" Furthermore, the law applied only to passenger steamboats and their officers.

Towing vessels were exempt until some of them blew up alongside passenger packets, destroying both. Revisions and additions to the law established rules for running lights; examinations for masters, pilots, engineers, and mates; and criminal penalties for negligence or disobedience.

Meanwhile, in addition to the never-ending effort to attain lightness, steamboat designers began to give considerable thought to aesthetics. The disparate and awkward elements of paddle wheels, smokestacks, pilothouses, and various appurtenances were difficult to organize in a unified design. The steamboat designers of the United States, Britain and, to a lesser extent, Germany were alone in the world in achieving this concept. The steamboat architects of Asia, South America, Africa, and most of Europe never managed it. Their boats seem to have been gathered instead of designed.

Starting in the mid-1840s American naval architects began to adjust the incongruous masses into an integrated whole. Sheer curves (that graceful upward sweep at the ends of decks) were laid out with the mathematical precision of parabolas and ellipses. Side bulkheads and stationaries (vertical posts) were sloped inboard at precise angles to lend an appearance of stability to the superstructure. The spring lines of paddle-wheel housings were set at the level of the boiler deck, not at the wheel-shaft center. Smokestacks were made normal to the curve of the roof and sloped outboard at an eighth of an inch per foot to overcome the effects of perspective. Deck lines were softened by jigsawed drapery. Elaborate decoration and adornment kept pace with the finest Victorian buildings and dwellings on land. By the end of the Civil War, the steamboat had developed into the fabulous form Americans recognize. Very little change occurred after that time.

Americans, especially those of the Mississippi River system, were justly proud of their steamboats. Behind all of the colorful décor, there was a real boat beautifully adapted to the waters on which it ran. The steamboat, as the first self-propelled vehicle, not only carried the freight and the passengers in a totally untamed environment, it also created an industrial empire to create and support it. Within two decades after the introduction of the *New Orleans*, the American West was transformed from a wilderness into a cultural and industrial entity of incalculable worth.

The change from wooden to steel construction was marked by the same reluctance to innovation that Fulton and Roosevelt experienced regarding engine and hull design. The transition was a gradual process that began in 1873 with the building of the towboat *Alex Swift*. This boat demonstrated the advantages of ferrous hulls: strength, lightness, and longevity. Connections

*The* Senator Cordill *shows the charming beauty of the vessels that were made from the rough lumber strewn about the Howard Shipyard and Dock Company at Jeffersonville, Indiana.*

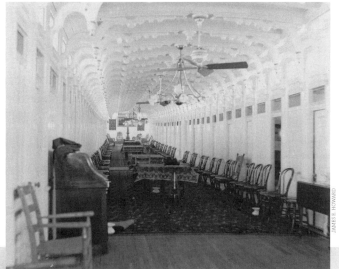

JAMES E. HOWARD

Steamboats were not built entirely by the shipyards indicated in the records. Subcontractors did much of the work. This view of the cabin of the Belle of the Bends *shows a desk and other furniture, electric lights and fans, carpets, spittoons, and transom glazing, all done by specialty firms. The cabin's elaborate woodwork could have been made by either the Howard mill or an outside firm.*

JAMES E. HOWARD

*The* E. R. ANDREWS *was a towboat built at the Howard Shipyard and Dock Company during the transition from wood hulls to steel hulls. The hull frame, sides, and deck were made of steel, the bottom of oak. The boat sits on the launching ways, ready to slide into the Ohio River upon completion. Although the lumber in the foreground seems to be scattered randomly, it was to be used for construction.*

*Beautiful packets and doughty towboats were not the only products of boatyards. The* Fort Chartres *was a snag boat used for clearing trees and wrecks from the river bottom and banks.*

between members of steel frames were much more rigid and easier to make than with wood. Iron and steel did not become waterlogged and gain weight over the years. A thin skin of these metals was far stronger than the thick planks needed for wooden hulls. The thousands of feet of caulking required to make watertight the joints between wooden planks was not necessary.

Despite the advantages of steel, the mariners' resistance to change and the extra costs associated with iron and steel construction delayed the transition for decades. The cost of the metal and especially the cost of the machinery and training needed to fabricate it were disadvantages to steel construction. Tools and equipment had to be devised and purchased. Lifting, carrying, and placement of large, heavy steel plates could not be done manually. The shipyards were obliged to acquire efficient powered mobile cranes to do such work. Drilling, punching, and cutting of iron and steel demanded specialized and expensive equipment. Shipwrights had to be retrained.

By the end of the 1890s steel hulls became larger and more common. Yet, the techniques of wooden design lingered on for many years. Hulls were built of wood with iron or steel reinforcing frames, steel frames with wooden bottoms, and steel bottoms with wooden sides. The hog-chain system of bracing was gradually replaced by trusses within and above the hull. By the 1930s the hog chains were totally eliminated.

Concurrent with the transition from wood to steel was a revolution in hull subdivision. In the wood-hull era boats were ordinarily built with but one watertight bulkhead near the bow to isolate damage from collisions. The rest of the hull was wide open and subject to flooding when breeched anywhere aft of the collision bulkhead. With the advent of steel construction, designers realized that longitudinal bulkheads added much

stiffness to hulls. Common practice divided the hull into four longitudinal compartments, and a number of lateral bulkheads further subdivided those compartments into spaces small enough that flooding one, two, or more of them would not sink the boat.

The days of design "in the wood" were past. No longer could an owner or a builder make a sketch on the back of an envelope and build a boat from it. Extreme care became the norm in construction planning. Analyses of stresses and strains on the frames and skin now were performed by trained engineers. Rivet holes had to be accurately measured on both the skin and the frames to which it was attached. Rivets in seams connecting sheets of the skin were equally difficult, especially where plates and sheets were curved. Detailed blueprints were required to locate all of those holes. Draftsmen and engineers had to be trained. Heavy boring, punching, and shearing machines replaced the saw, the adze, and the plane. The techniques of handling and securing white-hot rivets had to be mastered. Riveted construction was the norm until the beginning of the 1940s.

The development of electric-arc welding during the late 1930s and the active stimulation of its techniques during World War II virtually eliminated the rivet as a connection. Where rivets had been used, connections became either bolted or welded. Welding had the advantage that it eliminated the necessity for caulking seams between sheets. Following the lead of the airplane industry, stressed-skin design improved the rigidity of the entire hull structure.

For many decades wooden cabins continued to be built on steel hulls. Today cabins are both framed and sheathed with steel. Wood is commonly used for interior finishes, but on certain classes of vessels (warships and passenger-carrying boats)

JAMES E. HOWARD

*The transition from wood to steel construction was not easy. This was a gore made by curving a flat steel plate. Seamstresses used the term "gore" in exactly the same way. The holes to receive rivets presented a difficult problem in both drafting room and seamstress shop.*

they have been largely replaced with fire-resistant artificial materials to protect the steel framing. This is necessary, for while steel does not burn at the temperatures of ordinary fire, that heat is sufficient to cause early failure in catastrophic fires.

Today boat and ship design must meet many requirements of the United States Coast Guard and the American Bureau of Shipping. These include not only the basic structural strength to hold the vessels together, but the designers must prove that the boat will remain afloat and upright under stringent conditions of wind, wave, and loading. Before the vessel can be certified for operation, many tests must be performed and passed. The days of empirical "by guess and by golly" design are gone forever.

*Captain Alan L. Bates is a naval architect, author, and columnist for the* Waterways Journal. *He supervised the restoration of the* Belle of Louisville, *and his book,* Str. Belle of Louisville *(1964),*

remains a standard source on the history of the boat and the crews who worked on her. All of his books have been cited as authoritative sources on naval architecture. In 2010 Bates received the National Achievement Award from the National Rivers Museum and Hall of Fame in Dubuque, Iowa.

*The author gratefully acknowledges the assistance of Captain James E. Howard, owner and president of the Howard Shipyard and Dock Company in Jeffersonville, Indiana. Howard taught Bates the practices and materials of steamboat architecture and building during a series of interviews from 1953 until Howard's death in 1958. The meetings were informal. Howard allowed Bates to see and handle many of the drafting tools used during his time at the business, he answered the author's questions in detail, and he showed many photographs of the work at the boatyard to Bates. These discussions are the source of much of the author's knowledge. As Bates comments, "To 'sit at the knee' of such a man was a great privilege."*

## SELECTED BIBLIOGRAPHY

Flexner, James Thomas. *Steamboats Come True: American Inventors in Action.* New York: Viking Press, 1944. Repr., Boston: Little, Brown, and Company, 1978.

Hunter, Louis C. *Steamboats on the Western Rivers: An Economic and Technological History.* Cambridge, MA: Harvard University Press, 1949. Repr., New York: Octagon Books, 1969.

Way, Frederick, Jr. *Way's Packet Directory, 1848–1994.* Athens: Ohio University Press, 1994.

Way, Capt. Frederick, Jr., and Capt. J. W. Rutter. *Way's Steam Towboat Directory.* Athens: Ohio University Press, 1990.

# 3

## A Synoptic History of Towboating and Its Origins

JACK E. CUSTER

### Early River Coal Movement

The records of early river coal shipments are so sparse that our total knowledge of the river coal industry from 1789 to 1799 is the vague awareness that there was such a trade. The earliest river shipment of coal on record is a small quantity brought down by a flatboat from Pittsburgh, Pennsylvania, to the Falls of the Ohio in 1789.

Towing, not towboating, in a rudimentary sense began early in the steamboat era. Keelboats were tied to the guards of the primordial packets and taken in tow on their upstream runs to expand the packets' freight-carrying capacity without increasing their draft. Towboating, such as we know it now, came ca. 1845–55. From the 1840s through the 1860s, nonpowered coal boats brought coal down the Ohio River from Pittsburgh as far south as New Orleans.

The flatboat was briefly used to transport coal. The increasing demand for the fuel in the young United States fomented the evolution of flatboats into coal boats similar to those used in the late nineteenth and early twentieth centuries. In the beginning, keelboats were used for coal shipment. After the keelboat

came the larger broadhorn, a variation on the basic flatboat, and from the broadhorn evolved the coal boat. The broadhorn evidently took its name from its bovine appearance from a distance, with the sweeps extended on each side at its stern. Generally, two coal boats were lashed together to form a pair, and the crew's quarters on each were aligned with one another. One could then be used for a kitchen and the other as a dormitory for both coal boats.

The only available motive power came from the river's current; and steering was provided by the immense sweeps, large oars, mounted on coal boats at their sterns. Handling coal boats was definitely a province of sweat and muscle power, not steam. The first coal boats were about 140 feet long and 22 feet wide and had a capacity of between 16,000 and 24,000 bushels of coal. The largest early coal boats measured 185 feet long and 32 feet wide.

The first recorded coal craft descended the Mississippi in 1829, when Captain George "Old Natural" Miller of Louisville, Kentucky, and others constructed two flats, 80 feet in length by 15 feet in width and loaded to 4 feet. Miller and his associates loaded the coal, mined at Bon Harbor, approximately three miles west of Owensboro, Kentucky, in the two flats and then took them down the Ohio and Mississippi rivers. The coal was sold to the LaBranche Sugar Plantation.

For about the first three decades of the nineteenth century, coal boats brought down mixed cargoes from Pittsburgh, which included coal as well as household utensils, agricultural implements, and sundry provisions that were peddled among settlers living along the river. During the early 1830s the increased demand for coal throughout the South became so great that it was the most valuable cargo that could be carried downstream. In New Orleans coal was exchanged for sugar and molasses, commodities not readily available in western Pennsylvania.

The early river shipments of coal depended totally on the rises in the unimproved, free-flowing Ohio River. Whenever there was sufficient water to create natural rises, coal boats would float down the Ohio from Pittsburgh, and towns and villages along the way would receive supplies of coal. During times of low water, coal could not be shipped, leading to times of privation, loss of income, discomfort, and stress.

*The packet* Golden Rule *at Cincinnati near the Roebling Suspension Bridge, ca. 1870s. Her hurricane deck is filled with barrels, buggies, and boxes. Alongside her starboard side is a freight barge loaded with more barrels. On her port side (barely visible at the bow) is a large covered model barge, which could handle approximately 1,200 to 1,600 tons of freight. The* Golden Rule *has expanded her capacity considerably by taking the two barges in tow.*

During the first half of the nineteenth century, nearly all the coal brought down the river was transported in coal boats. Although steamboats had already become a major factor for inland transportation, their arrival did not drive the manually powered flatboats, keelboats, and coal boats from the river immediately. A steamboat represented a huge capital investment for the time, and that investment could quickly be lost because of snags, boiler explosions, and a host of other factors that could destroy a steamboat within seconds. Steamboat operation required federal licenses from the Steamboat Inspection Service after 1852, whereas there was no licensing for flatboats, keelboats, and/or coal boats, and their operational costs and capital investment were much less than steamboats. Not until ca. 1860 did the towboat become sufficiently significant in transportation to affect the entrenched, manually powered coal boat trade.

The Falls of the Ohio at Louisville formed the dividing line for steamboat operations—steamboats that operated above the Falls were different from those that operated below the Falls. Boats that operated above the Falls tended to be smaller in order to go through the constricted Louisville and Portland Canal; whereas boats that operated only below the Falls were larger. Although side-wheel packets had been operating successfully for more than two decades in the 1830s, towboating came much later. In 1845 Daniel Bushnell, an early towboating pioneer, began towing coal down the Ohio with a stern-wheel towboat, the *Walter Forward*. His experiment was taking three coal flats, each loaded with two thousand bushels, to Cincinnati. However, as he discovered, towboats were not yet adequate for this job. It was not until five years later that the *Lake Erie*, a stern-wheel packet of 1845 that was better modified for towing, began towing coal down the Ohio.

We should note that the early downstream towboating tended to stay above the Falls of the Ohio at Louisville. Successful upstream towboating, such as we know it, came about by 1854. Three side-wheelers built in 1853, the *Joseph Landis*, *Dick Keys*, and *Peter Tellon*, brought their tows over the inundated Falls in early 1854.

However, the towboat had a minor role in the downstream movement of coal during the early 1850s. Initial attempts to use steam as a motive power for coal boats were not successful. One reason was that many early towboats were side-wheelers. Even though the side-wheeler was the predominant type of steamboat in the first half of the nineteenth century, it was not suitable for towing barges because of its inherent physical limitations in handling them. Trial and error led the early towboaters to conclude that the stern-wheeler was the most suitable type of steamboat for towing.

Gradually stern-wheelers supplanted the early side-wheel towboats because their multiple rudders provided much better handling. In 1856 Captain James A. Blackmore built the stern-wheel towboat *Coal Hill* at Brownsville, Pennsylvania, using the engines from the *Wheeler Boone*. Blackmore, one of the early towboat designers and builders, became a most important figure in the towboat's early development, especially in the 1860s and 1870s, and his *Coal Hill* became an archetype for early towboat design.

For a brief period in the early 1860s, the vanishing manual coal-boating industry and the nascent steam towboating industry operated side by side. The reason for their coexistence was the fact that the manual coal boats could operate in the shallow water of the unimproved rivers, while towboats had to lay up while the water level was down.

The transition from manual-powered coal boats to steam towboats taking tows of coal boats downstream occurred gradually. Twenty-eight years would pass after the first tow of coal was taken from Pittsburgh to New Orleans before the necessary piloting skills for handling large coal tows were developed and refined to the point that a single towboat could take an enormous amount of coal south, compared to the limitations of manually running coal in coal boats. No less important were the vast improvements in steam machinery and boilers that allowed larger and larger tows of coal boats to be handled safely.

The immediate result of the towboat's introduction to the river coal trade was a reduction in coal's cost for the consumer. This stemmed from a reduction in the number of crewmen needed to handle greater amounts of coal, and a reduction in the amount of coal lost in transit. In the heyday of manual coal boating, thirty pairs of coal boats manned by five hundred men could bring 1,250,000 bushels of coal down the river from Pittsburgh to New Orleans, and a loss of 20 percent was always anticipated before the matter of profit was considered. By 1902, however, less than one hundred men were required to move the same amount of coal in a towboat, and no more than 2 percent of the coal was lost between the shipping point and its destination.

The war period, 1861 to 1865, brought a huge increase in western Pennsylvania's coal production. Running coal to hostile regions, though dangerous, was enormously profitable. The Union defeated the Confederacy at places such as Fort Henry, Fort Donelson, Shiloh, and Vicksburg largely through the use of steam power on the rivers and rails. The increased need for coal during the war quickly rendered the old-fashioned manual coal-boating industry obsolete. Gradually, steam-powered stern-wheel towboats bringing tows of coal boats from Pittsburgh to New Orleans mechanized the industry.

Because of the towboat, the Union had ready access to coal for military purposes, whereas the beleaguered Confederacy did not. It took huge amounts of Pennsylvania coal for the Union forces to generate the steam needed to win the war. W. H. Brown, of W. H. Brown and Sons, one of the largest Pittsburgh river coal operators of the second half of the nineteenth century, acquired his immense fortune by supplying coal to the U.S. government during the war.

The postwar years saw the disappearance of the manual coal-boating operations and the rise of the expanding steam towboating industry. In 1863 Captain Richard C. Gray and Captain M. W. Beltzhoover organized Gray's Iron Line, the first major towboating operation, using the towboats *Little Giant* and *Rover*. During the remaining years of the nineteenth century, Gray's Iron Line added the towboats *Ironsides*, *Iron Mountain*, *Iron Age*, *Iron Duke*, and *Resolute*. Gray's Iron Line moved finished products as well as bulk commodities in thirty model (pointed bow) barges, which could each handle approximately 1,400 tons. On their trips back up the Ohio River to Pittsburgh, the Gray's Iron Line model barges carried iron ore from Missouri and/or iron from the Cumberland River iron furnaces. On their downstream runs from Pittsburgh, the same model barges were heavily laden with steel railroad rails, barrels of nails and spikes, cotton ties, barbed wire, and a variety of heavy hardware items.

In the years after the war, numerous men made sizable fortunes from the river coal trade.   Among the better-known names were J. N. and W. W. O'Neil, Joseph Walton, J. C. Risher, S. H. Crump, Thomas Fawcett, and W. H. Brown. Many opulent coal barons had started out in coal boating in the 1840s and gravitated toward towboating in the 1860s, when much money came from supplying the Union with coal during the war years. From the mid-1860s through the late 1890s towboating on the Ohio and Mississippi rivers was dominated by the coal trade out of Pittsburgh to New Orleans and by the grain trade in model barges from Saint Louis to New Orleans.

In 1866 the Mississippi Valley Transportation Company was organized to ship grain from Saint Louis to New Orleans. This was another model barge operation, whose guiding light was Henry C. Haarstick. In the 1880s the railroad mogul Jay Gould set up a similar model barge operation at the Saint Louis and New Orleans Transportation Company for shipping grain. In the wake of a depression during the 1880s, the two competing model barge operations were subsequently merged to form the Saint Louis and Mississippi Valley Transportation Company. The resulting consolidation was an operation with twelve towboats, approximately one hundred model grain barges, each with a 50,000-bushel capacity, and grain elevators in Belmont, Missouri, and New Orleans. The company also had marine ways at Mound City, Illinois. The huge grain operation died out by 1904, however.

In only about one decade the towboat evolved from being a "plain Jane" to one of the most handsome, powerful specimens of steamboating aesthetics, design, and architecture. By the late 1870s and early 1880s, some towboats were most impressive floating beasts of burden. They readily stood out from other boats in their mundane trade of transporting bulk commodities.

## Steps in the Towboat's Nineteenth-Century Development

There were eleven developmental steps in the towboat's evolution from 1860 to 1902:

(1) An important first step in the development of towboats was the standardization of the construction of a heavy generic bottom that could be used for a coal boat or a barge. From the 1840s until the late 1860s, coal boats were one-way entities, dismantled at their destinations. By the late 1860s and early 1870s, the amount of coal shipped from western Pennsylvania and from the Kanawha River Valley in West Virginia had increased so much that the one-way coal boat was no longer practical. As a result, coal boats became two-way conveyances for coal and were generally used until they were worn-out. In the twentieth century, coal-boat siding would be removed from worn-out coal boats in the New Orleans area and placed in the tows of empties being moved north. The siding would eventually be taken to the siding yards along the Monongahela River where it would be recycled and used on new bottoms.

(2) As tows of coal boats grew larger in the early 1870s, handling them safely became a paramount issue. The quantum leap in the towboat's early development was the transition from the rounded bow of the packets to the nearly rectangular head of the main deck on a coal trade towboat, which used a headlog, a heavy, squared timber, with nosing along it to cushion or pad the towboat's thrust against the pieces in her tow. The headlog's development allowed towboats to be hitched to a tow of loads or faceup to a tow of empties in a much tighter manner than had been possible in the early days when using a rounded bow. By using two to four capstans, winches used to pull in lines or to pull a steamboat into landings, at the head and using roller chocks, grooved wheels or pulleys horizontally mounted on the headlog, tows could be tightened up and kept under tension throughout a trip. In the 1870s additional capstans aft of the boilers were added on each side on the main deck to increase the tension that could be placed on a tow from the towboat. The tighter the integration with the tow a headlog and group of capstans provided, the more the towboat and

tow became a solid unit. That unification allowed pilots to have much greater control over their tows.

(3) The consequence of better control over tows led to the standard usage of heavy drivers, that is, stout coal barges in good to excellent condition, to cushion a towboat's thrust against a tow of coal boats. Without having stout drivers as buffers or idlers, powerful stern-wheel towboats could bash in coal boats' headlogs and their collision bulkheads. This was a problem for the larger and more powerful stern-wheel towboats, such as the *Joseph B. Williams* and the *Sprague*.

(4) The use of drivers in conjunction with headlogs provided much better control over tows of loaded coal barges and coal boats, and that improvement soon led to the adoption of stack knees, heavy steel plates, roughly triangular in shape, that were mounted at the corners of towboat headlogs. Although stack knees were used singly on the smaller towboats, they were used in pairs on the larger coal trade towboats to help the crew hitch their tows to their drivers. The stack knee was borrowed from the side-wheel cotton packets on the Lower Mississippi, where the stack knee was used to help roustabouts align their tiers of cotton bales. Timbers were also dropped down from the stack knees on side-wheel packets to keep flats from straying beneath their guards.

(5) After it became standard practice with loaded tows to use coal barges as drivers and stack knees at the ends of headlogs, the next developmental step was the duckpond method for handling loads. The duckpond, the space between the towboat and the first row of barges, was used to hitch a towboat to a tow in downbound movements. However, when towboats came upstream with empties, instead

of using the duckpond, they faced up to their empties and usually employed coal barges as drivers to cushion their thrust against coal boats.

(6) As a result of handling larger tows of empties, towing knees, set between the paired stack knees at each end of the headlog, gradually became the conventional means for towboats to face up to tows of empties. However, some towboats, such as the *Iron Mountain*, *Onward*, and *Volunteer*, never had towing knees and ran successfully with only stack knees.

(7) The significant structural entity that allowed towboats to grow in length and permitted their long, limber wooden towboat hulls to use more powerful nine- or ten-foot stroke engines was the development of the solid built-up footland, such as that used in the *Joseph B. Williams* of 1876. Footlands were heavy longitudinal timbers running from the bow area to the stern, used to stiffen the hull.

(8) One beneficial towboating operational technique that opportunely dovetailed with the footlands, used in conjunction with setting the hog chains, their posts, and clevises, which were iron yokes, into the heavy, solid, longitudinal footlands, was the towboat practice of filling the coal room, on the main deck between the boiler room and the engine room of towboats, with two hundred to five hundred tons of coal. This coal pressed down on the main deck and served as a shock absorber to damp the shock waves emanating from the towboat's long-stroke main engines, especially in the case of large, tandem compound engines, which used high- and low-pressure cylinders mounted end-to-end and center. Without an adequate supply of coal on board, a towboat's

engines could cause serious structural damage and even break hog chains. Normally, coal used for fuel on towboats came from fuel flats tied alongside their guards. The coal heaped in the coal room to suppress engine shock waves would not be used for fuel unless there were no other supplies of coal available and the destination was not far.

(9) From 1876 through 1899, the towboat's design remained relatively static, though with occasional aesthetic refinements and minor mechanical improvements. However, another quantum leap in the towboat's evolution came as a result of J. M. Hammett's use of double hog chains on the

*J. B. Finley* in 1899. Although the *Finley* came out with single hog chains, it was soon realized that her heavier engines would require double hog chains to supply additional structural support for her boilers, engines, and stern-wheel. The solid built-up footland running from nearly the bow to the stern on towboats, presumably dating back to the *Joseph B. Williams* of 1876, used together with double hog chains, allowed the safe usage of tandem compound engines on the largest towboats.

(10) The length of towboats visibly increased from the 1880s through 1902. That extended length placed the towboats'

*The* Tornado, *built by black steamboat builder, Cumberland W. Posey, sitting on the dry bottom of the Ohio River. The towboat left Pittsburgh on a rise, but the rise gave out and the* Tornado *had to remain here until the next rise came. As soon as her master realized that the boat was stuck, he would have had the engineer pump the hull full of water. If a wooden hull was allowed to dry out, the planking would shrink and the seams would open. By filling the hull with water, the* Tornado's *hull planking would remain tightly swollen and ready for operation. The reason for the blankets hanging down and for the canvas shroud is to keep the sun from drying out the towboat's planking and stern-wheel, respectively.*

rudders much further aft and gave them increased leverage in steering, allowing them to handle much larger tows over the years.

(11) Although the stern-wheel towboat appears to have reached its zenith with the *Harry Brown* in 1897 and the *J. B. Finley* of 1899, the last big step at the end of the nineteenth century was the gradual transition from skeg rudders to balanced rudders. A rudder is an underwater blade used to steer a boat. Skegs were triangular pieces that formed the front half of skeg rudders. Balanced rudders did not use these triangular pieces. They were larger and their added steering surface provided easier and more effective steering.

We have neither the exact dates for most of the developments listed above nor the names of those responsible for the steps. It is likely these changes were the result of towboat builders pooling their knowledge and experience while using trial and error over the decades. The towboats of the 1870s took on a more aesthetic appearance compared to their 1860s antecedents. The notable names of the towboat designers and builders of the early era were Isaac Hammitt and James A. Blackmore. In the ensuing decades, the main names of towboat construction were Peter Sprague, J. M. Hammett, James Elliott, and Andrew Axton. These were the men who brought the stern-wheel towboat to its fruition between 1876 and 1901.

## The Combine: The Upper Limit of Steam Towboating

Throughout the 1880s and 1890s, the seasonal nature of river transportation made the shipment of freight and bulk commodities especially challenging. Regular shipments and transportation were impossible without a constant stage or level of water on the Ohio River.

As the packets' business declined drastically in the latter years of the nineteenth century, the towboat came to the steamboat industry's forefront. The coal trade between Pittsburgh and New Orleans grew at a staggering annual rate because of the increased need for fuel. However, the fragmented nature of western Pennsylvania's supply chain for bituminous coal seriously hampered the river coal industry's success. There were approximately ninety coal dealers in the Pittsburgh area. Their coal was loaded in coal boats on the Monongahela River, and then towboats towed them south to Cincinnati, Ohio; Louisville, Kentucky; Cairo, Illinois; Saint Louis, Missouri; Memphis, Tennessee; Helena, Arkansas; Vicksburg, Mississippi; Natchez, Mississippi; and New Orleans, Louisiana. The river coal operation of the 1890s was complex because there were approximately ninety different companies shipping coal, and the unions involved for engineers, firemen, and others had accordingly ninety separate contracts or agreements. This excessive fragmentation led to operational chaos in the era's towboating business.

By the late 1890s a circle of astute businessmen from outside the coal industry contemplated the possibility of consolidating the coal operations. In June 1899 Colonel J. B. Finley, a Pittsburgh banker, and Charles L. McIlvaine, a Pittsburgh lawyer, took a tour of the river coal-shipping operations from Pittsburgh to New Orleans to survey the feasibility of consolidating the manifold Pittsburgh coal operations into a single corporate entity. The two men, however, did not have the intimate knowledge of towboating and the river coal business needed to evaluate the soundness of their proposed unification. They found a consultant knowledgeable of the river coal operation in Peter Sprague, a well-known steamboat builder, designer, and repair specialist. The unlikely trio headed south in June 1899 and surveyed the river coal operations at the various river cities.

*Pittsburgh Harbor on the Monongahela River, ca. 1901-2. Numerous coal boats are awaiting the next rise, which will allow them to be towed south. An "R. C."* stenciled on the ends of the coal boats indicates that these belong to the Combine. The towboats *Pacific No. 2, Jim Wood, Tom Dodsworth, Ed Roberts, Josh Cook,* and Iron Age *are laid up for repairs or awaiting the next river rise. The pump boat at right, spewing coal smoke, is supplying steam to siphons that pump out water accumulating in the leaking coal boats.*

Sprague explained the entire towboating operation in terms that Finley and McIlvaine could understand. They observed the towboats, landings, coal fleets, elevators, and innumerable other aspects of the coal business from the Smoky City of Pittsburgh to the Crescent City of New Orleans. After surveying the operations with Sprague's expert interpretation, Finley and McIlvaine presented their findings to their partners.

As a result the Monongahela River Consolidated Coal and Coke Company was started in October 1899, merging some ninety individual companies into a $40,000,000 corporate entity with holdings from Pittsburgh to New Orleans, coal land in Pennsylvania and Kentucky, and nearly ninety towboats and tugs, ranging from the mammoth to the minuscule. Because the company's official name was such a monstrous mouthful, most steamboat men referred to the operation as "the Combine." On the stock market the company was known as "River Coal." Many famous old towboats were brought together under one corporate flag—the biggest towboating operation of its day. Even a century later the sheer scope of the Combine's extensive towboating operation on the minimally improved Ohio and Mississippi remains most impressive.

Sprague had carefully explained to Finley and McIlvaine that their critical challenge was the ability to ship coal from Pittsburgh continuously because of the still nearly free-flowing Ohio River. This meant the Combine's future growth potential would depend on Mother Nature and her seasonal rises in the Ohio.

The other logistical issue Sprague had emphasized was the vital need for a constant supply of empties being returned to Pittsburgh in order to reload the empty coal boats with mined coal and be ready to move vast tows of loaded coal boats and barges south on the next rise. The immediate result of the Combine's formation was twofold: first, it quickly pushed contemporary towboating on the Ohio and Mississippi rivers to its

limits; and second, the lowly, empty coal boat instantly acquired an unwonted industrial celebrity status. The arrival of enough empty coal boats could quickly ensure the success of a coal run on a rise at Pittsburgh, or a shortage of empty coal boats could paralyze the river coal trade.

The Combine's challenge was having the number of loaded coal boats coming south balanced by the same number being towed back upstream as empties. This suddenly became a crucial logistical issue as the Combine boosted river coal shipments to levels previously unknown. As the Combine faced this challenge, it lost one of its towboats. On October 24, 1900, at Wood's Landing below Pittsburgh, the Combine's venerable *Smoky City*, built by Blackmore in 1872, unexpectedly went up in flames. Her total loss meant the Combine had one less towboat available to bring empties upstream. This towboat's fiery loss was catalytic in that it brought serious attention to the Combine's desperate need to deal with the imminent empty coal boat crisis. Although the Combine briefly deliberated over whether to build a replacement for the *Smoky City* using a wooden hull and conventional high-pressure engines, the company instead decided to build the largest towboat of all time, the *Sprague*. The Combine assigned *Smoky City*'s replacement to Sprague. His abundant knowledge and expertise would take the stern-wheel towboat to its upper physical limits.

In early 1901 Sprague drew up his towboat design. The idea for the proposed towboat came from Captain Augustus Jutte, one of the most knowledgeable men in the river coal trade and a member of the Combine's board of directors. Jutte proposed that instead of having the Combine's larger towboats slowed down by having to tow enormous tows of empty coal boats back upstream to Louisville from New Orleans, there should be one large, powerful towboat assigned to moving huge tows of empties upstream. Utilizing this one towboat to handle much larger tows of empty coal boats than was previously possible would allow the other towboats to head upstream faster because they would be bringing smaller tows of empties.

Pressing need superseded prudent planning and engineering for design of the proposed towboat. Sprague followed an outdated, inopportune steamboat-building philosophy of the 1870s: "Just build it bigger and stronger; and you won't go wrong." In his effort to design a towboat capable of bringing more empties upriver more quickly, Sprague exceeded all known physical and mechanical limits of contemporary towboat design. Despite the fact the Combine intended for this gargantuan towboat to revolutionize towboating and solve the empties problem, she did not do so immediately. Instead, two deficiencies in her engineering caused her to be a nearly dismal failure for about three and half years. William Hopkins, the chief engineer of the Iowa Iron Works in Dubuque, Iowa, failed to build her hull with the longer footlands that Sprague intended, causing her lengthy hull to be dangerously weak. As a result, her cylinder timbers, long timbers used to support a steamboat's engines and sternwheel, could not be adequately stabilized and required extensive reinforcement. Sprague also erroneously thought single hog chains, rather than double hog chains, would be sufficient. The insufficient hog chains, in conjunction with the inadequate footlands, caused serious mechanical and structural problems.

The Monongahela River Consolidated Coal and Coke Company announced its intention to expand its coal production by 33 percent in 1903. However, most of this coal would be hauled from the mines and delivered by rail. Previously, the Combine had used river shipment almost exclusively. As the fall of 1902 approached, the company drastically altered its operational strategy. Although the Combine towboats would handle more coal during times of rail congestion, the railroads would handle more coal when the Ohio was too low to allow coal shipments from Pittsburgh. This was the Combine's first acknowledgement of its increasingly difficult struggle to ship coal on the minimally improved Ohio River.

The railroads' superior shipping reliability eventually caused the Combine to move away from shipping coal by river. One significant latent factor in the company's abandoning river shipment was the Combine's irritation with the *Sprague*'s initial engineering flaws. Her structural and mechanical problems caused much of the initial enthusiasm for the consolidated river coal trade to dissipate as railroad interests took over the Combine.

However, the *Sprague*'s flaws were gradually repaired, and she began performing in the fashion Peter Sprague had intended. Eventually, the *Sprague* reversed her initial operational problems and redeemed her tarnished reputation with a vengeance. From 1905 on, the *Sprague* performed incredible work and established a series of records that remain astonishingly impressive, especially for handling, even in today's era of the powerful diesel propeller towboat.

The *Sprague*'s operational issues served as a harbinger of the desperately needed radical changes in towboat design that would come to fruition twenty-three years later. At the same time, the Combine's need to expedite the movement of empty coal boats from New Orleans to Louisville served as a catalyst for further towboat research. Because of the flaws in Sprague's finest and final design, steamboat builders and engineers eventually addressed the conventional stern-wheel steam towboat's inherent limitations, sought solutions, and ultimately developed a far superior towboat.

Instead of looking to the past for their answers, the unimproved rivers of the early twentieth century caused towboat builders to look for alternative solutions in propellers, tunnel hulls, hulls with a concave tunnel section under the steamboat's stern used to direct water to the propellers, and eventually the

*The* Sprague *at the Howard Yard in Jeffersonville, Indiana, in late October 1905. At 318 feet in length, she was the largest towboat ever built and was legendary for her inordinate size and power. The* Sprague *was the final design of Captain Peter Sprague (1827–1905), who designed seventy-eight steamboats. This photo reveals Sprague's penchant for precise proportions, balance, and harmonious lines. It also offers a look at some of the developments in towboat design. Note the rectangular nosing and headlog around the bow, the pair of stack knees at the corner, and the row of towing knees along the edge of the bow.*

*Captain Peter Sprague's* Joseph B. Williams, *built in 1876. By comparing the* Sprague *(above, designed in 1901) with the* Joseph B. Williams *pictured here, one can see the evolution of Sprague's design talent.*

*Ward Engineering Works of Charleston, West Virginia, built the* James Rumsey *in 1903. She was a small towboat with quadruple expansion engines, a tunnel hull, and twin propellers. She and the* A. M. Scott *of 1906 foretold the future of the towboat.*

MURPHY LIBRARY, UNIVERSITY OF WISCONSIN–LACROSSE

internal combustion motor. The solution came in stages with steam propeller towboats such as the *McDougall*, *James Rumsey*, *A. M. Scott*, *Inspector*, *Clairton*, and finally in penultimate fruition with the *Geo. T. Price* and *North Star*, the first two diesel-propeller towboats, built in 1925.

In the first decade of the twentieth century there was a growing dichotomy among steamboat builders, which can be seen perhaps most clearly in Charles Ward's erudite 1907 presentation in the *Transactions of the Society of Naval Architects and Marine Engineers*. Ward revealed that there were two schools of thought in boatbuilding along the inland rivers. The first consisted of the traditional steamboat men who had learned by trial and error. The second was the group of degreed engineers and experimenters, who were looking critically at the challenges of the minimally improved Ohio River and the limitations of the steamboats that had traveled for decades on the western rivers of the United States with minimal changes in their engineering and design.

For almost a century steamboats had been built to accommodate the unimproved rivers. As the beginning years of the twentieth century passed, two things were clear to steamboat men: the packet trades had plummeted, and the long-distance coal trade from Pittsburgh to New Orleans had not fared as well as expected back in 1899. Many steamboat men failed to see the limitations that conventional steam generation and steam power were causing for them. Many old-timers who had worked their entire lives on the unimproved rivers were not yet able to see those unimproved rivers were also strangling their industry's potential success. In addition, their towboats were representative of nineteenth-century technology and could not deal with the new century's challenges. By 1910 many previously accepted ideas were being questioned. Only a few forward-looking steamboat men could see that the future would be built on the internal combustion motor and propellers rather than steam engines turning side-wheels and stern-wheels. Yet the old ways were so entrenched in most steamboat men's thinking that new solutions were difficult for them to accept.

The year 1910 became the line of demarcation for accepting or rejecting the status quo of steamboats. Under the Rivers and Harbors Act of June 25, 1910, $500,000 was provided for testing towboats and barges on nontidal rivers. This funding provided study, research, and testing of many aspects of towboating that had essentially never been questioned. The University of Michigan would test barge hull lines with models—a radical break from the traditional thinking of towboat builders and operators.

The big question of the early twentieth century was the effectiveness of stern-wheels. Conventional radial stern-wheels were reliable and practical; however, few river men comprehended the enormous amount of energy lost in the massive wakes they created and in their slippage, the difference between a stern-wheel's peripheral speed and the forward speed of the steamboat's hull, which could be 15 or 20 percent. The U.S. Army Corps of Engineers also sought to know more about the types of rudders needed and the efficacy of different types of boilers, furnaces, diesels, internal combustion motors, and so on.

One unquestioned issue in 1910 was the preference for steel hulls. It had become clear to any steamboat owner that although the wooden hull might be cheaper to build initially, in the long run the steel hull's lower maintenance needs spelled the end of the day for wooden hulls. Although many steamboat men resented the government's intrusion into their bailiwick, many questions that should have been asked about towboating's operational efficiency long beforehand were finally addressed. The other value of the government investigation was that it asked for studies on towboat propulsion from a variety of people. The ideas eventually presented ran the gamut from conventional to questionable to absurd to nearly what was needed.

The leader of the innovators on the western rivers, Charles Ward, offered his company's *A. M. Scott* for testing on March 2, 1911. The *Scott*, with a tunnel hull and twin propellers, was able to demonstrate on the Kanawha River that her innovations and capabilities were the way of the future for towboats.

## Changing Times

The Combine's massive once-profitable river operation set up to move coal to New Orleans and bring empties back to the Monongahela River had become obsolete by 1908–9, in only a decade. Even though the Combine muddled on from 1910 to 1915, the operation became a shadow of the operational dynamo it had been from 1899 to 1903. The minimally improved nature of the Ohio River brought about the dissolution of the long-distance river coal trade, and that caused the fabled operation to become moribund by 1915.

As a result of the change in the fuel markets from coal to diesel, the big stern-wheel towboats that had been the backbone of the Combine's river operation rapidly fell into obsolescence. Their fuel consumption was excessive, the operational personnel required by the Steamboat Inspection Service was excessive, and the costs of their operation and maintenance escalated beyond what had been reasonable only ten years earlier. In a surprisingly short time, the nineteenth-century engineering and design philosophies for steam towboats had become impractical, and the towboats engendered by that thinking had become outdated. By 1915 it became clear that the towboats of the past were not meeting the needs of modern towboating.

*The* Inspector *of 1915, a Ward Engineering steamboat, as she appeared in her latter days. Larger than the* Rumsey *and the* Scott, *the* Inspector *was one of a series of Ward steamboats that shook the conventional thinking of the times and paved the way for the modern diesel propeller towboat that would come in 1925.*

The period 1915–16 was bitter for many who had worked in the industry for decades. The river coal trade had been a way of life and provided relatively steady employment for five thousand people in the Pittsburgh area for half a century. The subsequent changes were traumatic in their repercussions. Most of the Combine's fabled towboats were too large and costly to be transferred to other smaller, contemporary trades. Indeed, many famous old towboats became economic dinosaurs overnight. Some were permanently laid up and consigned to the infamous boneyards, where they quickly deteriorated in an ignominious requiem of rust, rot, and ruin.

Steamboat men watched their once-solid vocations and way of life fade away almost overnight. The heyday of towboating was summarily over, and there was little work to be had on the rivers. Towboating would nearly die out in the years after the Combine's demise, but the intervention of Standard Oil Company, Union Barge Line, Mississippi Valley Barge Line, and the United States government with the U.S. Army Corps of Engineers and Federal Barge Lines gradually resuscitated it.

While the diesel era of modern towboating actually began in 1925 in Charleston, West Virginia, and Nashville, Tennessee, the roots of the energy transition from steam to diesel go back to the first decade of the twentieth century. Many small gasoline-powered stern-wheel and propeller boats were built all along the rivers. Since their machinery was very light in comparison with steam machinery, they drew little water and could easily go to places steamboats could not reach. Some larger gas boats were used for maneuvering individual wooden barges or coal boats.

These small boats were homemade, inexpensive to operate, and especially dangerous because they did not have whistles to indicate their presence to larger steamboats operating nearby. Since these boats were not steam powered, they were exempt from the Steamboat Inspection Service's stringent documentation and periodic inspections. As a result, the records for these boats are limited, and we have minimal photographic documentation of their role in the gradual change from steam power to the internal combustion motor in the period from 1900 through 1925.

In 1900 the stern-wheel steam towboat had been the unquestioned backbone of the towboating industry for almost four decades. Although towboaters heartily embraced the status quo of steam power, the inherent limitations of stern-wheel steamboats were becoming clearer as the years passed. Two factors were involved in the changing attitudes: first, the realization that the Ohio River would have to become a series of slackwater pools from Pittsburgh to Cairo in order for towboating to become a viable mode of transportation year-round instead of seasonally; and second, the growing realization that the stern-wheel steam towboat had more operational drawbacks for twentieth-century towboating than most veteran towboaters could fathom.

One company was facing the challenge of developing a modern towboat and had been making strides in that effort. Since 1903 Ward Engineering Works in Charleston, West Virginia, had continued investigating and experimenting with towboating's challenges. The reason for Ward's advanced attitudes stemmed largely from its plant's physical location on the Kanawha River in West Virginia, an area that was an important source of bituminous coal's production (then second only to western Pennsylvania). Between 1880 and 1897, the Kanawha River had become the first completely improved tributary of the Ohio with ten locks and movable dams. The locks and dams allowed coal to be shipped down the Ohio to Cincinnati and Louisville on a surprisingly regular basis compared to the limited seasonal rises on

PLANT of
THE CHARLES WARD ENGINEERING WORKS
CHARLESTON, W. VA.
SHOWING: 720 H.P. DIESEL PROPELLER TOWBOAT "GEO. T. PRICE"
800 H.P. STEAM STERNWHEEL " E. D. KENNA"
9 - 500 TON COVERED BARGES

*Physical plant of Ward Engineering Works in Charleston, West Virginia, alongside the Kanawha River, ca. 1925. Ward built excellent boats, several of which saw service in saltwater and several of which are still in use nearly eight decades later. Near the center of the photo, the* E. D. Kenna *is nearing completion. At the right is the* Geo. T. Price *of the W. C. Kelly Barge Line. The* Price *was noteworthy as one of the two diesel propeller towboats built in 1925 that fomented the diesel revolution, which would begin supplanting steam power by the end of World War II.*

the Ohio that made coal shipments from Pittsburgh so erratic. Although the Kanawha is a small river, ninety miles in length, it was the first the U.S. Army Corps of Engineers transformed from a free-flowing unimproved river to a contained river with the commercial benefits of a basic lock and dam system. The Kanawha's other strategic advantage was that it joined the Ohio River at Point Pleasant, West Virginia, 262 miles *below* Pittsburgh. That is to say, Kanawha River coal was 262 miles *closer* to the markets, and there were 262 fewer miles of the unimproved Ohio River for Kanawha River coal operators to contend with as towboats moved their coal to consumers.

Charles Ward had emigrated from England and first lived in Cincinnati, Ohio. By 1871 he moved to Charleston, where he joined in building the Kanawha Valley's first gas plant. In 1872 Ward began his own business in Charleston. By the end of the nineteenth century, Ward's company was fabricating water-tube boilers for the U.S. Navy, compound steam engines, and steamboats. The *Mascot*, a steam launch the company built in 1893, was the first tunnel-hull boat on the western rivers.

Unlike the conventional boatbuilding operations of Pittsburgh, Cincinnati, Jeffersonville, Indiana, and Paducah, Kentucky, Ward Engineering routinely carried out extensive experimentation with hulls, engines, boilers, and means of propulsion. The advantages of improved rivers were literally demonstrated every day for the company's engineers and designers—in their operation's backyard along the improved Kanawha. The river's perquisite of a constant six-foot channel persuaded the Charleston boat builder to consider using propellers on steamboats instead of stern-wheels long before any other boatyard contemplated such thinking. Ward Engineering built two propeller steam towboats, the *James Rumsey* in 1903 and the *A. M. Scott* in 1906. Although innovative, these towboats did not gain immediate acceptance because of their limitations on the unimproved Ohio River.

While Ward Engineering was working toward solutions to the problems presented by the nineteenth-century style of towboating, Mother Nature stepped in to wipe out many nineteenth-century steamboats. In January 1918 an unexpected cold siege caused the Ohio River to freeze. At Paducah, many steamboats had been taken to Duck's Nest, a short distance up the Tennessee River. Duck's Nest had been used as a safe winter haven for steamboats for years, and steamboat men had never thought the place would be vulnerable to ice.

When the thaw came, heavy ice came down the Tennessee in prodigious amounts and shredded large steamboats to pieces within moments. Steamboat men were stunned. It was as though everything on the Tennessee River had been targeted for destruction, and almost nothing of the steamboats was left as the ice moved downstream and obliterated nearly everything in its path. The loss of steam towboats and packets in the 1918 ice at Cincinnati, Paducah, and Memphis was more devastating than anyone had expected. The tonnage lost was staggering, and many river men wisely decided to look elsewhere for more secure jobs. The United States government came to the rescue shortly thereafter and began experimentation to remedy the many problems of the towboats.

## Post–World War I Changes

The post–World War I era on the Ohio and Mississippi rivers was one of rapid change. Cargoes for towboats became diversified, and Pittsburgh no longer dominated towboating's coal supply chain in the manner it had for decades. Packets could not operate year-round because of the unimproved rivers, and that made them extremely vulnerable to railroad competition as well

*The J. M. Leithead, ca. 1940s. Another futuristic Ward towboat, she began as the* Clairton *in 1918 in Charleston, West Virginia. This steam propeller towboat, built nearly one hundred years ago, has a surprisingly modern appearance. Everything in her design is totally functional and bland. Although the* Leithead *was supposed to have been converted to diesel in the early 1950s, this pioneering towboat was scrapped instead.*

as competition from large trucks, which had gained greatly from improved tires. The competition would wipe out the remaining packets by the mid-1930s.

After World War I, more steam towboats were built, stern-wheel as well as propeller driven. They were smaller and no longer reflected the design and engineering that created many sizable famous towboats of the late nineteenth and early twentieth centuries.

During the 1920s Carnegie–Illinois Steel of Pittsburgh built a fleet of modern steel-hulled, steam, stern-wheel towboats. These were functional pool boats, boats whose pilothouses were positioned at the forward end of their cabins instead of above, and their aesthetics were hardly remarkable. However, their designers sought economical operation and specified the novel utilization of standard parts, whereby the machinery on one was identical to the others. Standard parts and identical specifications seldom had been a concern of nineteenth-century towboat construction. Few things were standard, and rarely was one steamboat like another. Mechanical and design individuality had prevailed.

The Carnegie–Illinois boats, on the other hand, were designed for economy and versatility, using four return-flue boilers and a 750-horsepower engine. They could deliver reasonably sized tows of steel to Memphis and return with much less per ton-mile expense than their predecessors.

The gradual canalization of the Ohio River slowly brought a year-round operation, which was a welcome change from the previous seasonal operation for towboating. From the 1860s through 1916, coal had been the main cargo on the rivers, and the majority of towboating was involved in shipping coal. By 1915, however, coal's near-total domination of towboating had become a thing of the past. In place of coal, cargoes became diversified.

The Rivers and Harbors Act of 1910 provided $500,000 for research and experimentation to develop a better towboat under the aegis of the U.S. Army Corps of Engineers. Ward Engineering then began building a number of propeller steam towboats, which gradually solved the various operational problems of steam stern-wheelers. Beginning with the *Inspector* of 1915 and the *Clairton* of 1918, Ward developed the modern towboat, though steam powered. Gradually several other boat builders, such as Dravo, followed Ward's lead and gravitated toward building steam propeller towboats. Even so, the propeller-driven towboat did not supplant steam stern-wheelers overnight.

By 1920 World War I was over, and Federal Barge Lines was created to resurrect the moribund river industry. With government money available, more boatbuilders joined in the movement to build modern towboats. Steam engines still prevailed because diesel technology was in its infancy. In the early 1920s diesels were slow and unable to develop much power. The turning point in the towboat's evolution came in 1925, when Ward Engineering built the *Geo. T. Price* and Nashville Bridge Company built the *North Star*, both diesel powered with twin propellers.

During the 1920s Ward Engineering was in the vanguard of diesel experimentation, though it built both steam- and diesel-powered boats. Although the early diesels were far from impressive in their appearance, they were able to turn the long-ailing towboating industry around and systematically solve every operational problem the steam stern-wheel towboat had bequeathed to the industry. In 1930 Ward built two marvelous twin propeller-driven steam turbine (rotary instead of piston-driven engine) towboats for the Mississippi Valley Barge Line, the *Indiana* and the *Louisiana*. A year later the engineering firm built the twin-prop steam towboats *James A. Rankin* and *Vesta*. After these successes, though, Ward Engineering unfortunately

*The new towboat* Indiana *undergoing her trial run at Charleston, West Virginia, in 1930. The* Indiana *was novel because her power was steam electric. Instead of steam reciprocating machinery, she had steam turbines. She and her sister, the* Louisiana, *were examples of the advanced towboats Ward Engineering Works produced. The* Indiana *was converted to diesel in the 1940s.*

succumbed to the financial ravages of the Great Depression, and the most advanced boatbuilding operation along the western rivers disappeared.

There was a brief period, approximately 1925–35, during which there was an operational parity for diesel and steam. That is to say, diesel propeller towboats with smaller crew requirements and lower operational costs required slightly more depth to operate than was generally available on the unimproved rivers. On the other hand, the steam stern-wheel towboats, despite their higher operational costs, could go almost anywhere because of their shallower draughts.

However, the completion of the Ohio River's locks and dams in 1929 gradually brought about a new operational environment for towboating. The slackwater pools between dams provided deeper water, precisely what the diesel propeller towboats required to show their advantages and potential. Suddenly, the few previously valid reasons for continued use of steam towboats disappeared. Perhaps more than any other factor, the completion of the Ohio River's low-lift locks and dams accelerated the acceptance of diesel power and propellers for towboating. With a guaranteed nine-foot channel, there was no reason to rely on steam and stern-wheels any longer.

The Ohio River's lock and dam system was an engineering marvel whose completion was inopportunely synchronized with the disastrous beginnings of the Great Depression. An incomparable American engineering triumph deserved to bask in the contemporary limelight but instead was usurped abruptly by a national economic disaster that would not be relieved until World War II.

Nevertheless, in light of the Ohio's conversion to a contained river in 1929, why was there not a more rapid transition era during which the diesel totally supplanted the steam towboat? The lack of money during the Depression era kept businesses from having the surplus needed for capital investment in new equipment. However, when steamboat operators looked at, for example, Union Barge Line's *Peace* and *Neville* in the 1930s, it was impossible not to envy the lower operating costs and benefits of changing from steam to diesel power. There were no firemen, and the required operating licenses were incredibly few when compared to steamboat licensing.

No further massive advances were to come to steam machinery. Steam engines required heavy maintenance and long layups. With steam power, there were seldom any minor repairs. Virtually everything about a steamboat, even those kept in excellent mechanical shape, routinely involved intensive manual labor and extensive costly repairs. Everything about maintaining a steamboat took far too much time for the modern era.

Whereas steam had already reached a point at which there was neither a chance for reducing operational costs nor increasing efficiency, the diesel towboat of the 1920s and 1930s rapidly moved in the opposite direction. Significant changes came almost yearly in diesel operations. A quantum leap in diesel power came when improved injectors were able to better atomize diesel fuel. Early low-speed diesels were gradually supplanted by high-speed diesels that used reduction gears, which lowered a motor's revolutions per minute and provided a mechanical advantage by lessening the amount of slippage. As a result, the power generated per cubic unit of displacement with diesel power increased in leaps unheard of previously and impossible with steam power.

Compressed air also came to the forefront of power generation as a result of diesel research and development. Countless applications of compressed air around diesel machinery made life easier and more convenient for diesel engineers. The Air-Flex clutch also allowed a direct reversal of propellers without having to rely on the added step of an engineer's manual reversal in the outdated fashion of steamboats.

Even though steam was on the way out as a motive power on the rivers by 1937, many operations such as Standard Oil, Federal Barge Line, and Union Barge Line were still mostly steam powered; their operations were not yet ready for the coming era. World War II brought a temporary reprieve for steamboats and simultaneously revolutionized towboating. In 1942 the available diesel motors were installed in landing ship tanks (LSTs) heading abroad for World War II, and that left new diesel power unavailable domestically. The majority of river and rail transportation during the World War II era was carried on by steam power. The steamboats ranged from floating antiques of the early twentieth century to the most modern steamboats of the late 1930s and the last stern-wheeler built in 1940. The surprising arrivals were twenty-one modern steam propeller towboats ordered by the Defense Plant Corporation. They were originally planned as diesel powered, but the urgent material demands of World War II caused them to be built as steamers.

Although steam stern-wheel towboats did yeoman work during the war years, they were barely able to keep up with demand and their operational limitations were demonstrated daily. The situation was identical on the rivers and the rails: steam stayed in place because the war effort abroad postponed the diesel power transition. However, when the war came to an end in 1945, the river industry embarked with alacrity on its delayed transition from steam to diesel power. As American industry could finally shift from wartime to peacetime manufacturing by 1946–47, the shift from steam to diesel on the rivers acceler-

ated as soon as diesel manufacturers could supply the domestic market once more.

Steam's biggest stronghold was at Baton Rouge, where Standard Oil had an impressive fleet of six steamboats, ranging from a 1902 antique to a modern 1937 stern-wheel towboat. Dravo carried out dynamometer testing on the Standard Oil steamboats in 1946. These tests measured a steamboat's thrust and could show the amount of energy lost in the wakes created by a stern-wheel. The results were humiliating for the staunchest steam advocates: two modern diesel towboats were easily able to replace five of the six steamboats Standard Oil had used throughout World War II, and the reduction in operating personnel was astounding.

Another advantage for Standard Oil in switching from steam to diesel was a reduction in the time needed to pump out oil tows at terminals. Whereas aging primitive steam reciprocating pumps would require nearly two days of pumping in Memphis, modern diesel-powered pumps could do the same work in slightly more than one day. Changing to the diesel motor cut costs drastically overnight.

The subsequent transition to diesel came in several waves. The first and most devastating to steam came in 1948, the second in 1951, and the third in 1953. During these years, many steamboats were retired and replaced with diesel towboats. The steam strongholds were U.S. Steel in Pittsburgh; Amherst Barge Company in Charleston, West Virginia; Armco Steel in Huntington, West Virginia; and the Ohio River Company's Huntington operations. The handful of remaining steamboats were retired between 1954 and 1959.

*The brand-new* Jim Bernhardt *at Hartford, Illinois, on June 5, 1976. This handsome towboat has three propellers, each turned by a 3,500-horsepower (hp) diesel, with a total of 10,500 hp. It turned out that the 10,500-hp towboats built by Dravo and the Nashville Bridge Company were more powerful than needed. Soon it was realized that 6,000-hp towboats with twin propellers could provide as much power as needed at a considerably lower operational cost.*

## Conclusion

Few leaders of twenty-first century towboating have any idea that their industry originated with the Union army's need for coal to fuel its military operations against the Confederate States of America in 1861. The towboat remains one important advantageous result of that terrible war.

The towboat mechanized the manual coal boating industry that had gone on for nearly three decades. It went through five decades of development from 1852 through 1902 and reached its fruition through men such as James A. Blackmore, Isaac Hammitt, Peter Sprague, James Elliott, J. M. Hammett, and Andrew Axton. It is difficult for us to appreciate the enormous challenges of towboating on the unimproved free-flowing rivers of the nineteenth century or how rugged a career early towboating was. The temperature in an engine room of a steamboat was normally above 105 degrees Fahrenheit. Steamboats were cold in winter and miserably hot in summer. Though steamboats were fascinating, living on a steamboat as part of its crew was seldom pleasant.

On the other hand, there are few things more delightful than seeing a stern-wheel steamboat kicking up a big wake. That wondrous wake was in reality, however, lost energy, and lost energy translated into lost time and money.

In the twenty-first century it may be tempting to scoff at the limitations of archaic steam towboats in light of the marvels of contemporary diesel power, propellers, and so on. However, steam stern-wheelers handled big tows of wooden model barges and coal boats on the unimproved Ohio and Mississippi rivers in a remarkable fashion for years.

Modern towboaters are incredulous when they learn that lead lines were used on the Mississippi up until the late 1940s. Although tying up for all except the worst fog and becoming windbound with a tow of empties may seem preposterous nowadays, a world of primitive steam towboating went on successfully for many decades before radio and radar arrived on the rivers.

It would be most interesting to have a time machine to take deckhands from the twenty-first century back to the Pittsburgh harbor of 1902 on the Monongahela and see if they could hitch up a tow of wooden coal boats to a towboat's headlog with a duckpond using stack knees and their appurtenances. They would be baffled at the complexities and labor-intensive nature of old-time towboating! The difference is that the Ohio is now a contained river with locks and dams.

Since 1929 slackwater navigation has been a major factor in the acceleration of the diesel towboat's evolution. The marvels of modern river transportation also came about through the far-sighted efforts of Ward Engineering and Nashville Bridge Company. Now, eight decades after the completion of the original fifty-two locks and low-lift movable dams, they are being replaced with larger locks and dams, and only two of the original are left. The reason for their replacement and expansion is the diesel towboat.

*Jack E. Custer is a process writer/redactor for UPS-Supply Chain Solutions in Louisville, Kentucky, whose research on steamboats has appeared in numerous publications. He is a coauthor of the Rock Island District of the Corps of Engineers' 1996* Steamboat Wreck Sites on the Upper Mississippi and Illinois Rivers. *He was editor of the* Egregious Steamboat Journal *from 1991 to 1998. Author of research documents for the Mississippi River Museum in Memphis, Tennessee, and the River Heritage Museum in Paducah, Kentucky, Custer also has built four models for two museums. His specialties in steamboat research are the mechanical and architectural evolution of the towboat and the steamboats of Captains James A. Blackmore and Peter Sprague. He has taught at Tulane University, the University of Tennessee, the University of Louisville, and Bellarmine University.*

## SELECTED BIBLIOGRAPHY

"The Coal Business," *Elizabeth (PA) Herald*, Centennial Edition, June 7, 1900.

"Coal Towing from the 'Broadhorn' to the Present Powerful Towboat," *Louisville Courier-Journal*, November 16, 1902.

Gould, E. W. *Gould's History of River Navigation*. Saint Louis: Nixon-Jones Printing, 1889.

Hunter, Louis C. *Steamboats on the Western Rivers*. Cambridge, MA: Harvard University Press, 1949.

"Isn't That Steamboat About to Sink?" *Egregious Steamboat Journal* 32 (January/February 1998).

"News of Rivers and Steamboats," *Memphis Commercial Appeal*, February 16, 1910.

"News of the Rivers," *Memphis Commercial Appeal*, March 28, 1901.

"News of the Rivers," *Memphis Evening Scimitar*, November 5, 1908.

*Report Covering a Survey of the Standard Oil Company of New Jersey (Baton Rouge Branch) Floating Equipment*. Pittsburgh: Dravo, 1947.

"The River," *New Orleans Daily Picayune*, October 21, 1902.

"River and Weather," *Louisville Courier-Journal*, October 24, 1902.

"River Intelligence," *New Orleans Daily Delta*, February 2, 1854.

"River News," *Memphis Daily Appeal*, June 15, 1870.

"River News," *Pittsburgh Post*, November 4, 1901.

Rosskam, Edwin, and Louise Rosskam. *Towboat River*. New York: Duell, Sloan, and Pearce, 1948.

U.S. Congress. House. *Experimental Towboats*. 63rd Cong., 2nd sess., 1913–14, H. Doc. 587. Washington, DC: Government Printing Office, 1914.

# 4

## The Era of Town Building Below the Falls
## "Whatever will benefit a part—will benefit the whole"

RICK BELL

Even as Nicholas Roosevelt's pioneering steamboat, the *New Orleans*, arrived at the Louisville waterfront on October 28, 1811, other dramatic events were taking place at the Falls of the Ohio. Just three miles west of the fledgling town of Louisville, Kentucky, the new communities of Portland and Shippingport, located at the lower end of the Falls, were beginning to emerge. Products of ambitious goals during the era of town building in the Ohio Valley, both communities were dramatically impacted by and influenced the development of early American steamboats and the national economy.

An exposed limestone shelf, known as the Falls of the Ohio, is the only natural impediment in the 981-mile passage between Pittsburgh, Pennsylvania, and the Mississippi River. At this point the river gradually descends twenty-six feet in elevation over a three-mile distance, dividing the Ohio into the upper river and the lower river. Only at times of seasonal flooding, usually occurring in the early spring, was the dangerous rock shelf covered with enough water to make passage safe for cargo-bearing vessels. Even then the rapidly moving river poured through narrow rocky chutes, making the Falls of the Ohio a

necessary stopping place for all navigators. The earliest water-born travelers, Native Americans and early French fur traders, dealt with the navigational barrier by unloading their canoes and bateaux (small, flat-bottomed boats) and portaged around the barrier, most frequently using the Kentucky shoreline.

Until the development of practical steam-powered craft, there was little need for harbors at the lower end of the Falls. In early 1811 the *Niles' Register* estimated that nearly 1,200 flatboats, barges, and keelboats had passed over the Falls at Louisville in the previous six months, usually bound for New Orleans. Only a handful of hardy traders attempted the backbreaking trip upstream, against the current, pulling or rowing keelboats. The small town of Louisville, then only the fifth-largest community in Kentucky, boasted an ample harbor formed by the entrance of Beargrass Creek, which during this era emptied into the Ohio River at Third Street. Self-propelled vessels floating westward were able to pull into Beargrass Creek and wait until water in the chutes was deep enough to safely accommodate their passage.

As the volume of shipping steadily increased, entrepreneurs including General William Lytle (1770–1831) of Cincinnati,

Ohio, and two French brothers, Louis and John Tarascon, recognized the economic opportunities made possible by developing new communities just below the Falls. The towns they created, Portland and Shippingport, located on the Kentucky shore, form an instructive chapter in the birth of the great American steamboat era—an era characterized by the growth of a new economy based on river transportation, boatbuilding, and inland maritime commerce.

Lytle and the Tarascons represent a breed of American developers and town proprietors who flourished during the early nineteenth century, profoundly impacting the growth of the American West. Many ambitious planners, motivated by visions of future commercial empires, would—as in the case of Portland and Shippingport—see their plans fail. The new towns below the Falls would end in recrimination, bankruptcy, suicide, and despair, but they were started with high hopes in the "Era of Good Feelings."

The first two decades of the nineteenth century brought unprecedented economic prosperity, political stability, and industrial innovations; thus, the period was remembered as the Era of Good Feelings. The dramatic expansion of American geography made possible by the Louisiana Purchase in 1803 opened vast new lands for settlement and freed the Ohio and Mississippi rivers from colonial dominance by Spanish and French overlords. The Battle of Tippecanoe, on November 7, 1811, ended the continuing threats of Indian warfare in Indiana and the Northwest Territory. The War of 1812 and subsequent embargo of British imports proved a powerful stimulus to American manufacturers in New England and the trans-Allegheny frontier, especially in Pittsburgh and Lexington, Kentucky.

Nicholas Roosevelt's practical demonstration of a viable steam-powered craft was the final ingredient in a heady mixture of need and opportunity for Ohio River commerce. When the *New Orleans* arrived in Louisville in late October 1811 it caused a sensation, which was only amplified during its necessary layover awaiting a rise in the river. In the monthlong sojourn before the vessel eased over the Falls during the last week of November, Roosevelt used the time to demonstrate the final piece of the inland river navigation puzzle. The *New Orleans* proved its true worth by cruising upriver, back to Cincinnati, to show that the inland river system had become a two-way street. Raw materials, farm products, and manufactured goods subsequently flowed south to New Orleans and the Gulf of Mexico, while imported goods moved freely back upriver to eager customers in Saint Louis, Missouri, Louisville, Cincinnati, and Pittsburgh. Steamboats on the western waters provided the foundation for a new economic order.

—•—•—

Two weeks after the *New Orleans* cruised back upstream, three miles to the west of Louisville a young surveyor, Alexander Ralston, was ready to report a different kind of progress to his employer, Lytle, in Cincinnati: "On Friday last we finished the plan of your Town as proposed by you. Mr. Barclay shewed me a sketch of the work which he tells me he has forwarded to you which will serve to guide you in your sites &c. Would it not be well to know whether you intend any buildings between Water Street and the river—and whether you intend that the whole shall be public ground or not—if public ground who will wharf it?"

Ralston's report touched on several key elements in the genesis of the new Ohio Valley community. The town to which he referred was Portland, its name chosen to emphasize its nature as an eligible landing place. Joshua Gill Barclay (1784–1851), a cousin of Lytle's brother-in-law and partner Senator John Rowan, was the agent selected by Lytle to represent his interests in developing his property. The surveyor's question as to a wharf location at the site presents one of the central issues of town building and development: Who would decide and control the new communities springing up in the Ohio Valley—the proprietors or the citizens of the towns?

Lytle was one of the earliest and most experienced land developers in the Ohio Valley. The son of an early Kentucky pioneer, in his youth Lytle became a veteran Indian fighter, surveyor, and speculator who developed a set of skills greatly prized on the American frontier, those of a land locator. These hardy souls—Daniel Boone and Simon Kenton are the best remembered—braved the western wilderness when it was the land of the Shawnee and Cherokee, located eligible places for future townships, and staked their claims. In 1801 Lytle left his home in Lexington and moved to the new town he founded in Williamsburg, Ohio. During this same period, Lytle also established the communities of Point Pleasant and Fort Clinton, Ohio. In 1806 Lytle relocated to Cincinnati, where he and his family became community mainstays and leaders in that rapidly developing river town.

Kinship and family ties were important considerations in pioneer Kentucky. As business opportunities grew, kinship became one of the determining factors in business partnerships, employment, and commerce. In 1794 Lytle's sister Ann married a young Bardstown, Kentucky, lawyer, John Rowan, and they built an impressive new home on land given to them by her father, Captain William Lytle (1728–1797). This house, officially known as Federal Hill, has come down in folklore as "My Old Kentucky Home." William Lytle and John Rowan would be close personal friends and business partners throughout their lives,

and their relationship would have a profound impact on the new town of Portland.

In the decisive year of 1811, Lytle obtained more than three thousand acres lying just west of Louisville, which shared a common sequence of land ownership with the town. Land adjacent to the Falls of the Ohio, owned by King George III of Great Britain, was awarded to Charles DeWarnsdorf in 1773. The following year, British agent John Connolly and American patriot John Campbell purchased the DeWarnsdorf grant. During the Revolution both men were captured and imprisoned by their enemies. Connolly's lands were escheated by Virginia. Campbell's land was subdivided into the site of Louisville, and following the war he was compensated for his loss by the presentation of land just west of the rapidly developing upper river town.

Judge Fortunatus Cosby purchased three thousand acres, below and adjoining the Ohio River, from Campbell's sister and heir, Mrs. Sarah Beard, in 1806 for a total of $10,000. The next year Cosby deeded one-third of his newly acquired land to Henry Clay for "$1 dollar and other consideration." It was commonly held that the other "consideration" was the payment of a large gambling debt owed to the Kentucky congressman and legendary cardsharp. In May 1811 Clay accepted $45,000 and title to land in downtown Lexington from his old friend General Lytle. With this trade and additional land purchases from Cosby, Lytle began to formalize his plans for a new real estate development project that would dwarf all his previous efforts.

Personal letters during this period were frequently a mixture of business and family matters. Relatives could usually be trusted to work for the common good of the family, and trust was an important attribute during these times of unprecedented population mobility. Lytle needed a dependable person to serve as his agent, and brother-in-law Rowan provided such a

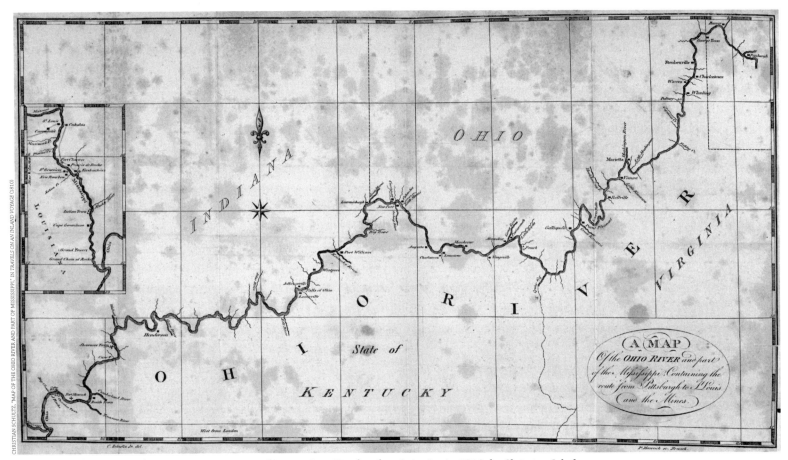

*Map of the Ohio River to the Mississippi containing the route from Pittsburgh to Saint Louis, 1810, by Christian Schultz*

candidate. Rowan wrote to Lytle in February 1811, "I have prevailed upon Mr. Barclay a cousin of Mine, to ride over and bear the letter. I beg leave to introduce him to you and family and recommend him to your Attention and politeness—He is a young man of much intelligence and much Honor."

Four months later Rowan repeated his endorsement of Barclay. He included some practical advice on establishing duties and benefits expected by Lytle's new employee:

> I applied to Mr. Joshua Barclay to attend to your business at Louisville—He agreed to do so very readily—when I spoke about compensation he said you and he would fix that—He set out on friday last for Louisville, where he will wait your instructions—I could give him no special instructions. My directions were that he should repeatedly and almost constantly traverse the land, notice any trespassers that had been, or might be committing, and drive off the trespassers—As soon as you can make the arrangements that new wooden house should be fixed up for lodging and some trusty old Negroe woman hired or bought, as a cook washwoman &c and be placed there—The business would be better and more cheaply attended to.

In the early years, what was known as Portland "proper" was defined by the Ohio River on the north and today's Northwestern Parkway six blocks to the south. It extended from today's Thirty-third Street west to Thirty-ninth Street and was laid out in the regular grid pattern known as the Philadelphia model. Surveyor Ralston made the main streets very broad to accommodate the expected heavy traffic of hackney cabs, wagons, and dray carts, the transportation vehicles common in a maritime community. Using the standard surveyor's chain of precisely 66 feet, the streets were 1.5 chains, or 99 feet, in width, interspersed with alleyways of 33 feet, or one-half chain length.

Barclay was a sound choice as the first resident of Portland. He developed into a practical and responsible businessman and lawyer and a successful farmer. Barclay also had the unusual distinction of being related to two of America's most beloved artists. He was the cousin of songwriter Stephen Collins Foster, a relationship shared with his cousin Rowan. He was also, for a brief time, John James Audubon's nephew by marriage through his short-lived first wife, Julia Berthoud, niece of Audubon and his wife Lucy (Bakewell) Audubon.

The job of managing the new real estate development at Portland was more than one individual could handle, and again the proprietor reached into his family circle for assistance. In June 1811, Lytle received a letter from an applicant for the job: "Dear Uncle—Since I saw you I have conversed with uncle Parker and Dr. Ridgely about discontinuing the study of medicine and they both have advised me to quit it and turn my attention to something less injurious to my health, which I am very anxious to do for I assure you I am very tired doing nothing." The letter's author, Robert Todd R.S., would soon join the small band of developers located on the Portland site. Todd (who was designated by the patronymic R.S. to indicate he was the son of Robert Todd) was a Lexington blue blood of the highest circle. His mother, Jane Lytle, was another of Lytle's sisters, who in 1788 married Robert Todd, a military aide to Colonel George Rogers Clark. The elder Todd died at the hands of Indians four years after his marriage, and four years later Jane followed him to the grave. Young Robert Todd R.S. became a ward and particular favorite of Lytle.

Not all of the earliest citizens of Portland were Lytle relatives. Ralston is one of those fascinating individuals who float down the stream of history and bob up to appear occasionally in the record. A man of mystery, Ralston is a shadowy participant in the American saga. In 1791 Ralston arrived in America from Scotland to work as a rodman and assistant to Pierre Charles L'Enfant on the project to survey the future site of Washington, DC. He remained on that important project until 1794. By 1806 he had worked his way westward, and he became so deeply immersed in the Aaron Burr conspiracy he would be one of three men indicted for treasonous activities. With the apparent goal of establishing a new western empire, disgraced former Vice President Burr had recruited Ralston and sent him and two others ahead of his expedition downriver for scouting purposes. After a confusion of legal jurisdictions, unproven accusations, and botched prosecutions, Ralston escaped punishment for his involvement. Thereafter, he was available in November 1811 to conduct the initial land survey of Portland for Lytle.

Ralston appears once more in the historical record, again using his skills as a surveyor and town planner. In 1821 the site for Indiana's new capital was selected at the junction of Fall Creek and the West Fork of the White River, and Ralston was chosen as its planner. Working with Elias Pym Fordham, he proposed a dramatic town layout based on the geometric circle, similar to Washington, DC. The design of Indianapolis was Ralston's brainchild. He remained in the new city and in 1827 died in relative obscurity. Ralston was buried in a pauper's graveyard provided for schoolteachers and sank quietly beneath the currents of history.

The man most responsible for the successful development of the American steamboat industry would become involved in Portland's earliest stage. Captain Henry Miller Shreve

(1785–1851), the future superintendent of the western waters, is generally regarded as the single most essential figure in the development of American steamboat design, river improvement, commercial application, and the establishment of maritime legal precedent. He transformed the role of river transportation in the United States.

Shreve began his maritime career in 1807 as a skilled keelboatman on the Monongahela River. In 1814 he entered American history on several fronts. Roosevelt's *New Orleans* was owned and operated by the Robert Fulton–Robert Livingston partnership, who used their vast wealth and political influence to claim an exclusive monopoly on steam-powered craft on the lower Mississippi River. Although many westerners protested this arrangement, Shreve defied their monopoly by cruising from Pittsburgh to New Orleans. His initial voyage came at a crucial moment in American history. In December 1814 Shreve piloted downriver the *Enterprise*, a seventy-five-ton capacity steamboat equipped with an oscillating cylinder engine designed by Daniel French. It was filled with a cargo of munitions and military supplies, sent by Pittsburgh merchant William Foster (another cousin of John Rowan and father of songwriter Stephen), to aid the American army in New Orleans commanded by General Andrew Jackson. When the *Enterprise* arrived, Jackson commandeered the vessel and sent it on various scouting and delivery missions, marking the first time a steam-powered vessel was used in warfare. Shreve not only served as pilot, but also helped operate a cannon battery during the Battle of New Orleans, a decisive American victory over the British on January 8, 1815.

Thereafter, when the New York-based firm of Fulton and Livingston ordered the *Enterprise* seized, Shreve had the boat released on bail and set forth on his decisive voyage in defiance of the Eastern monopoly. On June 1, 1815, the *Louisville Western Courier* made an announcement that rocked the people of the Western river systems:

> COMMUNICATION—Arrived in this port, in 25 days from New-Orleans, the Steam-Boat, *Enterprize*, Capt. SHRIEVE. The celerity and safety with which this boat descends and ascends the currents of these mighty waters, the improvement of the navigation of which is so advantageous to the western world, must be equally interesting to the farmer and the merchant. The facility and convenience of the passage, in ascending the rivers, are such as to give a decided preference to this mode of navigation, while the size and construction of the boat entitles it to all the advantages which the *Aetna* and *Vesuvius* have in vain tried to *monopolize* over the *free* waters of our common country.

Shreve's masterful achievement of piloting a steamboat upriver to Louisville revolutionized western commerce and is perhaps the single most pivotal economic event in the history of the Falls communities. His practical and profitable demonstration of upriver navigation meant that manufactured goods, passengers, information, and capital could travel upstream as well as down. From that moment the Louisville area began its rapid ascent and would soon become Kentucky's largest community and dominant economic engine.

The next year, 1816, Shreve built his own boat, the *Washington* (400-ton capacity), a craft that marked a fundamental change in steamboat design. The early Fulton-designed vessels were ships, with the engines and boiler located in the well of the keel, below the waterline. This arrangement was effective on lakes or deepwater rivers such as New York's Hudson, but the Ohio and Mississippi were entirely different challenges. A

*Captain Henry Miller Shreve, ca. 1815*

GARNETT LAIDLAW ESKEW, *THE PAGEANT OF THE PACKETS* (1929)

new craft was needed to navigate the shallow and often nearly dry western waters. Shreve developed a flat-bottom boat with very little draft, designed to ride on, rather than in, the water. He placed the engines, boilers, and machinery on the first deck and then added a second deck above to accommodate passengers and freight. Above that a third deck hosted a pilothouse that commanded a sweeping view of the river, making visible the obstructions, sandbars, snags, and sawyers that were the bane of steamboat pilots. With the *Washington*, Shreve fathered the western steamboat and set the stage for the "Palmy Days of Steamboating," a popular phrase of the 1850s used to describe the profitable and exciting era, when the great river vessels ruled commerce and stimulated the American imagination.

After those dramatic events Shreve moved to Portland in December 1817 to start a more routine maritime enterprise by purchasing the ferry rights from Lytle. In the days prior to bridges crossing the Ohio, dependable ferry service was a necessary and profitable business. Shreve's Ferry, located at Lot Number 12 in Square 92 (today's Thirty-fifth Street), ran at regular intervals to the new community of New Albany on the Indiana shore. When Shreve made the purchase it was his understanding that Lytle was granting him the exclusive privilege of ferry ownership in Portland. However, as events would prove, this question would occupy both men for decades of controversy, legal actions, and bitter accusations.

Shreve continued to be the major creative force in river navigation. In 1826 he was named superintendent of the western waters by the federal government and given the task of solving a fundamental problem of river navigation. One of the greatest dangers to boatmen was the presence of snags and sawyers on, or just beneath, the river's surface. These floating or embedded logs and trees routinely punctured the wooden bottoms of boats and destroyed countless craft. Shreve invented a practical snag boat and developed techniques and trained crews in the removal of these dangers. His great accomplishment of clearing more than one hundred miles of snags from the mouth of the Red River in Louisiana opened that river to navigation. When a town was built at the junction of the Red and Mississippi rivers, it was given the name Shreveport to honor the master of the western rivers.

———— ·•·•· ————

It would seem that William Lytle had every possible advantage in developing his property below the Falls. He had practical experience, business and family associations with powerful merchants and politicians, the services of men with exceptional talent, access to capital, and a sterling reputation. But he did not have the field entirely to himself.

Decades before Lytle, one of the original owners of the land below the Falls sought to develop part of his property. The northernmost point of Jefferson County, Kentucky, juts toward the Indiana shoreline and pinches the Falls into its most precipitous series of rapids. A township at this place, called Anonymous, was incorporated by the Virginia legislature on October 10, 1785, but little was done to advance its interests. After his release from prison by British authorities following the American Revolution, John Campbell established a village on the site that he named Campbell Town, in his own honor. It was here he erected the first tobacco warehouse, marking the genesis of the tobacco-wholesaling industry in Kentucky. Very little was accomplished at the location, and with Campbell's death the land passed to his brother Allan Campbell.

Recognizing the advantage of such an eligible location, another set of proprietors began to develop an alternative vision for a future town at the foot of the Falls of the Ohio. It is difficult to imagine a more different, or unlikely, set of rivals for Lytle. In 1806 the Tarascon brothers, with their agent James Berthoud, commenced the formation of the new town they would call Shippingport.

The Tarascon brothers, Louis Anastasius (1759–1840) and John Anthony (1765–1825), and Berthoud were French nobles who escaped persecution and death in their native land during the turmoil of the French Revolution. Louis was born near Avignon and became a successful merchant in Marseilles. A volatile, idealistic, and energetic character, Louis was actively engaged in the royalist cause and fled France at the time of the beheading of King Louis XVI (ironically, the namesake of Louisville, Kentucky). Younger brother John is remembered as a more cautious and reserved figure with no interest in politics, but his name alone would have doomed him in revolutionary France. The Tarascon brothers landed in America in 1797 and settled in Philadelphia. They prospered economically through their import of fine silks and luxury goods from Europe. Louis married Nanina de LaPointe, the orphan niece of Gabriel de Colemesnil of New Jersey, and John married her sister Elizabeth. In America the brothers abandoned claims of nobility and European conventions and devoted their energies to capitalist plans to restore their family fortunes and to gain security in their new homeland.

More highly placed in the French nobility was the man known as James Berthoud (died 1819), whose actual name was Bon Herve' de Belisle, Marquis de-Saint-Pierre. His wife, Elizabeth, was *dame d'honour* to the ill-fated Queen Marie Antoinette.

Family tradition reports that he and his family escaped France with the assistance of his Swiss coachman, a servant named Jacques Berthoud. The marquis and family were saved when the coachman secured a passport in his own name. Upon reaching America in 1794, the former marquis adopted the more democratic moniker of James Berthoud in appreciation of his loyal servant.

Encouraged by their commercial success in Philadelphia, the Tarascons looked westward for new entrepreneurial opportunities. In 1799 Louis sent two trusted clerks, Charles Brugiere and Berthoud, down the Ohio River to scout locations to establish shipyards capable of building oceangoing vessels. Their goal was to use the abundance of hardwoods available in the Ohio Valley and build ships capable of sailing down the Ohio–Mississippi systems and through New Orleans to the West Indies. Upon Berthoud's recommendation they located a shipyard in Pittsburgh.

In 1800 the Tarascons brought "a large force of ship carpenters, joiners, calkers, riggers and other expert workmen" from the East Coast to Pittsburgh. They built at least five sailing ships and seven packet boats at the location. Even forty years after the fact, Louis would boast of his accomplishments in a September 1838 letter to Robert Lytle: "Pittsburgh (was) the place of my creation of the western navigation by building at it in 1801 the first ship for sea and the first keel Boats of 25 tons for the Missouri." Their 120-ton schooner, *Amity*, was built and loaded with flour for Saint Thomas. Things looked promising for the Tarascons.

In September 1802 the firm of Tarascon Brothers, James Berthoud and Company was formed. A year later Berthoud purchased forty-five acres of land, the site of Campbell Town, from Allan Campbell for $2,306.25. Because all goods and cargoes had to be carried, they renamed the town Shippingport to emphasize its role in the shipment of materials. To their new Kentucky home, they brought other French immigrant families, including the Berthouds, Offands, Schraders, Avalonds, Fouches, and Cerfs. A lively French community began to form and flourish. In *Sketches of Louisville*, the area's first history published in 1819, Henry McMurtrie provides a vivid description of the geographic advantages enjoyed by the site:

> Shippingport is the natural harbor and landing place for all vessels trading on the western waters with New Orleans, the Missouri, and upper Mississippi, the lower and upper Ohio, and in fine, in conjunction with Louisville and Portland, which, in some future day, will be all one great city, is the center port of the western country. Nature has placed it at the *head* of the navigation of the lower Ohio, as it has Louisville at the *foot* of the upper one, where all ascending boats must, during three-fourths of the year, of necessity, be compelled to stop, which they can do with perfect safety, as, immediately in front of it is a basin called Rock Harbor, that presents a good mooring ground, capable of containing any number of vessels, of any burthen, and completely sheltered from every wind.

Along with the signs of progress demonstrated below the Falls in Portland and Shippingport, the older community of Louisville was reaching an unprecedented level of success thanks to the increasing number of steamboats on the Ohio River. Founded in May 1778 by Colonel George Rogers Clark, Louisville was the westernmost outpost of the new American republic and the launching point for invasion of the British forts in Illi-

nois territory. With Clark came about 150 soldiers and twenty civilian families who established themselves on Corn Island, a small point of exposed limestone resting just off the Kentucky shore. The island location helped protect the population from Indian attack and kept Clark's feisty volunteers gathered together.

New forts were soon built on the mainland Kentucky shore, and settlers began to arrive at this site. For several years threat of Indian attacks forced the settlers to remain in Fort Nelson, located at today's Main and Seventh streets, or in the fortified stations scattered throughout the adjacent countryside. By 1779 the Indian threat had abated, and the land that still belonged to British agent John Connolly was escheated, clearing the way for an equitable distribution. The Court of Kentucky County (then still a part of Virginia) had Connolly's one thousand acres surveyed and laid out in an orderly street plan. In 1800 the citizens of the new town of Louisville, so named by Clark to honor the French alliance during the American Revolution, elected trustees. The Virginia Assembly vested the trustees with legal title to the land. Louisville became its own proprietor and began to divide and sell property based on the purchaser's agreement to build a dwelling house within two years of the sale.

More than topography, natural resources, or any other element, it was the self-governing nature and administration of the trustees, serving as proprietors, which marked the difference between Louisville and its two lower-river neighbors. By spreading decision making among elected officials, rather than concentrating all authority in a single person or business partnership, better choices were made. In emphasizing the needs of the common good, rather than the profits of a single developer, Louisville emerged as the leading community at the Falls of the Ohio and would eventually envelop the downriver towns. During the Era of Good Feelings at the Falls, the political power of democracy trumped the economic influence of capitalism.

———— •–•–• ————

By 1814 all the elements were in place for Lytle to implement his master plan for Portland. He had acquired title to the land, placed his agents on the site, and witnessed the beginning stages of the steamboat boom. His efforts were directed at more than merely starting a new town and making a modest profit from selling real estate, and steamboats were the key to his plans.

Historian Louis C. Hunter effectively summarized the unparalleled growth in the new maritime endeavors:

> The first successful runs were between Louisville and New Orleans, there being little activity on the upper Ohio until after 1820. Following the *Velocipede's* first regular trips between Pittsburgh and Louisville in that year, however, steamboats multiplied rapidly. Both in number and tonnage the increase was remarkable. In 1817 there were 17 steam craft on Western waters with an aggregate tonnage of 3,290. Within the next five years over 60 more were added, and by 1830, 187 steamboats totaling 29,481 tons plied the lakes and rivers of the new country. This represented about half of all American tonnage and roughly equaled the volume of merchant steam shipping in the entire British Empire.

Traffic on the river was still thwarted by the physical obstruction posed by the rocky Falls of the Ohio. For many the solution to the problem was obvious—build a canal to bypass the rapids. Public discussion about a canal began as early as 1804, but despite periodic starts and stops on both the Kentucky and Indiana shores, Lytle held the key. Writing to a potential partner, Baltimore's David McClelland, in 1817 Lytle revealed his plans and frustrations:

> The scite [*sic*] of the Canal at the Falls of Ohio near Louisville, Shippingport and Portland being all-together on my land—it is so throughout the whole extent which is 465 rods in length. . . . The Toll for passing a flat boat through the canal would be from 4 to 10 dollars, and the merchants of Cincinnati and else where assure me they would prefer paying me from 4 to 600 dollars per barge or steam boat rather than <u>unload below the Falls</u> and drag their boats over the rapids, and I think more than forty in that business have offered to bind themselves and heirs to pay it for every load. Barge or steam boat coming up-which would amount to a vast sum in the round of 12 months, and, they are increasing every year beyond calculations—and in a more moderate rate for those that are descending—
>
> If I could command my debts now due me <u>I would open the canal my self</u>, as I am of opinion it offers a fairer prospect for accumulating a vast and inexhaustible source of wealth beyond any thing either Europe or America can offer at this day and which will increase for perhaps 1000 years to come—If I take on any partners in this scheme with me they must be of few and plenty of cash to open the canal and pay me a good price for the land.

His was a grand scheme, and for it to succeed many of his associates urged Lytle to move from Cincinnati to the Louisville area and personally supervise the project. Rowan encouraged Lytle to relocate as early as 1811:

> I still remain of the Opinion that it would be your interest to reside upon your Louisville estate, if Mrs. Lytle could be

*General William Lytle, ca. 1820*

reconciled to it.—But would not advise it unless it were in perfect accordance with her Wishes—*Happiness in life is a primary object*—and no man can be happy unless his wife is happy also—The attachment of Mrs. Lytle to Cincinnati is of the tender kind, particularly those connected with the death and burial of her dear departed daughter; and ought to be regarded with the most delicate attention—if it should ever be your united inclination, as we believe it to be your interest, to settle at Louisville, we will hail it as a matter of much comfort to ourselves, as we can then occasionally at least, see and enjoy the society of each other.

For his initial land offering in 1814, Lytle used the *Louisville Western Courier* and other regional newspapers to trumpet his holdings:

Will be sold at public auction on the 3rd day of September ensuing, a number of half acre lots in the town of Portland, on the Ohio River, about two miles below the town of Louisville. . . . The plan of the town of Portland—its situation upon the river immediately below all difficulties and hazards of passing the falls—its contiguity to Louisville, and its being directly on the nearest and best road from that place to Corydon and Vincennes, all conspire to promise the purchaser ample compensation for any funds he may vest in that way. . . . There is already a large and convenient Warehouse erected, and a ferry established at the place.

The sale sparked an optimism that nearly reached the point of financial hysteria. On September 13, 1814, F. Berthault ecstatically wrote to his friend William Wainwright in Boston, "This place is rising in importance in a commercial point of view every Day.—A Canal, to turn perpetual Mills, is to be dug shortly, 2 ½ miles long around the Rapids.—The land has been bought by the Company for $250,000.—in consequence of which the adjacent lots of ground have risen 150 (percent) in three months! making the acre worth 1000!" Despite all the high hopes, this particular canal scheme did not come to fruition. No company purchased land, but everyone expected the grand event to occur in the near future, and many were eager to hazard their money.

Lytle saw another moneymaking opportunity in laying out a turnpike to provide a direct link between the Louisville wharf and the wharf in Portland, bypassing the Falls. In 1817 he had platted "The Enlargement of Portland," stretching from today's Thirteenth Street westward to join Portland "proper" at Thirty-third Street. Along the street, which would become Portland Avenue, rows of five-acre lots called "country seats" were surveyed and prepared for sale. The avenue became, and would remain, the dominant commercial and residential corridor of the community. Newspaper advertisements again spread the advantages of investing in Lytle's development:

> Will be offered for sale, on Monday 27th of October (1817) next, at the Union Hall Hotel, in Louisville, Kentucky: A Number of Valuable lots in the town of PORTLAND, Situated on the Ohio river and about two miles below Louisville and a half a mile below Shippingport; at the main harbor and anchorage below the falls. . . . The plan is contemplated to Unite Louisville and Shippingport with Portland, in one great and general plan of a city, which appears at this time to be increasing in extent, population and opulence, more rapidly than any other west of the Alleghany Mountains; and as nature has given it ascendancy in point of locality, there is no doubt of its being in a few years a great and Commercial City.

Businessmen and investors flocked to Lytle's sales to get a piece of what everyone believed would be a great real estate bargain. In his diary, Congressman Robert Clough Anderson Jr. of Kentucky reflected the giddy optimism:

> General Robert [sic] Lytles sale of lots in Portland and along the avenue and bottom commenced yesterday. They sell very high. He has sold to the am(oun)t of $100,000. There have been this week sales of property in Louisville at a price we think enormous. It is still rising. I buy a lot of 5 acres at the extravagant price of $2,000. I think it prudent to invest some money where the public attention is so highly excited. Some contend that the town will go down stream and render the late purchase very valuable. I believe they may be valuable on account of their vicinity to Louisville, but I do believe the town (the valuable part) will rather go up.

Lytle's 1817 real estate clients represented a who's who of blue-blood families with both social prominence and business experience. Purchasers included James D. Breckinridge, Arthur Lee Campbell, James D'Wolf, Dr. William Craig Galt, Craven P. Luckett, Anderson Miller, William Pope, Henry Miller Shreve, and Robert Wallace. Relatives of the eminent Clark family were George C. and Owen Gwathmey, James A. Pearse, John Croghan, and Paul Skidmore. Captain Aaron Fontaine and his successful sons-in-law, Fortunatus Cosby, Alexander Pope, and Cuthbert Bullitt, were also among the investors.

The initial sales netted more than $100,000, and Lytle was well on his way to raising the estimated quarter million dollars needed to construct a 2.5 mile canal. (These estimates were grossly inaccurate. The Louisville–Portland Canal, when finally completed in 1830, took four years and nearly $700,000 to complete.) Lytle's insistence on raising construction capital from sales of individual parcels of land was beginning to bear fruit as the economic boom that was the Era of Good Feelings was reaching its pinnacle.

Other investors and potential partners lined up to be a part of Lytle's plans. Skidmore was one of the earliest investors and in 1812 erected the first iron foundry in the area. Robert Steele wrote to his uncle Lytle about the sale on March 30, 1811:

> Mr. Cosby has this day disposed of about 15 acres of your joint lands to Mr. Paul Skidmore, for the sum of one hundred dollars per acre all payable in 12 months. . . . Being myself extremely anxious to see Mr. Skidmore establishment . . . flourish, have undertaken on my part to say that an establishment of that kind will greatly enhance the residue of your lands in the neighborhood.

The smell of immense profits attracted investors from across the nation. Back in Baltimore, spurred by the potential revenues made possible by private ownership of the only canal at the Falls, McClelland proposed a grand partnership to Lytle in early 1818:

> If Capitalists would at all be <u>convinced</u> that <u>18</u> per cent would be divided on the Stock, from the proceeds of the tolls, or by combining, that source of emoluments, with any other that could be connected with it, or Water works, to be supplied by the canal, a Bank &c, &c, . . . there would be no kind of difficulty in raising the Capital you wish, or over <u>five million</u> of dollars if necessary in a day or two or three gentlemen to whom I have mentioned the subject, concur with me in this opinion.

> It would give me pleasure, Sir, to be useful to you in this place, but I cannot be so unless you come to a definite determination on some plan you want carried into effect, and then give me authority to make the arrangements you wish—*Full power and authority to act is indispensible, if you would wi*[s]*h me to raise a large sum of money;* I think I could very easily if you take all the Canal stock, devise a plan by which you could and their interest monied men have and by this means raise the requisite funds to execute at your plans, or if you preferred it, (and I would) to have no partners, to get you <u>on loan</u>, from ½ to a million of dollars, for 10 to 20 years, by paying an interest not much above the legal note, but I need not sketch the plan without knowing whether you would wish it or not—*If you would monopolize it I think you have let the time for doing it go by*

As McClelland predicted, history would record that by demanding sole control, Lytle had let his chance to monopolize land development in Portland slip by. Even at the height of optimism, dire changes were coming to America's economic future, and these changes would have profound impact on both Lytle and his nearby rivals, the Tarascon brothers.

———— ·•·· ————

Initially, the move from Pittsburgh to Shippingport proved encouraging for the Tarascon and Berthoud partnership. They established a shipyard at the northern peak of Shippingport, opposite one of the small islands in the Ohio known as Rock Island, but produced only a limited number of small craft. They determined that their best path to financial success lay not in boat building, but in town building. With the growing number of steamboats docking at Shippingport, they erected a commission warehouse to serve the transshipping trade. They also constructed one of the largest ropewalks in America to turn Kentucky's ample hemp production into rope, cord, and bagging for the sailing and cotton industries.

Shortly after purchasing the original forty-five acres from Allan Campbell, Berthoud set about making legal the town he named "Shipping Port." As the original trustees, he recruited Cosby, Thomas Prather, Anthony Maquille, William C. Maquille, and his son Nicholas Berthoud. Tensions arose between the Tarascons and Berthoud, and in March 1807 they dissolved their partnership. Berthoud ended up with only fourteen lots in Shippingport, where he built a substantial house and warehouse. After his death in December 1819, his business interests were taken over by Nicholas. The will of James Berthoud, fallen marquis of France, revealed an estate worth less than $5,000, including slaves, music, French books, and a violin.

The life and career of Nicholas Berthoud would be forever linked to that of his famous brother-in-law, John James Audubon. Berthoud married Eliza Bakewell, and Audubon married her sister Lucy. Brothers of the sisters, Thomas and William Bakewell, established an early steam-engine factory in Shippingport. For many years, Nicholas helped support Audubon and his family, until the artist/author found world fame and financial success with the publication of his remarkable folio of bird paintings.

The 1810 census listed 98 citizens of Shippingport. Most were French immigrants drawn by the sympathetic embrace of the Tarascons, but others were drifters, boatmen, mechanics, and ship carpenters attracted by business opportunities. In 1814 Sarah Porter, a young widow with two young sons to support, opened a tavern serving the traveling public. Her youngest son, born in 1810, would gain international renown as "the tallest man in the world." Big Jim Porter, the Kentucky Giant, spent all but the last three of his forty-nine years as a resident of Shippingport.

The Tarascon brothers scored a significant commercial success in 1813 by defying the odds and importing a load of profitable luxury goods upriver. Louisville's *Western Courier* proclaimed the news: "Arrived from New Orleans, the Keel Boat, *Shippingport Trader*—Cargo Sugar, Cotton, Hides, Rice, Logwood, Spanish Indigo, Spanish Segars, Allum, Coffee—To John A. Tarascon." Cuban cigars, the "Spanish Segars" of the advertisement, along with the rare commodities of coffee, sugar, and dyes proved enormously valuable. Profits from these trade goods justified the effort and investment of a four-month trip up the inland river system. In a few years, regular deliveries by steamboat would make such luxuries commonplace.

The Tarascons' greatest venture, begun in 1815, was the erection of the Merchant's Manufacturing Mill, designed to harness the power of the Ohio River. Borrowing more than $70,000 from Philadelphia businessmen, they built an immense flour mill, powered by the undependable currents of the Ohio River. It was a scheme every bit as ambitious as Lytle's canal plans, and its fate would be similar. When first built, however, it was a marvel of engineering, technology, and architecture. In his 1819 history of Louisville, McMurtrie recorded his impressions of the mill:

> This valuable mill is remarkable, not only for its size and quantity of flour it is calculated to manufacture when completed, but for the beauty of its machinery, which is said to be the most perfect specimen of the millwright's abilities to be found in this or any other country. . . . The building is

divided into six stories, considerably higher than is usual, there being 102 feet from the first to the sixth. Waggons, containing the wheat or other grain for the mill, are driven under an arch, which commands the hopper of a scale, into which it is discharged and weighed, at the rate of seventy-five bushels in ten minutes; from this it is conveyed by elevators, to the sixth story, where, after passing through a screen, it is deposited into a <u>rubber</u> of a new construction, whence it is conveyed into a large screen, and thence to the stones; when ground, it is reconveyed by elevators to the hopper boy, in the sixth story; whence, after being cooled, it descends to the bolting cloths, the <u>bran</u> being deposited in a gallery on the left, and the <u>shorts</u> in another to the right. The flour being divided into fine, superfine, and middlings, is precipitated into the packing chests, whence it is delivered to the barrels, which are filled with great rapidity by a packing press.

John Tarascon announced in December 1819 that he was making fifty barrels of flour a day and expected to produce 250 barrels daily the next summer. He proclaimed the service would be available any time of the year, except for times of ice in the river. However, the rare occasions of a frozen Ohio River were less problematic than the normal yearly cycle of low water and the lack of a predictable and adequate river flow. At the same moment when American steam power was conquering the technological challenges of its age, the Tarascons reverted to the traditional, more European custom of producing water-ground flour. They plunged themselves deeply into debt to build a monument to yesterday's technology. It would prove a costly mistake.

The steady growth of Shippingport began to attract new citizens and amenities to serve them. An 1819 announcement in the *Louisville Public Advertiser* proclaimed the start of a professional class in the community: "Dr. J. Moser—Late chief Physician of the Hospital of San Juan de Dios in Madrid, having also practiced in the Baltimore Hospital, offers his services to the citizens of Louisville and Shippingport, in the different branches of Medicine, Surgery and Midwifery." In 1825 a new blacksmith, William Givens, proclaimed his craftsmanship to local citizens and offered to steamboat captains landing at the Shippingport wharf services such as "steam engine work, steam boilers, printing presses; large screws, of every description, mill irons, turning lathes, screw stocks, taps and dies, scale beams, coppersmiths' and tinners' tools; edge tools, of every description, of cast steel; mill picks, &c., &c."

An important role of the burgeoning steamboat trade was the contribution to nineteenth-century communications. Valuable government contracts were signed with boat owners to transport and deliver materials for the U.S. postal service. Louis Tarascon saw an opportunity in 1822 to supplement his income and provide an essential public service. Acting as postmaster, he proclaimed in an advertisement in the *Louisville Public Advertiser*:

The Post Master at Shippingport, to the Captains of Steam Boats, and of any other vessels arriving there, viz: By the 14th Article of the post-office act, every master of a vessel is bound, immediately on his arrival at a port, and before breaking bulk, to deliver, to the post office of said port, all letters directed to any person within the United States, which are under his care, and within his power, and brought by his vessel, except such letters as are for the owner or principal consignee: Therefore, all captains or masters of steamboats or other vessels, arriving at this place, are requested agreeably to said law, to deliver all letters at the Shippingport post office.

By the 1820s most Shippingport citizens had become wage earners and part of a cash economy. Unlike in pioneer times, residents now rarely raised and preserved their own food supply, but instead purchased it from a central marketplace. Inspection, licensing, and control of commerce were important functions of community life. In 1824 the trustees of Shippingport erected a market house and declared Tuesday and Friday to be the town market days, particularly inviting "the attention of the farmers, butchers and others, in the habit of attending market with produce."

In *Sketches of Louisville*, McMurtrie estimated Shippingport's population in 1819 to be six hundred and offered the following description of the town:

> Some taste is already perceptible in the construction of their houses, many of which are neatly built and ornamented with galleries, in which, of a Sunday, are displayed all the beauty of the place. It is, in fact, the *"Bois de Bouloigne"* of Louisville, it being the resort of all classes, on high days and holidays. At these times, it exhibits a spectacle at once novel and interesting. The number of steam boats in the port, each bearing one or two flags, the throng of horses, carriages, and gigs, and the contented appearance of a crowd of pedestrians, all arrayed in their "Sunday's best," produce an effect it would be impossible to describe.

*Louis Tarascon*

Portland, still under the control of its sole proprietor, Lytle, continued to prosper as large investors saw advantages in its prime waterfront location. In 1816 James D'Wolf Jr., of Rhode Island, purchased from Lytle, Robert Todd R.S., and Cosby a 106-acre lot for $10,600. Located at the extreme east end of Portland, adjacent to the Louisville boundary, D'Wolf planned to build and operate a steam-powered factory called the Hope Distillery. It was to be the largest whiskey producer in the world and the first to use steam engines in its operation. His goal was to produce 1,200 gallons of distilled spirits a day, an unprecedented industrial output. The residue of the sour-mash process was used to feed an estimated five thousand hogs at the site. After the factory was completed, the operation was poorly administered and was never able to acquire enough grain supplies locally to operate at peak efficiency. Although the hog raising and slaughtering operation proved successful, the Hope Distillery failed by 1826. Decades later D'Wolf's heirs profited when the land was purchased as the site of inexpensive housing for factory workers.

Developing the Portland property was a serious financial drain on Lytle's resources. He was increasingly having problems paying his bills, and Rowan was spending time defending Lytle against a series of lawsuits. Cash poor, Lytle paid his brother-in-law in property deeds. Still, Lytle persisted in advancing his canal plans without taking on partners.

For many years, merchants and businessmen in Cincinnati railed against Louisville's seeming unwillingness to build a canal bypassing the Falls. Louisville's economy, like those in Portland and Shippingport, benefited from the transshipping industries created by the navigational barrier. Travelers on the Ohio arrived in the Falls ports and stayed in local hotels, ate in local taverns, stored their goods in local warehouses, hired local hackney cabs and dray carts, and traveled on local toll roads. When they reached their destination, just three miles away, they repeated the entire process until the next steamboat was available for them to continue their journey.

As early as 1804, Indiana made noise to build a canal on the northern shore of the Ohio. The river made a dramatic curve around the Falls, going from the southern location at Louisville, turning northwest to round the point of Shippingport, and plunging southwest toward the Portland wharf. Three sides of Portland were bounded by the Ohio River. The shortest point between the upper and lower river was a 2.5-mile straight line cutting across the topographical elbow. The Indiana shore, however, required a much farther distance to bypass the barrier. From Jeffersonville on the east to New Albany on the west, the path of a canal would need to be cut through nearly seven miles of limestone and transect several streams.

Despite the logistical challenges presented by the topography of the Falls, as Kentucky delayed building a canal, Indiana persisted. In 1817 the Ohio Canal Company was chartered, and northern businessmen purchased stock and began planning the improbable task of creating a canal on the river's Indiana shore. Lytle's entire business model was premised on owning the only logical site for canal construction. McMurtrie's *Sketches of Louisville* was largely a subtle attempt to dissuade investors from the Indiana canal scheme. In correspondence during the summer of 1819, McMurtrie wrote continually to Lytle to thank him for providing financial support, for purchasing subscriptions to his book, and especially for "remembering their little <u>private agreement</u>." That agreement was apparently for McMurtrie's editorial emphasis on the impracticality of an Indiana canal.

McMurtrie also sought to encourage Lytle's sponsorship of his proposed infirmary in Portland: "Has Dr. Galt mentioned to you our conversation reflecting on Infirmary at Portland? Should encouragement be given me I should like to establish and conduct such an establishment, the benefits to Portland resulting there from would be incalculable." Had it been built, McMurtrie's infirmary would have preceded the 1822 establishment of the Louisville Marine Hospital and would have been a major enhancement for the community. Despite encouragement and financial promises, McMurtrie lacked the funds necessary to meet his expenses. Owing $350 to his printer, Shadrach Penn of the *Louisville Public Advertiser*, and a year's rent to his landlord, McMurtrie quietly slipped out of Louisville, leaving behind a trail of promises, invoices, and the city's first history book.

---

The War of 1812 stimulated an unprecedented economic boom in the Ohio Valley. Manufactured goods from Great Britain were embargoed, and new American factories began to produce objects for local use and international export. The newly invented steamboat moved produce down the rivers to New Orleans and the world. With Napoleon's armies at war, European agriculture was disrupted, and shipment of American commodities to the continent increased dramatically. These exports slowed when America's second war with England ended in 1815, and payment on a large national debt began to come due. Much of the cost of the war, and the four million dollars needed to purchase the Louisiana Territory, had been borrowed from abroad, and those creditors demanded species rather than bank notes.

To help control the nation's economy, the Second Bank of the United States was chartered in 1817. When a branch office was set up in Louisville, it followed the government's direction and began to call in loans to state and local banks, many of which had been profligate in their easy credit policies to friends and relatives of the bankers. Large numbers of loans in Louisville, Cincinnati, and other western urban centers had been used to expand industrial capacity, but much of the money went into real estate speculation, with new loans often being obtained using only other mortgaged properties as security. Land values in places such as Portland and Shippingport had expanded beyond reason, and when the banks began to demand immediate payment in cash, the boom went bust. America's first economic depression, the panic of 1819, gripped the nation as foreclosures, bankruptcies, and debtors' prisons became commonplace.

The lofty dreams of Lytle and the Tarascons faced new realities. Gone were the limitless opportunities, eager investors, and cagey entrepreneurs. Hard times had come to the Ohio Valley, and a time of retrenchment and disappointment began. What had been promising urban developments became the first western ghost towns, and personal fortunes and reputations were destroyed. Friends, even relatives, found relationships strained to the breaking point. On January 5, 1818, Todd lashed out at his uncle Lytle as his own business interests began to suffer:

> [Y]ou seem to have taken considerable umbrage at an expression contained in my last letter which was if I mistake not that your conduct in relation to the lotts No. 7 & 8 in the range of County seats was not correct—and I still contend that it was not and that you are not justified by the remark contained in my letter in returning such an answer—before I had any thought of moving to Portland I proposed to you to build a warehouse and designated the ground—I assured my acquaintances that I would have a warehouse built early in the year following on the best situation near the falls and obtained assurances of their custom.

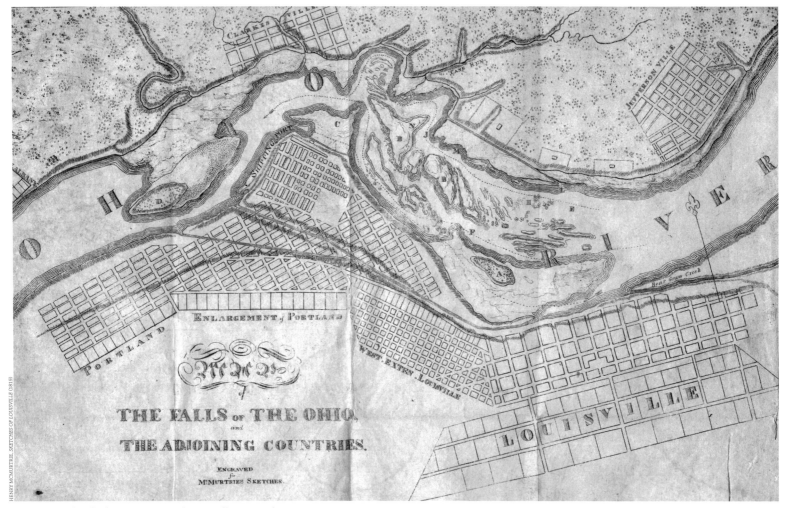

*Map of Portland, Shippingport, and Louisville, Kentucky, ca. 1819*

This ground not withstanding your agreement you sold to Captain Shreve without counseling me—I never intended to remind you of this circumstance—I will now ask my Uncle what he thinks of my situation and what to think, are my feelings on this subject.

Within two years Lytle hired Robert Wallace Jr., apparently as a replacement agent. Lytle sternly rebuked his new employee on January 7, 1820, for what he considered a dereliction of duty:

It appeared necessary to employ or unite with some person or persons to erect Wharf or Warehouse at Portland in order to promote the interest of the place—I am well aware you will have to employ one or two Agents or Overseers and it was for that purpose I gave you so high a Salary that you might have some person always on the spot when you were called off—Mr. Todd & Mr. Barclay did not receive more than one third what you are getting but finding it was necessary for the preservation of my property to have a Man constantly riding over it every day I was induced for that purpose to give you the high price.

In December 1820 Wallace wrote to Lytle with frustrations of his own:

I had almost accomplished a sale of Lot No. 1 in square 21 for 350$ in hand—which I thought would meet your approbations, but the man was persuaded to buy a lot in Shippingport for a smaller price.

Having excited the animosity of the Butchers and others by dunning them for rent &c—a party of them made an attack on Mr. Gallagher and myself on the 9th inst. At a time when we were rather unprepared—but we managed to beat them in such a manner, that I was compelled to pay 24.35$ damages & costs—our injury was trifling—tho' our risk was great—*It is utterly impossible to manage and preserve your property here without making enemies*—particularly in the outset—They have been so long accustomed to free plunder, that they consider me an intruder on their privileges.

---

Charles Sealsfield, an English tourist passing through the area in 1825, saw fit to comment on the characteristics of its inhabitants:

Below Louisville, are the two villages of Shippingport and Portland; the former is two miles from the town, with 150 inhabitants, the latter at the distance of three miles, with fifty inhabitants, mostly boatmen and keepers of grog shops, for the lowest classes of people. The environs of Louisville are well cultivated, Portland and Shippingport excepted, the inhabitants of which are said to extend their notions of common property too far.

The Tarascons also suffered economic woes and faced dozens of lawsuits demanding repayment of loans, especially from their former friends in Philadelphia. On March 14, 1821, as this notice from the *Louisville Public Advertiser* attests, they were forced to put up all their unsettled lots for public sale:

I am confident that any person acquainted with the importance of the commercial situation of the place, (truly the key to the commerce and navigation of the western country,) will find his interest at having so easily a share of it. For raise of property must always happen where commerce and navigation are to centre; and as to *the present hard times being the worst for sale, are the best to buy,* all chances of variations in prices decidedly for the purchasers.

Moreover, the hard times moved John Tarascon to reach out to Lytle in 1821 and propose an alliance for their common survival:

You will see by the within advertisement . . . there will be a public sale of about one half of the remaining unsettled lots of Shippingport and as the interests of Portland and Shippingport are co-equals—connected together that the raise of one raises the other; meanwhile the leaders of Louisville will always, or at least for a Time, do as much as they can to keep them Down, I have determined to let this lot go under the hammer for whatever they will, in order low prices and long credits may become an inducement for many people to bye and that an increased population may become a sudden and constant attraction for much more.

You conceive easily that more people in Shippingport will produce more people in Portland, as well as more people in Portland will produce more in Shippingport. On account of the situation you may consider Shippingport as a part of Portland and that *whatever will benefit a part—will benefit the whole.*

If I do succeed, next year you may do the same yourself for Portland and you will succeed also: but should I not succeed you could not either.

Time and fortune were running out for the brothers Tarascon. Their land sale was not enough to satisfy their creditors, and in February 1823 they surrendered possession of the great Merchants Manufacturing Mill to the firm of Berthold and Chouteau of Saint Louis. That firm turned over administration of the mill to John's brother-in-law, Joseph Barbaroux. The Tarascons, penniless and hopelessly in debt, depended upon the charity of Barbaroux for their daily living expenses.

On August 11, 1825, John could stand no more and committed suicide. In a life full of irony, none is more poignant than his finish. A devout Roman Catholic, he had donated the first church grounds and graveyard in Louisville to benefit his church. Because of his suicide, he was denied burial in the sacred ground he had so generously provided.

Louis lost political control of his property later in November 1827. The event was heralded by a news announcement in the *Focus*: "The citizens of Shippingport have had a meeting; have expressed a willingness to come under the jurisdiction of a corporation court for Louisville; and have appointed a committee to confer with the committee appointed by the citizens of that place."

Lytle had sunk all his capital into his scheme to develop and control a canal at the Falls. Cash poor, he began to sign away more land to Rowan for legal services, and the U.S. Bank seized and sold other properties. Earlier land deals soured, and former friends moved to protect their own interests. George C. Gwathmey represented the interests of the heirs of his nephew, Richard C. Anderson Jr., who had invested in Lytle's land with high expectations in 1817. Gwathmey, the former clerk of the Bank of Kentucky, did little to spare Lytle's feelings in a communication of May 9, 1827:

I reply much confidence on being able to satisfy you that <u>however strong</u> may be the <u>claims</u> of <u>your creditors</u> upon you to <u>restrain</u> you from making title to the children, for whom I now write. I have a stronger claim . . . and it is possible that in pursuance of my duty. I shall be obliged to go to law with <u>you</u> General: I shall have related the circumstances of this case, (which on bringing to mind having for my side the Books and papers of the Bank). . . . No sir, the transaction was open as any and at that time, well understood by you.

By 1824 the game was up for Lytle. Responding to an angry letter from Captain Shreve, one of Portland's first investors, Lytle renounced any further interest in his land at the Falls: "You must be aware I have no further control over Louisville or Portland property what I had not sold and conveyed before has subsequently fallen into John Rowan's hands by purchase at Sherriff's Sale and the U. S. Bank & Judge Rowan now control the whole." In 1832 the Kentucky Court of Appeals rendered a judgment against Lytle's heirs, and Shreve received compensation for his legal claims.

With Lytle no longer in the picture, the fortunes of a canal at the Falls improved. In 1825 the Kentucky legislature chartered the Louisville and Portland Canal Company. After a daunting four-year construction project, the dream of bypassing the Falls was finally accomplished. On December 21, 1830, the *Uncas* eased through the new locks. Completed with the financial support of the federal government, the Portland Canal was a tremendously successful commercial venue for its investors. History had turned a page. The day of the single proprietor was over at the Falls, and new chapters were ready to be written.

Building the Portland Canal, an essential link in America's inland maritime system, was a heroic achievement of innovative engineering and backbreaking labor. Original estimates projected construction time of six months duration with five hundred workers, mostly hired slaves, needed for its completion. However, when the engineers encountered solid bedrock just below the surface, the task was dramatically altered. Eventually more than three thousand workers, most Irish immigrants, were used to dig, blast, haul, and hammer the limestone into submission.

The original fifty-foot-wide canal had been designed for the small steamboats of 1825, but in the five years it took to complete construction, the average size of western boats grew considerably. Therefore, only about one-third of the Ohio River boats could fit through the narrow passage at the time of its opening. Nevertheless, the original canal proved successful for investors, shippers, and merchants.

The canal would forever impact the futures of Shippingport and Portland. During the excavation it was discovered that the limestone removed from the canal produced ideal hydraulic cement. This became the basis of a major manufacturing industry. The most dramatic impact to the topography was that Shippingport became a man-made island. Accessibility to the town was severely limited, with only two small bridges linking Shippingport to the Kentucky mainland. The canal's contractors sounded Shippingport's death knell with this 1828 announcement in the *Focus*: "TO THE PUBLIC—The subscribers having erected a bridge across the Lock of the Canal at Shippingport, for their own convenience, they are reluctantly compelled to refuse the

*Title page of the Charter of the Louisville and Portland Canal Company, 1825*

use of it to the public for horses or vehicles of any kind on the account of the inconveniences and interruptions caused by their transit. It is hoped due attention will be given to [t]his notice by persons having to pass in that quarter."

Shippingport's end came after a record-breaking flood in 1832, when the rising Ohio River swept over the low-lying town and destroyed nearly all the buildings. "The river is now about one foot higher than it has been within the recollection of our oldest inhabitants, and is still rising at the rapid rate of one inch per hour. The damage done to property in the lowest part of the city cannot fall short of twenty or thirty thousand dollars," reported the *Public Advertiser*.

Virtually all the original residents of Shippingport surrendered. Nicholas Berthoud, after selling his wharf and warehouse to brother-in-law William Bakewell, died of cholera the next year. Louis Tarascon drifted into utopian fantasies and as late as 1839 was still promoting dreams of model schools teaching democracy to immigrants and an elaborate series of perfect cities populating the Oregon Trail. He was also writing unsolicited letters of advice to American presidents. It is believed Tarascon died in New York City in 1840, virtually forgotten in the town he envisioned in Kentucky.

During the ensuing decades the glory days of Shippingport deteriorated into a memory. Roughly every fifty years the locks and canals were enlarged, each time taking more Shippingport land for its operations. In 1927 the Louisville Gas and Electric Company built a massive hydroelectric plant on the northern tip of the island at nearly the exact location of the old Tarascon mill. The rest of the property was preempted for operational support for the U.S. Army Corps of Engineers, and the final few fishermen, the last Shippingporters, were legally removed from the island in 1958.

Portland moved in the opposite direction. With the control of Lytle and Rowan removed, land was purchased and properties developed on a steady but more modest scale. Thousands of immigrants fleeing the Irish potato famine joined their relatives, who had stayed after helping to build the canal. Many Irish worked in the steamboat and railroad trades. German Catholics, leaving their homelands during and after a series of revolutions in 1848, reached Portland and became storekeepers, cobblers, basket makers, tavern owners, brewers, butchers, and builders. A burgeoning steamboat-building industry developed locally, and from the 1830s until the Civil War many of the great "floating palaces," such as the *Eclipse,* were completed in Portland.

Although lawsuits concerning Portland land continued until the early 1840s, the loss of Portland did not mean the end of William Lytle or his family. In 1830, a year before his death, Lytle's friend President Andrew Jackson named him surveyor-general of the United States. His son, Robert Todd Lytle (1804–1839), is remembered in Ohio history as "Orator Bob," a highly successful and popular congressman. Robert's son, General William Haines Lytle (1826–1863), the "poet-warrior" of the Union army, met a heroic and celebrated death at the Battle of Chickamauga.

The only memorial to Portland's founders rests in street names. Lytle and Rowan streets are modest residential areas running the width of Portland. Bank Street, the second-most prominent avenue in the community, got its name when the U.S. Bank foreclosed on Lytle and began selling the property to individual buyers. In essence, the bank was Portland's last proprietor.

Portland applied for annexation by the city of Louisville in 1834 to facilitate an arrangement to bring a railroad from Lexington to its wharf. When Louisville merchants ended the railroad's operation down Portland Avenue (the first steam-powered interurban service in America), Portland had itself de-annexed. The town of Portland flourished from 1842 until its final decision to join Louisville in 1852. Portland became Louisville's first West End neighborhood and still retains a sense of independence, pride, and identity.

The era of town building below the Falls was over, replaced by decades of steady growth for Portland and the ultimate decline of Shippingport. Louisville, with its trustee system of government and decision making, proved to be the better model of successful development at the Falls of the Ohio.

*Rick Bell serves as heritage consultant for Louisville's Waterfront Development Corporation on a project to research, archive, and publish a history of the city's riverfront from its pioneer days through the development of today's successful Waterfront Park. He has recently served as executive director of the U.S. Marine Hospital Foundation of Louisville, Kentucky. The foundation is dedicated to preserving and restoring the last remaining inland hospital, established to provide health care for Ohio River boatmen, built by the federal government in 1852. Bell is the former assistant to the director of The Filson Historical Society, where he supervised the design and installation of the Carriage House Museum. He was formerly the owner of a Navajo folk art gallery in Cortez, Colorado, and served as the interim executive director of the Gallup Inter-tribal Indian Ceremonial Association. Bell is the author of* The Great Flood of 1937: Rising Waters, Soaring Spirits, *in conjunction with the University of Louisville Photo Archives and Butler Books of Louisville. The book was recognized by the* Louisville Courier-Journal *as one of its top ten books for 2007.*

## SELECTED BIBLIOGRAPHY

Arthur, Stanley Clitsby. *Audubon: An Intimate Life of An American Woodsman.* Gretna, LA: Pelican Publishing, 1999.

Bader, Anne Tobbe. "Shippingport: A Historic Context of Shippingport Island, Jefferson County, Kentucky." Report by Corn Island Archaeology, Louisville, KY, 2007.

F. Berthault to William Wainwright, September 13, 1814, Manuscript Department, Filson Historical Society.

George M. Bibb to Caesar A. Rodney, December 11, 1807, Manuscript Department, Filson Historical Society.

Burnett, Robert A. "Louisville's French Past." *The Filson Club History Quarterly* 50, no. 2 (April 1976): 5–27.

Carter, Ruth C., ed. *For Honor, Glory, and Union: The Mexican and Civil War, Letters of Brig. General William Haines Lytle.* Lexington: University Press of Kentucky, 1999.

Cox, Isaac J. "The Burr Conspiracy in Indiana." *Indiana Magazine of History* 25, no. 4 (December 1929): 273.

Crnkovich, John J. "Tarascon Junr., James Berthoud & Co. and the Development of Shippingport, Kentucky." Thesis, University of Louisville, 1955.

Fatout, Paul. "Canal Agitation at Ohio Falls." *Indiana Magazine of History* 27, no. 4 (December 1961): 279–309.

Hall, Virginius Cornick, Jr. *From Tomahawk to High Finance: The Life of General William Lytle (1770–1831).* Cincinnati: Cincinnati Historical Society, 1957.

Hunter, Louis C. *Steamboats on the Western Rivers: An Economic and Technological History.* New York: Dover Press, 1977.

Johnson, Leland R., and Charles E. Parrish. *Triumph at the Falls: The Louisville and Portland Canal.* Louisville: U.S. Army Corps of Engineers, 2007.

Latrobe, J. H. B. *The First Steamboat Voyage on the Western Waters.* Baltimore: Maryland Historical Society, 1871.

Levi, Lily C. "Traditions of Shippingport." Paper read before the Filson Club, Louisville, 1906.

*Louisville Journal,* October 20, 1863.

Lytle Family Papers, Cincinnati Historical Society, Cincinnati, OH.

Morneweck, Evelyn Foster. *Chronicles of Stephen Foster's Family.* Pittsburgh: University of Pennsylvania Press, 1944.

Rice, Emmet A. "A Forgotten Man of Indianapolis." *Indiana Magazine of History* 34, no. 3 (September 1938): 286–87.

Sealsfield, Charles. *The Americans as They Are; Described in a Tour Thru the Valley of the Mississippi.* London: Hurst, Chance and Co., 1828.

Stone, J. William. "The Hope Distillery Company." *The Filson Club History Quarterly* 57, no. 1 (January 1983): 29–35.

Thomas, Samuel W., and Eugene H. Conner. "Henry McMurtrie, M.D. (1793–1865) First Historian and Promoter of Louisville." *The Filson Club History Quarterly* 43, no. 4 (October 1969): 311–24.

Tischendorf, Alfred, and E. Taylor Parks, eds. *The Diary and Journal of Richard Clough Anderson Jr. (1814–1826).* Durham, NC: Duke University Press, 1964.

Wade, Richard C. *The Urban Frontier: The Rise of Western Cities, 1790–1830.* Chicago: University of Chicago Press, 1959.

Wiley, Richard T. *Monongahela: The River and Its Region.* Butler: Pennsylvania Historical Association, 1937.

Yater, George H. *Two Hundred Years at the Falls of the Ohio: A History of Louisville and Jefferson County.* 2nd ed. Louisville: Filson Club, 1987.

# 5

## "Omen of Evil": Steamboats and the Colonization of the Ohio River Valley

THOMAS C. BUCHANAN

Benjamin Latrobe's famous account of the voyage of the *New Orleans* foreshadows many of the changes steamboats brought to the Ohio Valley region. He describes the *New Orleans* as having two cabins, "one aft, for ladies (comfortably furnished)" and another "larger one forward for gentlemen." With these words he conveyed new forms of river space, structured by gender in novel ways. He also noted changes in river work. He writes of "a captain, an engineer named Baker . . . the pilot, six hands, two female servants, a man waiter, [and] a cook." While he called the workers "unimaginative," Latrobe recognized the historic importance of these laborers. By the time he wrote his account, years after the historic trip of 1811, steamboat owners employed a vast new commercial working class. Differences that he noted on the *New Orleans*, between the cabin and deck crews, between male and female work, and between skilled and common laborers, endured as crucial divisions. This chapter will explore how ideas of gender and race molded the Ohio River steamboat economy, creating a crucial context for understanding the significance of the *New Orleans*.

Native Americans played an important role in Latrobe's narrative. Native peoples were amazed and awestruck by the

*New Orleans* and its crew; they were at once skeptical of and attracted to the new technology. Near the mouth of the Ohio River, "Chickasaw Indians" paddled out and raced the *New Orleans* before retreating "with wild shouts," which Latrobe felt were probably "shouts of defiance." At other points of the voyage native peoples shared the boat's labor, as when Chickasaw men helped cut wood for the *New Orleans*'s engines. It was during one of these stops when a native person "converse(d) in English with the men." During the exchange the crew learned that their steamboat was known by the Chickasaw as the "Penelore" or "fire canoe." They thought "it was supposed to have some affinity with the Comet that had preceded the earthquake,—the sparks of the chimney of the boat being likened to the train of the celestial visitant." They were convinced that the "smokey atmosphere of the steamer" and the churning waters from the paddle wheels were related to recent unusual geological and celestial events. All were evidence that the gods were unhappy with the loss of their ancestral lands to outside invaders.

Latrobe interpreted these early contacts in ways that are worth remembering as we commemorate the invention of the western steamboat. For the "native inhabitants," he asserted, who lived in "boundless forests," the first steamboat was an "omen of evil." It was a "precursor of their expulsion from their ancient homes." These early fears and concerns, Latrobe believed, influenced the Chickasaw as late as 1834, when during the Indian removals of Andrew Jackson's presidency, "hundreds refused to trust themselves to such conveyances, but preferred making their long and weary pilgrimages on foot." These trenchant observations suggest the way the steamboat economy remade native life. Steamboats encouraged European American and African American migration to the Ohio Valley, but their primary role in Native American history was one of marginalization and then removal. The steamboat era is thus intimately linked to the situation today where the memory of indigenous inhabitants has all but been erased from the region.

Latrobe's account gives readers a glimpse of how the steamboat revolution transformed the population of the Ohio Valley. He reminds us that the voyage represented more than a triumph of technological innovation; it signified the beginnings of a massive economic change that would be as much about new American ideas of gender and race as it was about machines and technological progress. Steamboats became microcosms and facilitators of a shift in ideals about domestic and racialized labor that transformed the Ohio River Valley. Latrobe's "female servants" represented new definitions of womanhood dependent on the wage, whose work was devalued both in the industry and the larger culture. While Latrobe does not mention African Americans, soon river work was racialized and intertwined with gender ideas. "Domestic" work on steamboats became associated with the cooks, chambermaids, and waiters of African descent at the same time that domesticity was being devalued as a source of productive labor. In these ways, the broad shifting of populations and redefinitions of work—characteristics of both

western settlement and industrialization—were very evident in the nineteenth-century Ohio River Valley.

Native Americans were part of this redefinition of work on the rivers only through their exclusion. This represented a huge shift. Native peoples had traditionally been central to river life and were integrated into the eighteenth-century flatboat economy. The Ohio River Valley in these years was what historian Richard White has called a middle ground, a place of cultural and economic accommodation. This was the land of the Shawnee, a people who had considerable control over early contact with American migrants. Their situation changed quickly in the revolutionary era—to a world where Native American and white settlers struggled over land, and race relations became increasingly typified by violence. After supporting the British in the Revolution, the Shawnee were forced to cede most of southern Ohio to the American government in 1795. As in the case of other native groups, the wars against the Shawnee would be an essential precursor to the steamboat era that followed. The violent dispossession of the lands along the Ohio River, so often separated from the story of the *New Orleans*, should instead be considered as a connected part of the western settlement process. The defeat of an intertribal army gathered (but not led) by the absent Shawnee leader Tecumseh at Tippecanoe in 1811, during the voyage of the *New Orleans*, suggests the link between formal violence and western economic development.

What were indigenous economies like before this dispossession? Despite a long history of interaction with the French, English, and then American empires, Ohio Valley Indians were able to maintain their distinctive cultures and staged various revitalization movements in the eighteenth and early nineteenth centuries. According to historian Stephen Warren, common ideas about gender roles linked various ethnic groups in the

*Native Americans are firing on a flatboat, which is loaded with livestock and domestic items, ca. 1830.*

*African American workers are loading empty barrels onto the* Queen City, *somewhere along the Ohio River, ca. 1906.*

region including the Shawnee, Delaware, and Miami. At a time when settler culture was broadly patriarchal with a woman's status legally subsumed under that of her husband, Native American women were responsible for their village's crop production and were seen to have a valued and complementary position in village life.

These ideas were directly challenged during the western expansion era in both agrarian and nascent industrial communities. The Quakers and some missionary groups viewed native women's roles as inappropriate and urged Indian families to take up family farming and men to take control over grain production, animal husbandry, and lumbering. European-American ideas of gender were also evident on the rivers, but here native peoples were pushed away rather than pushed to reform. In contrast with Latrobe's early account of native peoples' presence, by 1850 native peoples were virtually absent from steamboat life. On the lower Ohio, boats such as the *Time and Tide* (Louisville to Galena), the *Mountaineer* (Louisville to Saint Louis), and the *Alhambra* (Louisville to New Orleans), featured a new river working class. On the boats, there was a remarkable diversity of people including Americans and immigrants, European Americans and African Americans, slaves and free people, men and women. But there were no Indian names on steamboat crew lists. Travelers stopped recording observations of native peoples with any frequency. Native Americans, active on the waterways for hundreds of years, were now mostly absent from the region's growing cities and were not part of the region's newly invigorated trading economy. Indeed, steamboats were used to forcibly remove some Shawnee and other peoples to reservations on the Great Plains. They were deck passengers—cargo—in the remade Ohio Valley economy.

At the same time that native peoples were being excluded, African Americans were increasingly being included in western settlement structures. African Americans were incorporated over a wide-ranging geography, from slave territory south of the Ohio River to free land in the North. The river brought these worlds together, creating social tensions in the emergent, expansive nation. Free blacks from the northern banks of the Ohio traveled to the lands of slavery, down the Ohio and to the Mississippi. Enslaved people frequented the lower Ohio River, and the steamboat industry quickly became a site of considerable resistance as they "passed" their way to freedom. Changes in the experiences of river work thus created opportunities for westernized African Americans that were not available to the Shawnee and other native groups.

Above Louisville small numbers of African Americans worked in the steamboat industry, an industry associated with immigrant and white manhood. African Americans occupied mostly service and domestic roles amidst larger numbers of Irish and German immigrants and poor white American laborers. Despite their relative small size in the large river workforce, the workers were central to northern African American communities. Cincinnati's African American boatmen, for instance, composed about a quarter of the city's employed workers. They were drawn from a free black community (3,172 residents in 1850) that labored in racialized job categories. In "Little Africa" along the city's riverfront, urban and riverine black worlds blended together on the levee, facilitating the movement of workers. In Pittsburgh the black community, led by abolitionist Martin Delany, soon supplied small numbers of African Americans for service positions on western steamboats. These workers brought back important wages that helped sustain their enclaves.

William Wells Brown, who worked on both Ohio and Mississippi river packets, remembered the job requirements of a steamboat waiter very simply. "My employment on board was to wait on gentlemen," he recalled. This involved preparing the cabin table, carrying bags, serving food, filling the coal stoves, cleaning, running errands ashore, and generally catering to the individual needs of passengers. Waiters washed the cabin floor at night long after passengers had retired for bed, extending their hours of service. Such tasks had to be done while maintaining a respectable personal appearance. Waiters were expected to be well groomed and dressed (at their own expense) in suits or jackets. Though they were poor, they were expected to blend into the ambiance of the often well-appointed cabins.

African American cooks, such as thirty-five-year-old Anthony Hammonds and twenty-four-year-old Henry Hammonds, who worked on the *Illinois* out of Louisville, were also frequent fixtures on Ohio River steamboats. These cooks were responsible for the creation of a distinctive American cuisine that was noted for its variety, ranging from French-inspired pastries to savory local fare that blended African and English food traditions. The refined and copious food of western riverboats represented a departure from American food traditions or the frontier subsistence economies of eighteenth-century white settlers. To produce three meals a day, however, required hours of labor often in severe heat that stretched from the early hours of the morning, with breakfast preparation, to late in the evening when the final dinner dish was washed. This work, which helped create the boats' reputation among passengers, generally commanded higher wages than being a waiter. Cooks received as much as fifty dollars a month by mid-century on the larger boats.

Ann Davenport's working life demonstrates the intersections of gender and race in the Ohio Valley steamboat labor force. Davenport was born in Virginia in 1810 and was part of the migration of easterners into the Ohio River Valley in these years. She may well have migrated as an enslaved person, but by 1850 she was working as a free woman on the *Alhambra* on the lower Ohio and Mississippi rivers. She worked as the only woman amidst forty-one free workers and five enslaved ones. Her tasks would have been familiar to working-class urban women in the Ohio Valley: she washed table linen and bedding and towels from the staterooms, as well as officers' clothes. After hanging them to dry, she would have ironed these articles along the guardrails on the upper deck or in a small compartment at the rear of the ladies' compartment. Steamboat owners and officers hired women such as Davenport to re-create middle-class households, which became the civilized ideal in the era of national expansion.

Despite the devaluing of labor associated with domesticity, African American men could sometimes make a middle-class income as stewards and barbers. Stewards were known as the "captains of the cabin," a position that demanded managing the other cabin workers. Historian Carter G. Woodson called Cincinnati's stewards the "fortunate few" among river laborers. These workers procured foodstuffs from cities along the river network, using contacts with grocers and planters to supply cooks with necessary items. During travel, stewards managed waiters and cooks while also enforcing rules for cabin passengers. Barbers were also highly respected men. These workers, who were only employed on the larger boats, became the backbone of African American urban communities. They earned substantial tips and fees, money that gave them esteem when they went ashore.

While river work presented advantages to African Americans, they were still subject to the continuing exploitation of slavery and racism. Violence was common on steamboats, and

African Americans faced threats from all quarters. William Wells Brown found working as a steamboat waiter "better than living in the city," yet "anything but pleasant." "The Captain," Brown recalled, "was a drunken, profligate, hard-hearted creature, not knowing how to treat himself or any other creature." Passengers sometimes beat African American cabin-crew members for the slightest infractions. Chambermaids faced the added threat of sexual assault; the privacy of cabin rooms provided a dangerous opportunity for passengers and fellow workers. On-deck violence was routine. Mates drove their crews with all available weapons, though the whip was less common than it was on southern rivers. This violence spilled over into the levee districts of cities, where mobile African Americans were viewed with suspicion. On July 16, 1857, the *Cairo Times and Delta* editorialized, "How does it happen that so many colored blackguards are permitted to remain in Cairo? Where are these impudent niggers imported from Cincinnati or Shawneetown? We suggest the officers move them on." The change in racial geography noted in the newspaper article was significant. Shawneetown, founded by the federal government as an outpost to the Shawnee in the era of the middle ground, was now known by Cairo's respectable whites for its unruly African American workers.

Disease and injury were other key elements of the experience of African American laborers. While the era of flatboats and keelboats on the rivers was certainly very dangerous, industrialization brought new hazards that threatened the lives of all laborers. Snags, collisions, and fires killed or injured hundreds of workers on the western river system each year. The federal government listed 511 people as killed by boiler explosions in the Ohio Valley before 1848. Historian Robert Starobin estimated that several thousand slaves lost their lives in such accidents in the antebellum period. More commonly, river workers faced diseases, such as measles and influenza, which frequently trav-

eled along the rivers. These conditions were so threatening to the economy that the federal government built marine hospitals in Pittsburgh, Cincinnati, Louisville, Paducah, and Evansville in order to address the health conditions on the Ohio. These were historic efforts by the federal government to extend health-care benefits to working people, but river dangers always outran the ability of hospitals to manage the problem.

One of the ways African Americans survived under these conditions was through musical expression. Opportunities for singing and playing music were more limited on the Ohio River than on the Mississippi, where deck crew concentrations were more common. On southern rivers, plantation music could be heard in cabin bands; while on deck, collective songs, utilizing the call-and-response style for which African American culture would become famous, were frequently noted by travelers. Firemen sang as they loaded wood, and roustabouts sang while they loaded freight. One former slave recalled "de work went ahead easier when we was singin'." This expression had political implications. On the lower Ohio an enslaved crew reportedly bargained for more wages through song. Traveler Frederika Bremer heard enslaved workers incorporate "a hint that the singing would become doubly merry, and the singers would sing twice as well, if they could buy a little brandy when they reached Louisville, and that they could buy a little brandy if they could have a little money, and so on." Such demonstrations were a form of labor bargaining, while at the same time suggesting an influence on American musical culture, a dynamic on the river that would continue through the early jazz period.

The politics noted by Bremer were evident in a variety of other ways on board steamboats. The prevalence of racism and the context of a flourishing slave economy downriver provided the context for African American political expression. Black men, for instance, insisted on being called names of their own choosing. In this way they claimed the manhood generally associated with the industry but denied them through their confinement to domestic roles. In one revealing example, a waiter working on northern rivers refused to answer to the name "boy," the common term used for African American men in the South. The English traveler Henry Arthur Bright reported, "This morning we realized we were indeed on Free soil again . . . by the rudeness and impertinence of one of the Free Blacks who wait on board. Loch [his companion] asked him [the waiter] a question, and got no answer." Loch then proceeded with "Boy—what do you mean,—answer, sir." The waiter retorted, "I'll show you I'm a man." He continued his defiant speech, apparently knowing the free black steward would support his protest. Other political acts included work slowdowns, as in the case of one chambermaid whom a traveler reported was "languid," "indolent," and "diligently doing nothing." Another key element of African American political culture was the creation of reading networks, which took on particular meaning in the context of the lower Ohio, where free blacks had the opportunity to nurture literacy among enslaved people who were forbidden to learn to read.

This resistance is best understood as a response to the fissures in the expanding American empire. The settlement of the Ohio River Valley and the simultaneous growth of plantation societies along the southern rivers created tensions. The American nation was divided over slavery, a situation that stemmed from the Northwest Ordinance of 1787, which designated the lands north of the Ohio to be settled by free labor. In this context, steamboat laborers had an important political role in the nation. African Americans' politics were shaped by their experience as workers in an industrial environment but also as mobile maritime workers who worked on the boundaries of slavery and freedom. The cities and steamboats of the Ohio River Valley provided for a constant mixing of peoples that made determining labor status difficult. One enslaved barber from Louisville said, "It was just as though [I] was free," when he walked through the city's streets to visit his free family members and friends. Another enslaved Kentucky man, Milton Clarke, bargained with his master so that he could "pass up and down the river as [he] pleased," and "transact any business as though [he] was free." Such stories illustrate that abstract distinctions between slavery and freedom, between free land and slave land, were in reality blurry and contingent. People moved through the river economy constructing new identities as they went. This situation vexed slaveholders and boat captains (who were fearful of being sued for carrying away enslaved property), as well as southern police (who sometimes jailed northern free black steamboat workers in southern ports), but the mixing could not be effectively controlled.

In this context, northern African American steamboat workers were important in the resistance to slavery. Many of them were refugees from slavery and maintained contact with their southern brethren through river work, thus maintaining kinship ties in the process. Historian James Oliver Horton has documented several revealing cases of Cincinnati boat workers shuttling information to slave territory. These contacts were often crucial in helping runaway slaves negotiate their way to free land. In Saint Louis Henry Bibb was helped by a black steward who "very kindly aided him" in getting "into the land of freedom." Chambermaids would hide enslaved people in cabin rooms, while roustabouts would shelter them in small riverboat holds. In other cases river hands would testify to the freedom of runaways, helping them gain berths on north-bound steamboats. Such stories, which occur frequently in the historical record, indicate that the river—which always had a mythological place in African American oral culture—took on new meaning in the American antebellum period. In the words of historian Keith Griffler, the Ohio River was the "front line" of American freedom.

By the time the river freedom networks were well developed, the Shawnee and their brethren were a distant memory in the Ohio Valley landscape. Notably, it was at this time, mid-century, when middle-class river valley dwellers began to reconstruct the history of these peoples as part of the memory of western expansion and progress. Historian Thomas Ruys Smith analyzes how Mississippi and Ohio River Valley "panoramas" developed in this context. Panoramas allowed viewers to experience the immense size of the Mississippi River system by watching gigantic moving canvases, designed to re-create the experience of river travel. Physical movement was paired with intellectual movement, as viewers were encouraged to consider the advancement of societies as well as the changing geography. Native Americans were important to this process. Dr. Montroville Wilson Dickeson's *Panorama of the Monumental Grandeur of the Mississippi Valley*, an example of this style, was displayed in the years before the Civil War. It was about three hundred feet long and passed in motion before rapt audiences who paid twenty-five cents for admission. Dickeson's panorama began with the Ohio River and the prehistory of the "Red Man." The viewer was treated to an array of ancient "Mounds, tumuli, Fossas, etc" as well as chiefs in "full costume." Wars and violence were now forgotten as braves and "youths at their war practice" were presented as noble savages in bucolic settings. By the end of the panorama, the Indians had been fully consigned to their place as precursors to the civilization that now sprang from the banks of the western rivers. The Indian removals of the 1830s were entirely omitted. While Ohio Valley natives living on reserva-tions in Indian Territory would have had more scathing critiques of imperial expansion, the middle-class fare of the panoramas would serve as the dominant interpretation in American popular culture for years. This comforting narrative of the era of western settlement was reinforced by dozens of novels from this period that featured vanishing Native Americans as a noble part of the emerging national identity.

By the Civil War years, as relationships between Native Americans and the river increasingly lessened and art and memory provided a final erasure of the eighteenth-century middle ground, African Americans played an even more prominent role in the economy and society of the Ohio Valley riverboat world. During the Civil War thousands of free blacks and runaway slaves flocked to the riverboats of the Union's western flotilla, helping make the Union navy on the rivers into a force for liberation. The tradition of African American river work, and the shortage of white and ethnic workers in wartime, made it impossible for African Americans to be excluded from navy service. In addition to performing their customary domestic duties, Ohio River Valley African Americans fought next to whites in the heat of battle, loading guns and firing at the Confederates. They generally helped allow Union commanders to execute with success General Winfield Scott's Anaconda plan to strangle the South from the waterways. River workers were thus important in helping redefine race and labor in the nation. While gender continued to structure the labor force, as African American men found positions on deck, they claimed the physical manhood associated with roustabout culture.

The increase in the number of African American river workers only continued after the war. As Irish and German immigrants became less numerous on the docks of the Ohio Valley's river cities, African Americans, many recently emancipated,

*Lithograph of Ohio River at Hanover College, ca. 1850*

filled common labor positions. By 1870 African Americans composed 72 percent of deck crews in Saint Louis and Cincinnati and 53 percent of cabin crews. As one observer noted, "the calling now really belongs by rights to negroes, who are by far the best roustabouts and are unrivalled as firemen." The commercial districts of Pittsburgh, Cincinnati, and Louisville all became home to more African American river workers. The decks of steamboats and working-class urban wards suddenly became sites of African American music and song in ways that were typical of the lower Mississippi a few decades earlier. In some instances, greater advancement was possible in these years as well. By the turn of the century, Pittsburgh native Cumberland W. Posey rose from engineer to captain to boatbuilder to founder of the *Pittsburgh Courier*. Through the *Courier* Posey advocated African American civil rights, providing a tangible link with the river radicalism of the mid-nineteenth century.

Black labor had been part of the western extension of the nation, but men such as Posey worked to define that history on their own terms. Lacadio Hearn's remarkable ethnography of African American river life in Cincinnati in these years highlights the unique role of the river in African American memory. Hearn talked with old stevedores who had "wonderingly watched in their slave childhood the great white vessels panting the river's breasts." Other observers were less sanguine. Early river folklorist B. A. Bodkin recounted stories of hard-driving mates such as Lew Brown, Bull-Whip Shorty, and Mike Cartin. The surviving testimony of African Americans from the era illustrates the perception that tough working conditions prevailed on the rivers. As one steamboat barber testified, "I'd go to stealin' 'fo' I'd be a rooster [roustabout]. Certain su' I would, 'cause dey couln't wuk a man no harder in de penitentshuary." The river was thought about as a place of dangerous, low-paid work

even as it was remembered for its particular place in the African American freedom struggle. More recently, the Rivers Institute at Hanover College has continued to sustain the memory of ordinary river workers in its many projects to commemorate the 1811 voyage. In this way, the memories of African Americans, documented by travelers and recorded in interviews, have been revived in recent years and integrated into regional history.

As we remember the momentous voyage of the *New Orleans*, it is important to recall that this economic achievement was accompanied by a transformation in peoples' lives, changes that excluded some from the western expansion economy while bringing in others to work from distant lands. These changes, typical of human experience involving expansion and settlement, were made more dramatic by the industrial nature of work that steamboats helped bring to the Ohio Valley. The new class relations of industrialization were dramatically gendered and racialized, redefining the working roles of this formerly agrarian world. Free and enslaved African Americans took dramatic action in these years and thus entered the national debate about the future of race and nation. Two hundred years later, however, it is also worth remembering the lives of Native Americans, the forgotten and displaced, who were no less a part of this compelling and yet violent chapter in American history.

*Thomas C. Buchanan holds degrees from Oberlin College and Carnegie Mellon University. He served on the faculty at the University of Nebraska and has been at the University of Adelaide in Australia since 2005. He is the author of* Black Life on the Mississippi: Slaves, Free Blacks, and the Western Steamboat World, *published in 2004 by the University of North Carolina Press, and authored* "Race and (In)justice on the Mississippi: An Episode from 'The Journals of the* Davy Crockett'," *published in the March 2006 issue* *of the* Indiana Magazine of History. *His work has also appeared in the* Journal of Urban History, *the* Journal of Social History, *and* African American Urban History: Perspectives from the Colonial Period to the Present *(Palgrave, 2004), edited by Joe W. Trotter, Tera Hunter, and Earl Lewis.*

### SELECTED BIBLIOGRAPHY

Allen, Michael. *Western Rivermen, 1763–1861: Ohio and Mississippi Boatmen and the Myth of the Alligator Horse.* Baton Rouge: Louisiana State University Press, 1990.

Bennett, Michael J. "'Frictions': Shipboard Relations between White and Contraband Sailors." *Civil War History* 47, no. 2 (June 2001): 118–45.

Blassingame, John W., ed. *Slave Testimony: Two Centuries of Letters, Speeches, Interviews, and Autobiographies.* Baton Rouge: Louisiana State University Press, 1977.

Botkin, B. A., ed. *A Treasury of Mississippi River Folklore: Stories, Ballads, Traditions, and Folkways of the Mid-Century River Country.* New York: Crown Publishers, 1955.

Boydston, Jeanne. *Home and Work: Housework, Wages, and the Ideology of Labor in the Early Republic.* New York: Oxford University Press, 1990.

Brenson, Adolph B., ed. *America of the Fifties: The Letters of Fredrika Bremer.* New York, 1924.

Briggs, Harold E. "Lawlessness in Cairo, Illinois, 1848–1858." *Mid-America: An Historical Review* 33 (April 1951): 73n22.

Clarke, Lewis, and Milton Clarke, *Narratives of the Sufferings of Lewis and Milton Clarke: Sons of a Soldier of the Revolution, during Captivity of More Than Twenty Years among the Slaveholders of Kentucky, One of the So Called Christian States of North America.* New York: Arno Press, 1969.

Ehrenpreis, Anne Henry, ed. *Happy Country This America: A Travel Diary of Henry Arthur Bright.* Columbus: Ohio State University Press, 1978.

Feldman, Jay. *When the Mississippi Ran Backwards: Empire, Intrigue, Murder, and the New Madrid Earthquakes.* New York: Free Press, 2005.

Griffler, Keith. *Front Line of Freedom: African-Americans and the Forging of the Underground Railroad in the Ohio Valley.* Lexington: University of Kentucky Press, 2004.

Gudmestad, Robert H. "Steamboats and Cotton Kingdom." Paper at the 2004 Missouri Valley History Conference.

———. "Steamboats and Southern Economic Development." In *Technology, Innovation, and Southern Industrialization: From the Antebellum Era to the Computer Age.* Edited by Michele Gillespie and Susanna Delfino. Columbia: University of Missouri Press, 2008.

Hearn, Lafcadio. *Children of the Levee.* Edited by O. W. Frost. Lexington: University of Kentucky Press, 1957.

Hinderacker, Eric. *Constructing Colonialism in the Ohio Valley, 1673–1800.* Cambridge: Cambridge University Press, 1997.

Horton, James Oliver. *Free People of Color: Inside the African-American Community.* Washington, DC: Smithsonian Institution Press, 1993.

Horton, James Oliver, and Lois E. Horton. *In Hope of Liberty: Culture, Community, and Protest Among Northern Free Blacks, 1700–1860.* New York: Oxford University Press, 1997.

Hunter, Louis C. *Steamboats on the Western Rivers: An Economic and Technological History.* Cambridge, MA: Harvard University Press, 1949.

Kaye, Anthony E. "The Second Slavery: Modernity in the Nineteenth-Century South and the Atlantic World." *Journal of Southern History* 75, no. 3 (August 2009): 627–50.

Latrobe, John H. B. "The First Steamboat Voyage on the Western Waters." Maryland Historical Society Fund Publications, No. 6 (Baltimore: 1871), http://www.myoutbox.net/nr1871b.htm (accessed November 15, 2010).

Moore, John Hebron. "Simon Gray: A Slave Who Was Almost Free." *The Mississippi Valley Historical Review* 49, no. 3 (December 1962): 472–84.

Osofsky, Gilbert, ed. *Puttin' on Ole Massa.* New York: Harper and Row, 1969.

Ramold, Steven J. *Slaves, Sailors, Citizens: African Americans in the Union Navy.* Dekalb: Northern Illinois University Press, 2002.

Rawick, George P., ed. *The American Slave: A Composite Autobiography.* 19 vols. Westport, CT: Greenwood Press, 1972–79.

Smith, Thomas Ruys. *River of Dreams: Imaging the Mississippi before Mark Twain.* Baton Rouge: Louisiana State University Press, 2007.

Starobin, Robert. *Industrial Slavery in the Old South.* New York: Oxford University Press, 1970.

Trask, Kerry A. *Black Hawk: The Battle for the Heart of America.* New York: Henry Holt, 2006.

Ulrich, Laurel Thatcher. *Good Wives: Image and Reality in the Lives of Women in Northern New England.* New York: Vintage, 1991.

Warren, Stephen. *The Shawnees and Their Neighbors, 1795–1870.* Urbana: University of Illinois Press, 2005.

White, Richard. *The Middle Ground: Indians, Empires, and Republics in the Great Lakes Region, 1650–1815.* Cambridge: Cambridge University Press, 1991.

Woodson, Carter G. "Negroes of Cincinnati Prior to the Civil War." *Journal of Negro History* 1 (January 1916): 1–22.

Wortley, Emmerline Stuart. *Travels in the United States, etc., during 1849 and 1850.* New York: Harper and Bros., 1851.

# 6

## The Steamboat and Black Urban Life in the Ohio Valley

JOE WILLIAM TROTTER JR.

African Americans entered the Ohio Valley during the late colonial era, but their numbers remained small until the advent of the steamboat during the early nineteenth century. As the steamboat helped to transform the economy, politics, and culture of the Ohio Valley, it also stimulated the dramatic expansion of the region's black population. In addition to the major Atlantic seaport cities of New York, Boston, Philadelphia, Charleston, and others, increasing numbers of African Americans moved to the rapidly expanding Ohio Valley cities of Pittsburgh, Cincinnati, and Louisville. Although African Americans also moved to smaller centers of population along the Ohio River, this essay focuses on the rise of black communities in the three principal cities of the region. Beginning with the gradual movement of black people into the area during the late eighteenth century, African American communities developed in concert with European colonization and settlement of the Ohio Valley.

Like the history of blacks in the early New World, African American history in the Ohio Valley opened on a global stage within the larger context of enslavement. During the French and Indian wars, the Virginia Assembly enlisted free blacks, slaves, and Indians to fight in defense of the colony, but the law stipulated that they would serve "without arms, and may be employed as drummers, trumpeters or pioneers, or in such other servile labor, as they shall be directed to perform." As early as the 1750s, George Washington employed slaves and free blacks in his scouting expeditions to the Ohio River. In a letter to one captain in the colonial army, Washington urged the employment of "both mulattoes and negroes . . . as pioneers or hatchet men." By the early 1790s, 160 slaves lived in Allegheny County, where the Pittsburgh writer Hugh Henry Brackenridge claimed that they were owned "and abused" by devout Pennsylvanians who would not "for a fine cow have shaved their beards on Sunday." By the turn of the nineteenth century, fewer than two hundred blacks lived in the city of Pittsburgh; however, as Pennsylvania's gradual abolition law of 1780 took effect, all blacks in the city of Pittsburgh (about 185 persons or 3.8 percent of the total population) were free by 1810.

Some 450 miles downstream from Pittsburgh, the first European settlers arrived in Cincinnati during the late 1780s.

Unlike in Pittsburgh, however, blacks would only gradually move into Cincinnati during the early nineteenth century. As late as 1810, only eighty blacks appear in the city's official count.

From Pittsburgh to the Mississippi, the Ohio River flowed almost a thousand miles. Only the Falls at Louisville offered a major obstruction to downstream travel. At Louisville the river dropped between twenty-two and twenty-six feet within a distance of about two miles. Visitors frequently remarked on the violent character of the river at the Falls: "The ear is stunned with the sound of rushing waters; and the sight of waves dashing, and foaming, and whirling among the rocks and eddies below, is grand and fearful." Settlers moving down the Ohio River had to disembark at the Falls, travel overland to another spot on the river, and resume travel beyond the rapids. As early as 1751, two black men—one a slave and the other a "servant"—had entered the Louisville area. By 1792, when Kentucky gained statehood, it approved the institution of slavery and stimulated the immigration of slaveholding residents and black bondsmen. By 1810 Louisville's black population had increased to nearly five hundred. Enslaved blacks comprised more than 98 percent of the total black population, and about one-third of the city's total population.

Ohio Valley cities became major marketing centers for the region's agricultural and forest products. As settlements expanded along the Ohio River, farmers produced growing volumes of grain crops for markets at Cincinnati, Pittsburgh, and Louisville. Ohio Valley cities not only became processing and shipping centers for agricultural and forest products, but engendered and housed the development of new manufacturing industries as well. Such industries supplied the growing western markets and the increasing numbers of migrants who journeyed down the Ohio River. Under the influence of merchant capi-

talists and nascent manufacturing elites, the cities' wharves, warehouses, boatyards, artisan shops, hauling services, and coal and iron works expanded. By supplying settlers and traders as they moved down from Pittsburgh to New Orleans, these cities also slowly linked the region to national and international trade via the Mississippi River and the Gulf of Mexico. The value of western products, mainly from the Ohio Valley, entering the gulf port's inland trade rose from less than $3.6 million in 1801 to $5.3 million in 1806 and to $8 million in 1816.

Although diverse manufacturing enterprises developed in each of the cities, Pittsburgh emerged at the center of the early Ohio Valley economy. During the 1820s, however, the advent of the steamboat opened a new chapter in the economic and social history of the Ohio River Valley. Steamboats not only increased regional trade along the Ohio, but also intensified the oceangoing trade via the Mississippi Valley and the Gulf of Mexico. At the same time, transportation improvements—canals and railroads—connected the Ohio Valley to the Great Lakes and large eastern markets. The speed of steamboats lowered costs, particularly on the arduous upriver return trip from New Orleans, when workers used ropes to pull and drag keelboats upstream at the slow rate of ten to twelve miles per day. Whereas a barge set a record of seventy-eight days for the 1,500-mile return trip from New Orleans to Cincinnati in 1811, the steamboat cut the journey from New Orleans to Louisville, just ninety miles south of Cincinnati, to twenty-five days in 1817.

Although a variety of problems had to be ironed out, the steamboat soon proved its greater capacity over the earlier flatboats and keelboats. Under the growing impact of the steamboat, Cincinnati displaced Pittsburgh as the principal city along the Ohio River. Claiming the title of "Queen City of the West," Cincinnati built twelve of the seventy-one steamboats constructed before 1820, but thereafter it outstripped all competitors in the number of steamboats produced. The boat and shipyards also stimulated demand for steam engines, iron foundries, rolling mills, forges, machine shops, and machine tool shops. These industries not only produced spin-offs, such as the manufacturing of sugar mills for New Orleans sugar planters, for example, but also reinforced the city's foothold in earlier industries: flour milling, woodworking, whiskey distilling, slaughtering, meatpacking, and tanning. Indeed, by the 1840s, the

city's meatpacking business gave the "Queen City" its popular image—"Porkpolis." According to an English visitor, manufacturing was transforming Cincinnati into "one of the wonders of the New World."

Migration from the old northeastern states and the rapid influx of European immigrants transformed the demographic composition of the region. Between 1820 and 1850 Pittsburgh's population increased from an estimated 8,000 to 46,000; Cincinnati's rose from just more than 9,600 to 115,000; and

*An etching of the Falls of the Ohio River, 1811*

ZADOK CRAMER, *THE NAVIGATOR* (PITTSBURGH: CRAMER, SPEAR, AND EICHBAUM, 1811)

Louisville's increased from a little over 4,000 to 43,200. By 1850 German immigrants comprised between 10 and 15 percent of Pittsburgh's total, while the Irish increased to make up about 21 percent of the total. In Cincinnati the German-born population increased from 5 percent in 1820 to an estimated 15 to 20 percent of the total by the 1850s; by 1860 more than 40 percent of Cincinnatians were of German birth or German parentage. The Irish brought the city's immigrants or persons of immigrant parents to well over 50 percent of the total. Louisville also attracted a significant number of immigrants of German and Irish descent. By 1850 immigrants made up about 33 percent of the city's total population, much higher than most southern cities.

It was within the larger context of socioeconomic and demographic changes unleashed by the steamboat that the African American experience unfolded within the Ohio Valley. Although their numbers remained small during the antebellum period, the black population in Ohio Valley cities dramatically expanded during the era of the steamboat. Between 1820 and 1850 Pittsburgh's black population rose from less than 300 to more than 2,500; Cincinnati's from less than 500 to 3,200; and Louisville's from 1,100 to 7,000. As elsewhere, on the eve of the Civil War, Ohio Valley blacks were disproportionately mulattoes and women, with mulattoes making up well over half of the black population in Pittsburgh (74 percent), Allegheny City, which now comprises Pittsburgh's north side (60 percent), and Cincinnati (54 percent). By 1850 most blacks came to Pittsburgh from outlying rural and urban areas within the state, but a sizable minority, 25 to 28 percent, migrated from the upper South states of Virginia and Maryland. Nearly three-quarters of Cincinnati's black population came from the slaveholding states, mainly Virginia and Kentucky, which contributed well over 50 percent of the total. In Louisville, the majority of blacks were born in the South, and nearly one-third came from other southern states, particularly Virginia, the Carolinas, and Maryland.

Despite small numbers within the total populations of Ohio Valley cities, African Americans faced numerous obstacles gaining a foothold in the political economy of the region. From the outset, white political leaders, employers, and workers all hampered the migration, employment, and settlement of blacks in the Ohio Valley.  In Louisville white leaders described free blacks as "lazy, worthless, and less fortunate than slaves." Northern journalists and political leaders reinforced these views. They described free blacks and slaves alike as "depraved and ignorant." On one occasion, for example, the Ohio legislature reported free blacks as "more idle and vicious than slaves." One legislator urged the passage of "severe measures" to prevent their migration into the state. Similarly, an Indiana Supreme Court judge opposed the migration of what he called "a low, ignorant, degraded, multitude of free blacks" into the state.

Inflammatory racial commentary on the presumed character of black people was not simply rhetorical. Racially biased ideas and beliefs were translated into legislation and public policy. In 1786, although the Northwest Ordinance prohibited slavery north of the Ohio River, Ohio Valley legislators enacted a series of discriminatory laws against free blacks. In 1804 the Ohio legislature required free blacks and mulattoes to provide proof of their freedom upon entering the state. In 1807, while free whites could enter the state without restrictions, Ohio went a step further and required free blacks and mulattoes to post a $500 bond to guarantee their ability to support themselves. In 1815 and 1831 Indiana passed similar laws and in 1851 barred free blacks from its borders altogether. According to article 13 of the Hoosier State's new constitution, "no negro or mulatto" was to come into, or settle in the state, after the adoption of this constitution." Kentucky also prohibited the migration and settlement of free blacks within its borders, and, for its part, Pennsylvania disenfranchised free blacks in the state's new constitution in 1837.

Antiblack sentiment gained powerful expression in the formation of Ohio Valley chapters of the American Colonization Society (ACS). Formed in 1816, the ACS symbolized the movement to transport free blacks out of the country and back to Africa. Branches of the organization soon spread throughout the region. Although its constitution advocated "voluntary recolonization" of blacks in Africa, ACS members believed that blacks and whites could not peacefully coexist as free people on American soil. Moreover, according to some of its spokesmen, the removal of free blacks from the United States represented a viable program of racial uplift for African peoples on the continent. New World ex-slaves would presumably bring democratic institutions to Africa and open up the continent for American "civilization," commerce, and industries. While the ACS articulated the peaceful and voluntary removal of free blacks, as will be shown below, others adopted violent means to secure the same ends.

Despite the immense difficulties they faced, Ohio Valley blacks gradually gained a foothold in the urban economy. By 1850, in Pittsburgh, Cincinnati, and Louisville, between 66 and 85 percent of black men worked in five occupations—boatman, barber, cook, laborer, and waiter. As suggested by these figures, the steamboat itself became a key employer of enslaved and free black labor in the Ohio Valley. African Americans helped fill the labor demands of the steamboat world by loading and unloading cargo in river cities. They also worked as deckhands, cabin keepers, and cooks onboard steamboats as they plied both the Ohio and Mississippi rivers. Although they shared the harsh and ex-ploitative nature of this work with large numbers of American-born white and immigrant workers, they worked in a segregated environment and endured even greater levels of inequality and mistreatment than their white counterparts.

Steamboat captains and white workers developed a consensus on the subordinate place of free and enslaved black workers on the nation's inland waterways. Where blacks and whites worked in mixed crews, they were separated at mealtime, with blacks eating last "following separate sittings for [white] officers, cabin passengers, and white servants." Moreover, African Americans were not only workers on such boats, they were also literally cargo on steamers as the internal slave trade continued to redistribute the enslaved black population from the upper to the lower South. In 1834, at one Ohio Valley dock, a contemporary observer described the transport of human cargo on one steamer. The ends of "two long chains, extending from the forward to the rear of the steerage deck . . . were bolted to the sides of the boat about four feet above the deck floor. To these chains, at about equal distances apart, were attached twenty-five shorter chains with a handcuff attached to the loose end. The handcuff was attached to the right arm of each slave." The level of racial inequality and separation increased with the size of the boat. Still, as will be shown below, free and enslaved black steamboat workers gained access to a degree of freedom that would place them at the center of the emerging Underground Railroad.

In each city, along with black men, black women made up a significant segment of the workforce. As elsewhere in antebellum cities, they worked mainly as housekeepers, cooks, washerwomen, and seamstresses. The lowly position of blacks in the region's workforce elicited frequent comment. In 1815 the Cincinnati physician Dr. Daniel Drake described blacks as "disciplined to laborious occupations" and "prone to the performance of light and menial drudgery." Another observer, a local editor, believed that the "evils of slavery . . . infected" Cincinnati and relegated blacks to "certain kinds" of labor "despised as being the work of slaves." In 1827 a black visitor described his disappointment upon arriving in the city: "I thought upon coming to a free state like Ohio I would find every door thrown open to receive me, but from the treatment I received by the people generally, I found it little better than in Virginia. . . . I found every door was closed against the colored man in a free state, excepting the jails and penitentiaries." Although some white abolitionists encouraged the employment of black artisans, blacks repeatedly

*The* Loucinda *traveled between Madison, Indiana, and Louisville. In this photo, ca. 1900, African American men are loading whiskey barrels onto the packet.*

complained: "We have among us carpenters, plasterers, masons, etc., whose skill as workmen is confessed—and yet they find no encouragement—not even among [white] friends." During the 1830s a black cabinetmaker lost his job when white workmen threw down their tools and refused to work with a black man.

As employers and white workers limited the occupational mobility of black workers, African American men and women took jobs at the bottom of the workforce and challenged white rhetoric about their "improvidence," "depravity," and "ignorance." General labor and personal-service jobs provided an important if narrow avenue to freedom for many ex-slaves and fugitives. As early as 1834 a Cincinnati census revealed that an estimated 1,129 of the city's blacks had known slavery. Well over one-third had purchased their freedom at a total cost of $212,522 or about $450 per person. Others reported working and saving to purchase family members and friends.

In Pittsburgh and Allegheny City the value of black real estate property had increased to $110,015 in 1850. Laborers, stewards, cooks, and caterers accounted for seven and barbers accounted for three of the thirteen black property holdings in excess of $12,000. In 1850 Cincinnati listed the value of black property holdings at $1,317,000. At the same time, Louisville's black population listed real estate valued at $985,650. Louisville also claimed one of only nineteen blacks in urban America who owned property in excess of $20,000. African American property holders offered inspiring stories of individual and group success and entrepreneurship. According to the Rev. Charles B. Ray, a black New York minister and journalist, these men and women had the "proper materials in their character to become industrious, economical, and reputable citizens."

The barber trade provided black men their most promising opportunities to earn a living, purchase real estate, and increase their standing in Ohio Valley cities. The barber William W. Watson became the most well known property holder of antebellum black Cincinnati. In 1832 Watson received his freedom when a family member purchased him from his owner. Within less than a decade he owned a barbershop and bathhouse that catered to a predominantly white clientele in the central business district. He also owned two brick houses and lots within the city and another 560 acres of farmland in nearby Mercer County. His property holdings stood at an estimated $5,500. In her rationale for *Uncle Tom's Cabin*, Harriet Beecher Stowe, who lived in Cincinnati during her research for the book, named Watson and five other former slaves as examples of the race's capacity for "conquering for themselves comparative wealth and social position" by their "self-denial, energy, patience and honesty."

As African Americans gained a foothold in the economy, their industriousness did not insulate them from racial attacks. Their apparent progress generated as much resistance and hatred as did their alleged intemperance and inability to provide for their futures. In 1834 a white mob entered the Haiti district of Pittsburgh and threatened residents with violence. A decade later a white mob attacked members of a black band after a performance at the Temperance Ark in Allegheny City. An abolitionist paper, the *Spirit of Liberty Weekly*, blamed the incident on "alcohol and a deep-seated hatred" for black people. In Louisville patrols regularly conducted midnight raids on the home of free blacks and threatened inhabitants with bodily harm if they did not leave the city. When free black homeowners complained of such attacks, authorities advised them to "leave the state."

In 1834, according to an English visitor to Cincinnati, whites discussed African American self-help and self-improvement "with a degree of bitterness that dictated a disposition to be more angry with their <u>virtues</u> than their vices." In 1841 a white working man exclaimed that "White men . . . are naturally indignant . . . when they see a set of idle blacks dressed up like ladies and gentlemen, strutting about our streets." As early as 1842 Cincinnati's white residents mobilized to prohibit blacks and mulattoes "from purchasing or holding real estate" within the city limits. In the Queen City African Americans faced riots in 1829, 1836, and 1841. In the 1841 riot whites attacked black churches and businesses on Sixth and Broadway. When blacks

*The schedules to the sides of the photo of the* City of Wheeling *list the towns where the packet regularly stopped between Madison, Indiana, and Cincinnati.*

fought back, whites mounted an iron cannon and fired upon the black community. When officials finally declared martial law, authorities arrested some three hundred black men. Mobsters, guardsmen, and local law officers herded black people into the square at Sixth and Broadway, where they faced additional attacks on their persons.

As suggested by legal and extralegal forms of hostility, African Americans not only faced restrictions on their role as producers, they also confronted constraints on their access to citizenship. In 1837–38, the Pennsylvania constitutional convention restricted voting to white males twenty-one years of age and older. Until then, African Americans had voted in Pittsburgh and elsewhere in the state. In 1839 the Ohio legislature redefined the right of petition as a *privilege* for free blacks, proclaiming that blacks and mulattoes "who may be residents within the State, have no constitutional right to present their petitions to the General Assembly for any purpose whatsoever, and that any reception of such petitions on the part of the General Assembly is a mere act of privilege or policy and not imposed by any expressed or implied power of the constitution." Ohio modified its "black laws" in 1849. The state allowed blacks to attend separate schools and testify against whites in court but continued to deny them legal residence and the right to vote.

The line between freedom and bondage was even less distinct in the city of Louisville. Free blacks gained the right to vote in the constitution of 1792. Seven years later, however, the state constitution curtailed their rights considerably, applying much of the state's slave code to free blacks. Like slaves, free blacks were subject to death for crimes such as manslaughter, arson, rebellion, and rape of a white woman. Unlike whites, free blacks were also subject to the whip "well laid on" their bare backs; they could not testify in court against whites in capital cases; and

like slaves, they faced the slave patrols, which regularly searched their quarters without warrants. More so than blacks north of the Ohio, Louisville's free blacks also had to carry their "free papers" at all times. Otherwise, they could easily slip back into bondage.

Federal policies (particularly the Fugitive Slave Law of 1850) strengthened state and local restrictions on the lives of free blacks. In 1842 the U.S. Supreme Court strengthened the hand of slaveholders in *Priggs v. Pennsylvania*. At the same time, the court ruled that states could not enact legislation purporting to uphold or hamper federal statutes. This ruling resulted in passage of many personal liberty laws by state legislatures, which prohibited state and local officials from aiding southern slaveholders in recovering property in slaves. Such policies, however, were overshadowed by passage of the Fugitive Slave Act of 1850, which increased penalties for aiding and abetting runaways. On the pretense of seeking runaways, slave catchers and kidnappers regularly entered Ohio Valley cities seeking to entrap free blacks as well as runaway slaves for sale in the Deep South, where huge profits rewarded their efforts.

As hostility toward African Americans intensified, the black population failed to keep pace with the overall growth of Ohio Valley cities. Pittsburgh's black population declined from nearly 4 percent of the total population in 1820 to about 3 percent in 1840, before rising again to just over 4 percent in 1850. Cincinnati's black population dropped from a high of nearly 5 percent of the total population in 1840 to a low of about 3 percent in 1850. Louisville's black percentage of the total also steadily declined. As in other southern cities, however, African Americans continued to make up a large percentage of Louisville's total, about 16 percent in 1850, a decline from a high of 36 percent in 1810 and 28 percent in 1820.

African Americans developed a variety of institutions and social movements to address the spread of racial and class inequality in the community life of the Ohio Valley. In Pittsburgh blacks founded a Bethel African Methodist Episcopal Church (AME) in 1800. Named after "Mother Bethel" in Philadelphia, the Pittsburgh church represented the gradual spread of the AME Church into the Ohio Valley. In 1824 Cincinnati blacks broke from the white Methodist church and formed their own Bethel AME church. A few years later, Louisville blacks formed Quinn Chapel AME Church. As well, under the leadership of Henry Adams, a Georgia-born migrant who arrived in Louisville in 1829, African Americans broke away from the white First Baptist Church and formed the "Colored" or "African" Baptist Church in 1842. Later renamed the Fifth Street Baptist Church, it had 475 charter members at its formation. Although the church retained ties to the white body, it managed its own "internal affairs" in its "own way." By 1844 another group of Louisville blacks broke from the white First Baptist Church and founded the Second Colored Baptist Church. Although black Methodists outnumbered their white counterparts and pushed for independent congregations, they were less successful than their Baptist brethren. Nonetheless, blacks in Louisville founded the Fourth Street Methodist Church (later Asbury Chapel) in 1829.

The black church not only played a role in the religious life of the community, it also served as a springboard for the fight against racial inequality. African American church leaders and lay people repeatedly articulated their vision for black liberation in religious terms. As the statement of the board of managers of Cincinnati's Colored Education Society put it in 1837, "Ethiopia shall soon stretch out her hand to God, is the declaration of infinite goodness and wisdom. It must take place, and will doubt-

less be effected by human agency." Some contemporaries believed that black churches had "done more to educate the heart and mind for freedom's blessing . . . than every other means combined." Building upon the institutional foundation of the black church, itself rooted in the transformation of black class structure, African Americans established a plethora of fraternal orders, social clubs, militia groups, schools, newspapers, and social welfare, civic, civil rights, and political organizations. In 1845 attorney Salmon P. Chase of Cincinnati, a future senator, governor of Ohio, and chief justice of the U.S. Supreme Court, praised Cincinnati's black community for its institution-building activities: "Debarred from the public schools, you have established schools of your own; thrust by prejudice into the obscure corners of the edifices in which white men offer prayer, you have erected churches of your own. . . . Excluded from the witness box, you have sought that security which the law denies."

Using their expanding community institutions as sites of organization, planning, and strategy, African Americans resisted disenfranchisement, exclusion from public schools, slavery, and the activities of the ACS. When Pennsylvania disenfranchised black citizens in 1837, African Americans in Pittsburgh and western Pennsylvania filed their famous petition: "The Appeal of Forty Thousand Citizens, Threatened with Disfranchisement, to the People of Pennsylvania" (1838). Seventy-nine area blacks signed the petition, exhorting the state to restore the franchise to black people. The petition cited the contributions blacks had made to the state and argued forcibly that African Americans were as worthy and entitled as whites to exercise the vote. In part, the "Appeal" stated:

> Enough has been exhibited, to satisfy any unprejudiced mind that the colored population appreciates their pres-

*Eleutherian College was one of the first colleges in Indiana to teach black and white students together. The school opened in the 1840s just north of Madison, Indiana, between Cincinnati and Louisville.*

ent privileges; and are endeavoring to sustain themselves honorably, and respectably in the community in which they live. Whatever of ignorance or degradation there is among us, owes its existence chiefly to our former condition in life [slavery]. . . . The fathers of this commonwealth abolished this wicked system; and the wisdom of their deed is evinced in the fact that as we further recede from the fetters of the slave, we are better prepared to sustain the honours and high responsibilities of freemen.

In January 1841 John Peck became president of a new effort to gain the franchise. A week later the group met at Bethel AME Church and proposed a statewide convention to continue the fight for suffrage. In August 1841 a statewide convention met at the same church, with John B. Vashon, Lewis Woodson, A. D. Lewis, and Martin R. Delany taking leadership roles.

Ohio Valley blacks also waged a vigorous fight against the institution of slavery in the South. Their resistance gained powerful expression in the development of the Underground Railroad. Slave owners regularly passed through Pittsburgh and Cincinnati, where they often stayed overnight in local hotels or rooming houses with their slaves. Black riverboat employees played a major role on the Underground Railroad. They reported the arrival of planters and slave catchers, informed enslaved blacks of opportunities for escape, and facilitated contact with conductors. By the 1850s fugitive slaves regularly escaped through an elaborate communications and transportation network along the Ohio River. Blacks often referred to the Ohio as "River Jordan," a boundary line separating slavery and freedom. The black Pittsburgh leader Delany reinforced a focus on the river as a force in the black liberation struggle. In 1859 Delany published one of the earliest novels written by a black author. *Blake; or,*

*Levi Coffin (1798–1877). Coffin and his wife Catherine lived in Newport, Indiana, working for the Underground Railroad, from 1826 until they moved to Cincinnati in 1847.*

*the Huts of America, a Tale of the Mississippi Valley, the Southern United States and Cuba* revolved around the activities of a runaway slave who used his knowledge of steamboat culture to help organize a revolt against slavery and the plantation system.

African Americans linked their fight against slavery with an equally energetic struggle against the ACS. They held numerous mass meetings denouncing colonization, calling it "a scheme" of southern slaveholders to rid the nation of free blacks and to secure the institution of human bondage. In 1849, at a national meeting, Cincinnati's Rev. Wallace Shelton counseled blacks to reject colonization: "Stay where you are . . . and never leave this land, as long as one chain is to be heard clanking, or the cry of millions is to be heard floating on every breeze."

The struggle for social justice was by no means an exclusively African American phenomenon. African Americans gained the support of a small but influential roster of white allies. Whites assisted the fight against the ACS, slavery, and restrictions on black education. In Pittsburgh prominent supporters of African Americans included Jane Grey Swisshelm, editor of the *Saturday Visiter*, an abolitionist paper; F. Julius LeMoyne, president of the Pittsburgh Anti-Slavery Society; and Neville B. Craig, editor of the *Pittsburgh Gazette*, the city's first daily paper. In Cincinnati African Americans received the aid of Levi Coffin. A southern-born Quaker and renowned conductor on the Indiana Underground Railroad, Coffin moved to Cincinnati in 1847 and continued his abolitionist activities. Under the leadership of Connecticut-born Theodore Dwight Weld and Augustus Wattles, white faculty and students at Cincinnati's Lane Seminary published the antislavery *Philanthropist* and supported the Underground Railroad. The abolitionist movement also gained some support among Cincinnati lawyers and jurists. In 1841, for example, attorney Chase represented fugitive slave Mary

Towns in the Hamilton County Court. Before facing charges as a runaway, Towns had lived in Cincinnati for a decade. The judge accepted Chase's defense of Towns; "freedom and not slavery," he declared, was the rule in Ohio.

At the local level, whites offered their strongest support for black education. In addition to schools operated by Lane Seminary and the Ladies Anti-Slavery Society, Gilmore High School represented one of Cincinnati's most outstanding examples of white philanthropy on behalf of black education. In 1844 wealthy British clergyman Hiram S. Gilmore established the high school, employed five teachers, and taught some three hundred black students a variety of subjects, including Latin, Greek, art, and music. Some students paid fees, others attended free, and some received partial support to make their attendance possible. By 1848 Gilmore turned the school over to one of his teachers.

In Pittsburgh one of the most consistent supporters of black education was also a colonizationist. The cotton manufacturer Charles Avery, part owner of the Eagle Cotton Mill, not only supported efforts to recolonize blacks in Africa; he also funded Allegheny Institute and Mission Church, an institution of higher education for African Americans in Allegheny City. Built on land near Avery's home, the school combined education in the classics with training in the trades. Upon his death in 1858, Avery left $25,000 for the continuation of the school's work under the name of Avery College. A lay preacher in the Methodist church, Avery also articulated the view that blacks were "the biological and social equals of whites." More so than others in the ACS, he apparently took seriously the notion of voluntary recolonization.

Interracial cooperation sometimes included city officials. In Pittsburgh, when a white mob threatened the black community with violence in 1834, the mayor dispatched the Duquesne Greys, a white militia group, to disperse the crowd. After another racial incident in 1839, Mayor John R. McClintock, described as a "law and order" mayor, cooperated with black leader Delany to create special interracial teams of black and white officers to put down the disturbance. Whereas the mayor of Philadelphia feared black militia and fraternal orders and restricted their ability to use city streets for their parades, in Pittsburgh, the black Hannibal Guards and Freemasons paraded in the streets during the 1850s without incident. Moreover, Allegheny City and Pittsburgh blacks regularly and publicly celebrated British Emancipation Day on August first.

In Cincinnati African Americans regularly commemorated West Indies Emancipation Day. On such occasions, speakers spoke boldly and clearly about the need for liberation. In August 1841 one speaker warned "all oppressors in every nation that the day is at hand when the hand of Almighty God will sunder the chains of the oppressed in every land." For their part, Cincinnati authorities sometimes upheld the claims of blacks over whites. In the racial outbreak of 1829, for example, the police arrested ten blacks and seven whites for their part in the conflict, but the mayor fined the whites and released the blacks, affirming that they had acted in self-defense. As one historian concluded, "In this instance, at least the black community appears to have been totally victorious."

Even as African Americans worked to build interracial alliances, they confronted a variety of internal tensions and conflicts. Class, color, gender, cultural, ideological, and political differences repeatedly threatened racial solidarity. As elsewhere in America, in the Ohio Valley African Americans of light-skinned color gained economic opportunities and privileges denied to their darker-skinned counterparts. Although the vast majority of all blacks worked in jobs at the floor of the urban economy, dark-skinned blacks occupied a notch below lighter-skinned blacks. This light-skinned privilege was not only revealed in economic and class terms, but in legal and political status as well. On two occasions during the 1840s, the Ohio State Supreme Court sanctioned the right of mulattoes to vote, arguing that they were not "Negroes." When Democrats gained control of the Ohio legislature and passed a law in 1850 disenfranchising anyone with a "distinct and visible admixture of African blood," the Ohio Supreme Court again defended mulatto men, insisting that the law could not disenfranchise males with more than 50 percent white ancestry.

In addition to the internal color line, African Americans faced significant gender conflicts. Along with their church-based activities, African American women spearheaded the formation of antislavery societies, temperance unions, and sewing circles. They also raised funds for black male-dominated fraternal, religious, social, and political organizations. In Cincinnati, under the leadership of Elizabeth Coleman and Sarah Earnest, for example, the Anti-Slavery Sewing Society produced clothing for runaway slaves and aided their escape from bondage. African American women also swelled the ranks of those attending the black political and civil rights conventions. Yet, black women were often disenfranchised. Consequently, at one of the early conventions, black women passed and delivered a resolution to the men: "Where as we the ladies have been invited to attend the Convention and have been deprived of a voice, which we the ladies deem wrong and shameful. Therefore, resolved, That we will attend no more after tonight, unless the privilege is granted." As a result of the women's protest, the men introduced and passed a resolution "inviting the ladies to share in the doings of the Convention."

Ohio Valley blacks also faced important ideological and political differences. Some blacks eschewed protest despite worsening conditions. When a group of Cincinnati blacks petitioned the legislature for redress and protection during the riot of 1829, leaders of the Methodist Episcopal Church abstained from endorsing the document. As one spokesperson explained, "All we ask is an continuation of the smiles of the white people as we have hitherto enjoyed them." Other blacks moved to Canada.

Between 1843 and 1847 Delany published a black newspaper called the *Mystery*. Although living in Pittsburgh, he also served as coeditor of the *North Star* with Frederick Douglass. In 1849 Delany and Douglass parted ways. While Delany moved increasingly toward a black nationalist stance, Douglass retained his commitment to an interracial abolitionist movement, including close cooperation between blacks and whites such as William Lloyd Garrison and Harriet Beecher Stowe. Delany advocated pride in blackness, independent actions, and the notion of emigration to a new homeland for African Americans. In his book on the question of black "destiny," he repeatedly claimed that "Mexico, Central America, the West Indies, and South America, all present now, opportunities for the individual enterprise of our young men, who prefer to remain in the United States, in preference to going where they can enjoy real freedom, and equality of rights." Delany insisted that African Americans act independently on the question of emigration: "Go or stay—of course each is free to do as he pleases—one thing is certain; our Elevation is the work of own hands." Although Delany would eventually advocate the Niger Valley area as a site of settlement, he rejected the ACS and resisted settlement of Liberia as a viable solution to the problems facing African Americans.

As Delany moved toward emigration ideas, other blacks broke ranks with Douglass and Garrisonian abolitionists on different grounds. As early as July 1850, Rev. Lewis Woodson opposed the abolitionists. When Douglass visited Pittsburgh and spoke at the Wylie Street Methodist Church, Woodson disrupted the antislavery gathering with persistent challenges to Douglass's ideas, calling the renowned abolitionist an infidel. Woodson objected to the Garrisonian belief that the church aided and abetted slavery and that abolitionists should abrogate religious affiliation. He later became president of a new Christian antislavery society formed in Pittsburgh during the late 1850s.

At the same time that African American leaders such as Delany and Woodson worked to reconcile emigration, civil rights, and abolitionist ideas on their own terms, some blacks accepted the overtures of the ACS. Between 1846, when Liberia became an independent republic, and 1849 more than a thousand blacks left the United States for Africa. Nearly two hundred of these settled in Pennsylvania's Bassa Cove colony, founded by the Pennsylvania Colonization Society in 1835. In November 1857 five Pittsburgh blacks left for Africa on the ship *M. C. Stevens* from Baltimore. Three years later fifteen Allegheny County blacks departed for Africa on the same ship.

Although African Americans faced significant internal conflicts and differences, their difficulties securing a position in the urban political economy as a group helped to mitigate such friction. While blacks catering to white elites amassed resources, power, and prestige that enabled them to protect themselves better than their working-class and poor counterparts, their industriousness and social contacts failed to fully shield them from class and racially motivated attacks. Only the onset of the Civil War, emancipation, and the rapid expansion of industrial capitalism would bring blacks more fully into the economy and polity as citizens as well as producers. In gaining a greater measure of freedom for themselves and their children in the

*Frederick Douglass (1818–1895), ca. 1850s*

wake of the Civil War, the African American community would build upon its antebellum foundation. Thus, the growth of black communities during the era of the steamboat would influence African American life and history well into the late nineteenth and twentieth centuries.

*This essay is based upon Joe William Trotter Jr.'s* River Jordan: African American Urban Life in the Ohio Valley *(Lexington: University Press of Kentucky, 1998). The author wishes to thank the University Press of Kentucky for permission to reprint excerpts from this book.*

*Joe W. Trotter is the Giant Eagle Professor of History and Social Justice and heads the department of history at Carnegie Mellon University. He is also the director of Carnegie Mellon's Center for Africanamerican Urban Studies and the Economy (CAUSE), founded in 1995. In addition to books on African American life and labor in Milwaukee, West Virginia, and the Ohio Valley, Trotter is the author of a two-volume textbook on the African American experience from its African beginnings through recent times.*

## SELECTED BIBLIOGRAPHY

Allen, Michael. *Western Rivermen, 1763–1861: Ohio and Mississippi Boatmen and the Myth of the Alligator Horse.* Baton Rouge: University of Louisiana Press, 1990.

Baldwin, Leland D. *Pittsburgh: The Story of a City, 1750–1865.* Pittsburgh: University of Pittsburgh Press, 1937.

Balfour, Stanton. "Charles Avery, Early Pittsburgh Philanthropist." *Western Pennsylvania Historical Magazine* 43 (March 1960): 19–22.

Berwanger, Eugene H. *The Frontier Against Slavery: Western Anti-Negro Prejudice and the Slavery Extension Controversy.* Urbana: University of Illinois Press, 1967.

Bigham, Darrel E. "River of Opportunity: Economic Consequences of the Ohio." In Robert L. Reid, ed., *Always a River: The Ohio River and the American Experience.* Bloomington: Indiana University Press, 1991.

———. *On Jordan's Banks: Emancipation and Its Aftermath in the Ohio Valley.* Lexington: University Press of Kentucky, 2006.

———. *We Ask Only a Fair Trial: A History of the Black Community of Evansville, Indiana.* Bloomington: Indiana University Press, 1987.

Blackett, Richard J. M. "Freedom or the Martyr's Grave: Black Pittsburgh's Aid to the Fugitive Slave." *Western Pennsylvania Historical Magazine* 61 (April 1978): 117–34.

Brown, Eliza, et al. *African American Historic Sites Survey of Allegheny County.* Harrisburg: Pennsylvania Historical and Museum Commission, 1994.

Buchanan, Thomas C. *Black Life on the Mississippi: Slaves, Free Blacks, and the Western Steamboat World.* Chapel Hill: University of North Carolina Press, 2004.

Curry, Leonard P. *The Free Black in Urban America, 1800–1850: The Shadow of a Dream.* Chicago: University of Chicago Press, 1981.

Dabney, Wendell P. *Cincinnati's Colored Citizens: Historical, Sociological, and Biographical.* Cincinnati: Dabney Publishing, 1926. Repr., New York: Negro Universities Press, 1970.

Delany, Martin R. *The Condition, Elevation, Emigration, and Destiny of the Colored People in the United States.* N.p., 1852. Repr., New York: Arno Press, 1968.

Gerber, David A. *Black Ohio and the Color Line, 1860–1915.* Urbana: University of Illinois Press, 1976.

Green, Constance McLaughlin. *American Cities in the Growth of the Nation.* N.p., 1957. Repr., New York: Harper and Row, 1965.

Hays, Samuel P., ed. *City at the Point: Essays on the Social History of Pittsburgh.* Pittsburgh: University of Pittsburgh Press, 1989.

Larsen, Lawrence H. *The Urban South: A History.* Lexington: University Press of Kentucky, 1990.

Levine, Bruce. "Community Divided: German Immigrants, Social Class, and Political Conflict in Antebellum Cincinnati." In Henry D. Shapiro and Jonathan D. Sarna, eds., *Ethnic Diversity and Civic Identity: Patterns of Conflict and Cohesion in Cincinnati Since 1820.* Urbana: University of Illinois Press, 1992.

Lucas, Marion B. *A History of Blacks in Kentucky: From Slavery to Segregation, 1760–1891.* N.p., 1992. Repr., Frankfort: Kentucky Historical Society, 2003.

Miller, Floyd J. *The Search for a Black Nationality: Black Colonization and Emigration, 1787–1863.* Urbana: University of Illinois Press, 1975.

Miller, Zane L. *Boss Cox's Cincinnati: Urban Politics in the Progressive Era.* New York: Oxford University Press, 1968.

Nieman, Donald G. *Promises to Keep: African-Americans and the Constitutional Order, 1776 to the Present.* New York: Oxford University Press, 1991.

Quillen, Frank U. *The Color Line in Ohio: A History of Race Prejudice in a Typical Northern State.* N.p., 1913. Repr., New York: Negro Universities Press, 1969.

Ross, Steven J. *Workers on the Edge: Work, Leisure, and Politics in Industrializing Cincinnati, 1788–1890*. New York: Columbia University Press, 1985.

Share, Allen J. *Cities in the Commonwealth: Two Centuries of Urban Life in Kentucky*. Lexington: University Press of Kentucky, 1982.

Staudenrous, Philip J. *The African Colonization Movement, 1816–1865*. New York: Columbia University Press, 1961.

Taylor, Henry Louis, ed. *Race and the City: Work, Community, and Protest in Cincinnati, 1820–1970*. Urbana: University of Illinois Press, 1993.

Thornbrough, Emma Lou. *The Negro in Indiana: A Study of a Minority.* Indianapolis: Indiana Historical Bureau, 1957.

Trotter, Joe William, Jr., and Ancella Radford Bickley, eds. *Honoring Our Past: Proceedings of the First Two Conferences on West Virginia's Black History*. Charleston, WV: Alliance for the Collection, Preservation, and Dissemination of West Virginia's Black History, 1991.

Turner, Edward Raymond. *The Negro in Pennsylvania: Slavery, Servitude, Freedom, 1639–1861*. Washington, DC: American Historical Association, 1911. Repr., New York: Arno Press, 1969.

Wade, Richard C. "The Negro in Cincinnati, 1800–1830." *Journal of Negro History* (January 1954): 43– 57.

———. *The Urban Frontier: Pioneer Life in Early Pittsburgh, Cincinnati, Lexington, Louisville, and St. Louis*. Chicago: University of Chicago Press, 1959.

Woodson, Carter G. "The Negroes of Cincinnati Prior to the Civil War." *Journal of Negro History* 1 (January 1916): 6–7.

Wright, Richard R. *The Negro in Pennsylvania: A Study in Economic History*. Philadelphia: n.p., 1912. Repr., New York: Arno Press, 1969.

# 7

## Steamboat Music

SANDRA M. CUSTER

There are two kinds of steamboat music: music made by and on the steamboat that was recognizable up and down the rivers, and the songs inspired by the majestic steamboats that traveled the Ohio–Mississippi River system during the past two hundred years. Steamboats were a part of the wharf scenes all along the Ohio and Mississippi rivers, arriving and departing with bells tolling, whistles blowing, calliopes playing, paddle wheels churning, and steam pluming.

One of the earliest sounds on the stern-wheel packet steamboats was the bell-pull system. Hanging from the ceiling in front of the pilot was a series of brass rings and wooden handles. These were attached to lines that ran from the pilothouse over a series of small wheels down to the engine room, where they were connected to an array of bells suspended from the ceiling. Each of the three bells—a stopping bell, a backing bell, and a gong—had a different tone and two or more signals. The stopping bell would indicate to come ahead full when the boat was stopped. If the boat was running in either direction, it would mean stop. The backing bell would signal to back, full when stopped, or slow when running. Ringing the backing bell twice would signal dead slow when running. Ringing the gong once

when stopped would indicate to change direction. When running, the gong would indicate half speed. Ringing the gong twice when running would mean to run her as fast as she would go. When the boat was stopped, ringing the gong three times would either indicate for the engineer to warm up the engines or that the day's work was over. Some upper Ohio River boats also had a chestnut bell that was used to signal "hold the boat where it is, otherwise known as the dead slow signal." On this signal the engineer would look out of the window and balance the boat's speed exactly against the current.

This bell system was later replaced by the engine room telegraph. The telegraph's dial in the pilothouse read Full Ahead, Half Ahead, Slow Ahead, Stand By, Stop, Finished with Engine, Slow Astern, Half Astern, and Full Astern. By moving a pointer on the dial, the pilot caused the telegraph's internal bell to ring down in the engine room, and a corresponding pointer would move to the identical position on a duplicate dial in the engine room.

The roof bell dates to the beginnings of the steamboat. It was required by law for the exchange of passing signals, one tap for right, two for left, the same signals later used with the

*Eisenbarth-Henderson calliope, ca. 1900. Set on sawhorses, the calliope had twenty whistles connected to steam by bellcranks and wires. Showboats used calliopes to attract audiences—a most effective tool for increasing box-office receipts. After the 1850s calliopes became standard fare for circuses, showboats, and excursion steamboats.*

steam whistle. The roof bell's use was borrowed from church bell soundings, that is, to gather the flock, to celebrate, or to toll a death. After 1855 it was also required for giving a fog signal while tied at shore and for fire and man-overboard alerts. The pilot also used the roof bell when requesting lead-line soundings: one tap for starboard bow, two for port, or one followed by two for both.

The *S & D Reflector* describes the wharf scene at 5:00 p.m. one Saturday afternoon in the summer of 1906:

> Within the hour the deep-toned roof bell will notify all and sundry that the *Queen City*'s departure may be expected within thirty minutes. There was a ritual about this "30 minute bell" rung out with cadence and precision. It was tapped bong—bong—bong; then a pause. Again the bong—bong—bong. Another pause. Then a final bong—bong—bong. The *City of Louisville* chimed in for her Louisville departure. The *Island Queen* by then was lapped down outside the *Queen City* and Homer Denney was on the roof playing the calliope.

Such were the sounds of the wharf for the entire city to hear.

Captain J. Stout of Pittsburgh saw a steam whistle on a trip to Philadelphia and took the idea to Andrew Fulton in Pittsburgh. Fulton was a bell and brass man. While the side-wheeler *Revenne* was being built at Wheeling in 1844 for Captain Andrew Bennett of Wheeling, Stout had a whistle installed. This was one of the first whistles installed on a steamboat. The sounds of the whistles were so individual that everyone on the riverbank could tell what steamboat was arriving or departing by the sound of its bell.

In 1855 Joshua Stoddard, a farmer from Pawlet, Vermont, invented the steam calliope. The calliope, which made its formal debut on July 4, 1856, in Worcester, Massachusetts, was sometimes called a steam organ or steam piano. Steam blasts through a series of whistles were controlled by a keyboard. A calliope's keyboard required strong fingers and its music was usually harsh. The first steam calliope appeared on a steamboat in 1857 and quickly became standard equipment on the luxury steamboats and showboats of the period. The *New Orleans Daily Crescent* reported on January 12, 1857: "The steam musical apparatus recently put on board the circle packet *Natchez* has not answered the expectation of the officers of the boat." While being played it would let out the "most fearful screams."

Yet the calliope went on to become one of the greatest advertising devices for showboats, excursion boats, circuses, and carnivals. It was the best announcer for a showboat's arrival, notifying townspeople that the boat had arrived and calling them to the wharf. When "Oh Dem Golden Slippers," "Turkey in the Straw," or "Dixie" echoed across the countryside, there was no doubt that a showboat was at the landing. Ruth Williams, Joe Baird, Harry Sutton, Charles Tredway, and Clint Cole were known all along the river system for bringing music to the landing. Some favorite tunes were "My Old Kentucky Home," "I'm A Yankee Doodle Boy," "Goodbye, My Lover, Goodbye," "The Blue Alsatian Mountains," and "Out of the Wilderness." Fate Marable could get more pretty music out of the calliope than anyone. During the early 1900s the four highest-ranking calliope players were Marable, Homer Denny, Bill Foley, and George Strother. Some of their old favorites were "The *Robt. E. Lee*," "Way Down Yonder in New Orleans," "Here Comes the Showboat," and "Happy Days Are Here Again."

When the steamboat landed and the landing stage went down, the roustabouts went into action. Shuffling on and off the steamboats and loading and unloading heavy freight such as bales of cotton, barrels of salt, or crates of fruit, the rousters would improvise rhythms to match the bouncing movement of their freight. The songs they sang would keep them in step, that is, a shuffle to maintain their rhythm. Musician Mary Wheeler felt these roustabout songs needed to be preserved, and she recorded the words and melodies of more than sixty of their songs. The songs reflected life as they knew it. Some were songs about the steamboats they worked on, such as the *Macombrey Queen* or the *Kate Adams*:

> Oh, I thought I heard the *Kate Adams* when she blowed,
> She blowed jes' lak she ain't goin' to blow no mo'.
> The reason that I lak the *Kate Adams* so,
> She carries a chambermaid an' a watch below.
> Come on boys with yo' neck out long,
> Show me what shoulder you want it on.

Others were love songs, such as "Alberta, Let Yo' Hair Hang Low," or songs of homesickness, such as "I'm Wukin' My Way Back Home."

When the Anchor Line's *City of Bayou Sara* burned in 1885, one of her roustabouts, Colin Robinson, was taken on board the *Arkansas City* and immediately composed a song about the disaster:

> B'y' Sara Burned Down
> Way down the rivuh an' I couldn't stay long,
> B'y' Sara burned down.
> She burnt down to the water's edge,
> B'y' Sara burned down.
> The people begun to run and squall,
> B'y' Sara burned down.
> When they begin to look they wuz about to fall,
> B'y' Sara burned down.

> Look away over yonder, what I see,
> B'y' Sara burned down.
> The captain an' the mate wuz comin' after me,
> B'y' Sara burned down.
> Tere's two bright angels by my side,
> B'y' Sara burned down.
> 'Cause I want to go to Heaven when I die,
> B'y' Sara burned down.

Showboats brought music and theater to the towns along the Ohio-Mississippi river system, performances people had never seen before. Noah Miller Ludlow, an actor from Albany, New York, built one of the earliest showboats—a keelboat outfitted for an audience. Its journey began at the headwaters of the Cumberland River and drifted down to New Orleans in 1817.

The 1820s brought Sol Smith to the Mississippi River and many tributaries by keelboat. William Chapman and his family floated down the Ohio and Mississippi rivers in the 1830s using the name *Floating Theater* for their craft. Showboating remained very popular prior to the Civil War. While most of the floating theaters remained on flatboats or barges, they were among the first craft to use towboats regularly and were considered floating palaces. They provided entertainment for everyone, complete with banjo playing, vocalists, and performers. In *Showboats: An American Institution*, Philip Graham describes showboating during the pre-Civil War era on the upper Mississippi:

> On the upper Mississippi the principal showboat during the pre Civil-War period was the steamer *Banjo*, which belonged to "Dr." G. R. Spaulding, the owner and manager of several circuses of the time. She first appeared in 1849 at Cape Girardeau on her way upstream to Saint Louis and Alton. She was last recorded ten years later at Saint Paul. The little

*A group of African American roustabouts on the* City of Cairo *in the late nineteenth century. Roustabouts moved in concert, often to the rythm of songs or chants, to move heavy loads on and off steamboats.*

steamer, only eighty feet long, was fitted up in theatre fashion, with a stage fully equipped with drops, scenery, and footlights, and with a pit seating an audience of two hundred. She carried what was then termed a "nigger show."

This last fact is significant. First, it meant the activity of the boat would necessarily be restricted to the northern rivers, for with such a program on board the *Banjo* would not dare play south of Cairo, Illinois. Second, it meant some of the showboats had picked up the newest in American entertainment, the fast-developing minstrel show. Thomas Dartmouth "Daddy" Rice in 1831 had created his character "Jim Crow" from a black livery stable boy with a queer old tune and a ludicrous limp. Soon all the northern portions of the United States, as well as England, were singing and jumping:

Wheel about, turn about,
Do jis so,
An' ebery time I wheel about
I jump Jim Crow.

In 1853 in the Terre Haute, Indiana, area, the Spaulding and Rodgers Circus Company was on board the *Floating Palace*. Daddy Rice was Spaulding's rival from 1851 to 1865 and again after the Civil War from 1868 to 1886. During this time Rice composed "Rochester Song," which regaled many. One stanza runs:

In blowing up Van Orden I never will cease
As long as my name is Dan;
He had me arrested for saying he's a thief,
Which I am to prove it I can.
For he knows full well that it's the truth I tell,
A greater villain than he never run;

So now on my fortune he cuts a great swell,
Which money was made by my fun.

The Civil War transformed the entertainment scene along the Mississippi River system. Rice reappeared in 1869 on a tour from Saint Paul to New Orleans with his circus loaded on the steamboat *Will S. Hays*. He traveled by steamboat, though he performed his shows on land. This launched the biggest circus afloat in America until about 1877.

Captain August Byron French dominated showboating from 1878 to 1902 with a series of boats, *French's New Sensation No. 1* and *French's New Sensation No. 2*. Early on French teamed up with a Mr. Church who did magic tricks and his daughter, Celeste, who sang and danced. French had a banjo, and for two years they traveled. In 1878 he met and married Callie Leach in Waterloo, Iowa. They put together a team including Ned Martin, a comedian; French's cousin Maurice Dolen, a blackface minstrel; Callie's cousin Newton Mowry, a comic singer; and the husband-and-wife team of Ed and Caroline DeHass. French was a magician, ventriloquist, and banjo player, and Callie was housekeeper, chief cook, and mate. Their variety show consisted of music, dancing, singing, a stump speech, globe rolling, sleight of hand, and ventriloquism, with a finale featuring the banjo and a chorus. In 1897 *French's New Sensation No. 2* staged *Uncle Tom's Cabin*, which was presented only on the upper Mississippi River.

Captain Billy Bryant's first showboat experience was with Captain Edwin A. Price's *New Water Queen* in 1900. He joined as a member of the "Famous Four Bryants." The other three members were his mother, Violet; father, Samuel; and sister, Florence. Billy later built his own showboat, the *Princess*, which was towed by the *Florence* and later by the *Valley Belle*. Some of Billy's plays were *East Lynne*, *Hamlet*, *The Drunkard*, and *Ten Nights in a Barroom*. Some of Violet Bryant's most popular songs were "The Fatal Rose of Red," "The Wedding of the Lily and the Rose," and "The Green Grass Grew All Around." In 1929 Billy tied up at Cincinnati for a three-night stand and was asked to stay a few more days. He ended up staying for seven years. During one of those years, the showboat offered performances for thirty-eight straight weeks. His *Hamlet* became a hit on Broadway and on the *Goldenrod* at Saint Louis. Billy's showboat operated until 1942.

Captain John William "Bill" Menke and his brother Ben built a twin-screw gasoline yacht, named the *Cincy* during the winter of 1904–5 and set out from Cincinnati on their first showboat venture, a moving picture show. They played river towns, schools, churches, and store rooms with *The Great Train Robbery*, *The Sinking of the* Maine, and other early movies. The equipment consisted of a bedsheet, picture projector, and gas engine and generator.

At this time, the showboats were using an advance man who would distribute handbills, with advertising such as: "A Clean Performance—No Coarse Jokes, No Double Entendres, Nothing the Most Perfect Lady Will Object To—A Good Show, A Big Show, A Moral Show." Also emphasized were "the Best Actors of the Nation, Musical Artists Galore," and "An Evening of Dramatic Surprises." The Menke brothers became advance agents for Captain French's *New Sensation*, then switched their affiliation to Ralph W. Emerson's *New Grand Floating Palace*, and then to John W. Cooley and James Hagen's showboat *Wonderland*.

In 1905 the Menkes bought an interest in W. R. "Double R" Markle's *Sunny South*. Her seating capacity was 1,200, and her specialty was musical comedy and full-length drama. The first performance in Gallipolis, Ohio, featured the musical comedy *Trip Around the World*, starring Joe K. Kelley. By 1931 the

Menkes' audiences had many favorites among the melodramas including *St. Elmo*, *The Fighting Parson*, *Mysterious Intruder*, *The Woman Pays*, *The Sweetest Girl in Dixie*, *The Old Homestead*, *Tildy Ann*, *The Skin Flint*, *The Rio Grande Romance*, *East Lynne*, and *Lena Rivers*.

During the first season of the Eisenbarth-Henderson floating theater, *The Modern Temple of Amusement*, owned by Captain Elsworth Eugene Eisenbarth, two plays were presented, *Musical Toys* and *The Little Wild Cat*. The first was scarcely more than an act, though good music filled the periods between the acts. Julia Henderson Eisenbarth insisted on better entertainment, so during their second season *The Merchant of Venice* and *Hamlet* were added. Within six months every showboat on the river had added a full-length play, which was in most cases a melodrama.

Throughout the Ohio Valley the Eisenbarths' *Modern Temple of Amusement* featured *Human Hearts* and *Uncle Tom's Cabin*. Captain Eisenbarth was always willing to pay for good band members and insisted that his bands play good music. Under the direction of Harry High, the E-H band included Norman Hanley, baritone and euphonium player; Dick Mitchell, trombonist; Howard Tozier, cornetist; Raymond Sillito, drummer; and Bert Potter, bass player. The band would give an hour-long concert immediately preceding the evening performance. All the musicians doubled as actors.

The showboat *Princess* that was owned by Norman Thom and ran from 1907 to 1917 was a real family affair. Thom was captain, leading man, and director, and his wife, Grace, was leading lady and calliope player. They were assisted by Grace's friend Ruth Williams and their daughter, Norma Beth, who played the juvenile roles. Grace's grandmother was in charge of the kitchen. The *Princess* had full-length plays, usually melodramas, such as *The Tenderfoot*, *Heart of Kentucky*, *The House of Fear*, and *Way*

*Performers and band members on stage of the Eisenbarth-Henderson* Modern Temple of Amusement *showboat, ca. 1900. Captain Elsworth Eugene Eisenbarth is seated next to his wife Julia Henderson Eisenbarth, who is holding their baby daughter.*

*Down East.* The vaudeville acts were considered refined. Plays were selected in accordance with local interests, for example, *Hearts of Blue Ridge* was performed near the Blue Ridge Mountains and *Along the Missouri* was played on and near the Missouri River.

Some other showboats were Charlie F. Breidenbaugh's *Theatorium*, Markle's *Goldenrod* (sold to Emerson in 1914), John and Wiley Preston McNair's *New Era*, Emerson's *Cotton Blossom*, and Al Cooper's *Dixie Queen*. In 1917 Bill Menke and a partner bought the *Greater New York Show Boat* from Edwin Price. In 1922 Menke acquired the *Goldenrod* from Emerson; and the Menke brothers bought the *Hollywood* in 1928 from Price. The *Hollywood* sank in the ice at Paducah, Kentucky, in 1939. By 1931 shows performed on board included *Grandmothers and Flappers*, *Gossip*, *Mr. Jim Bailey's*, *The Girl Who Ran Away*, *Peg o' My Heart*, and *S'manthy*.

In more recent times there was a showboat performance on board the *Sprague*, a retired towboat at Vicksburg, Mississippi, from 1949 through 1973. Captain Thomas J. Reynolds used the diesel towboat *Attaboy* to tow the showboat *Majestic* on the Ohio and Monongahela rivers. The *Becky Thatcher* at Marietta, Ohio, offered showboat performances during the late 1970s and 1980s. Although the itinerant showboat ended with the *Majestic* in the 1960s, the *Goldenrod* offered *Ten Nights in a Barroom* into the 1980s at the Saint Louis riverfront. She was subsequently moved to Saint Charles, Missouri.

Opryland's *General Jackson* on the Cumberland River at Nashville, Tennessee, continues the tradition of entertainment afloat. However, the *General Jackson's* performances are far more refined than anything ever offered on showboats.

Throughout the years Streckfus Steamers of New Orleans and Saint Louis offered all forms of entertainment, and the Streckfus approach to music afloat outshone all others. Lily Streckfus hammered out tunes on the calliope onboard the first boat *J. S.*, and the best of jazz and Dixieland music, featuring black musicians Fate Marable and Louis "Satchmo" Armstrong, was featured on the *Sidney*.

In 1901 Captain John Streckfus Sr. hired Charlie Mills, a black piano player from Quincy, Illinois, plus three white men, Emil Flint, Rex Jessup, and Tony Catalano, for one of the first excursion seasons on board the *J. S.* Mills was talented at the piano and the calliope. It was Mills who introduced Marable to Captain Streckfus in 1907. Marable was born at Paducah, Kentucky, about 1890 and was a shoeshine boy in Paducah when he took his first job with the Streckfus line, playing the piano on the first *J. S.* Marable, along with a white violin player, beat out ragtime on board the *J. S.* for one season. Then, a trumpet player and drummer were added to make a four-piece orchestra. This group played on board the *J. S.* until she burned in 1910.

Marable was by far the most colorful steamboat musician in the country, and he had a major positive influence on black musicians of his time. On the *Sidney* in 1915 Marable played an air calliope, built in Muscatine, Iowa, instead of a piano, in the ballroom. He called it a "Tangley Air Calliophone."

The Streckfus line ran their boats according to the rhythms of the times, so they decided to let Marable organize his own black jazz band. Some of the musicians in Marable's band were Warren "Baby" Dodds on the drums and George "Pops" Foster on bass, from 1919 to 1921; David "Davey" Jones on the mellophone and Johnny St. Cyr on banjo and guitar, 1918 to 1920; and Joe Howard on cornet, William Ridgely on trombone, and Boyd Atkinson on violin from 1918 into the early 1920s.

Charles Creath and Dewey Jackson, who both played trumpet on the *Capitol* with Marable in the early 1920s, also both went on to lead their own bands and make records. Jimmy Blanton was on bass with Marable during the first year the *Saint Paul* ran on the Ohio River. He later became a featured soloist with Duke Ellington. Arthur James "Zutty" Singleton, a drummer, was with Marable on the *Capitol* in 1923 and 1924.

And then there was Armstrong, an eighteen-year-old cornet player and vocalist. Armstrong had a natural talent for "picking up a tune." Fellow musician Davey Jones quickly taught him how to read notes after both were hired by Marable. Armstrong later stated, "Lots of people made a good living working on the boats of the Streckfus Line." Some of the finest white bands "anyone could ever want to hear graced Capt. Joe's bandstands, as well as the very best colored musicians." When Armstrong visited a local dance in Saint Louis, he realized the musicians were doing things that had been done in New Orleans years before. Armstrong worked on the Streckfus boats from 1918 until the end of the season in 1921. Homesick for New Orleans, he then went to work at Tom Anderson's cabaret on Rampart Street in his beloved city.

"Dixieland" or early jazz music originated in New Orleans and became very popular before 1920 and gained in popularity through the Roaring Twenties. The original Dixieland Band, from New Orleans, was an all-white band, which played in Chicago in 1916 and then in New York, starting something of a craze.

Dixieland music and jazz were also popular on the showboats. Captain Streckfus was very particular about music on the Streckfus excursion boats. He recruited New Orleans players and sent them north on his boats. On one trip the *Sidney* made to Burlington, Iowa, Marable was playing Dixieland music. The *Sidney* was attracting large crowds with the music from New Orleans, while the competing *G. W. Hill* was about to go broke

on excursions with a local orchestra, poor music, and poor pay. None of the other excursion boats had what was called good, solid-beat rhythm music with the Dixieland flavor. The *Island Queen* had a big orchestra, and the *Homer Smith* had Everett Merrill as its leader and saxophonist. However, neither of the boats' owners recognized the value of southern musical influence.

In the early days most of the jazz bands did not play from sheet music. Band members would all sit down around a Victrola, learn the melodies, and then improvise their parts. Everybody knew the old "standards" from New Orleans. "High Society" was one of Captain Streckfus's favorites, and every new clarinet player auditioned with that song. If he could pass the test with "High Society," he was good enough for anybody. As a rule, the steamboat orchestras played four-beat rhythm Dixieland. Some of the standard tunes were "Dixieland One Step," "Millenburg Joys," "High Society," "Panama," "Clarinet Marmalada," "At the Jazz Band Ball," and "Muskrat Ramble."

As late as the 1960s, crowds of more than three thousand passengers on board the *Admiral* in Saint Louis danced to the music of a twelve-piece orchestra under the direction of Russ David. Entertainment consisted of Joe Schirmer's banjo and Dixie Land Band, a barbershop quartet, and a Parisian cancan by the Lalla Bauman Dancers.

Besides the music played by and on steamboats, there is another type of steamboat music—songs written about the steamboats that have plied the Mississippi River system for two hundred years. Samuel L. Clemens, as Mark Twain, is usually credited with doing more than anyone else to promote steamboat history and create an interest in the subject through his *Life on the Mississippi* and his other works set on the river. However, steamboat historians and river men of the nineteenth

*The band on the Streckfus Steamer* Sidney *during the 1918–21 era. Louis Armstrong is fourth from the left, next to Fate Marabel at the piano.*

century know that this credit should go instead to Colonel William Shakespeare Hays of Louisville, Kentucky. Hays was born in Louisville on July 19, 1837. From childhood, he could play almost any kind of musical instrument. With his boyhood home so close to the Ohio River, his love for rivers and steamboats soon became a major influence in his music and writing. Hays received a liberal arts education at Hanover College in Hanover, Indiana, and at Georgetown College in Georgetown, Kentucky. In 1856, while he was a student at Hanover, he wrote the words to his first song, "Little Ones at Home." He wrote the words and music to "Evangeline," one of his most beautiful and long-lived productions, in 1862. More than 300,000 copies of the song have been printed.

Hays first went to work for George D. Prentice as one of the editors of the *Louisville Democrat* in 1856. He then went on to write a wonderful series of river and steamboat columns in the *Democrat,* the *Journal*, the *Courier-Journal*, and the *Times* from the 1860s through the early years of the twentieth century. Working as the Louisville river columnist for more than fifty years put Hays in the position to know and be known by all the steamboat men from Pittsburgh to New Orleans. His knowledge of the industry and the people who worked in it was encyclopedic. While working at the various newspapers, Hays was able to continue writing his poems and songs. His newspaper work also gave him the ability to travel, maintain a license to work aboard steamboats, and pursue other activities he enjoyed.

After establishing himself with John L. Peters of New York, a native of Louisville who was affiliated with the publisher Oliver Ditson and Company in Boston, Hays published his ballads with the firm in the United States and England for ten years. The combined circulation of his songs exceeded that of any other American author's composition at that time. Nearly four million copies of songs such as "Mollie Darling," "Nora O'Neal," "Driven from Home," "Write Me a Letter," "Little Old Log Cabin in the Lane," "Susan Jane," "We Parted by the Riverside," "My Southern Sunny Home," "Nobody's Darling," "You've Been a Friend to Me," and "Shamus O'Brien" were printed and sold. Hays also dabbled in blackface comedy; on the back of the 1886 edition of his book *Songs and Poems* is an advertisement for "Will S. Hays' Great Southern Minstrels, The Crème de la Crème of Negro Minstrelsy, Season 1886–1887." Although the song "Dixie" has traditionally been attributed to Daniel Emmett, there is evidence to indicate it was none other than Hays who wrote this famous song. However, the scholarly question of the song's origin and its author remains unanswered and controversial.

Hays was a consummate Southerner, and his political sentiments were naturally aligned with the Confederacy. Union General Benjamin Butler, a noted looter of New Orleans homes, took particular umbrage at Hays for his song "My Sunny Southern Home" and had the songwriter jailed. During the Civil War, Hays was a pilot on the packet *Grey Eagle* between New Orleans and Vicksburg. He continued working on steamboats during the 1860s and 1870s. Two steamboats were named for Hays, one in 1865 and the other in 1882.

Hays's love of and connection with steamboats showed through the years in his sheet music. "Down in De Co'n Fiel'd" was respectfully inscribed to "Capt. Jas. O'Neal, General Superintendent of the St. Louis and New Orleans Anchor Line Steamers." One of Hays's best-known steamboat songs, "The Last Trip," is inscribed as "a descriptive song written in memory of the late Capt. J. M. White." The notation in *Will S. Hays' Songs and Poems* explains: "The following lines were written in respect to the memory of the late Capt. J. M. White, who for many years commanded steamboats in the Vicksburg and New Orleans trade. One of the distinguishing traits in his nautical career was, that, no matter how turbulent the river, he never failed to respond to a hail from shore":

Mate, get ready down on deck,
I'm heading for the shore,
I'll ring the bell; for I must land
This boat, forevermore.

Say, pilot, can you see that light—
I do—where angels stand?
Well, hold her jackstaff hard on that,
For there I'm going to land.

That looks like Death a-hailing me'
So ghastly grim and pale;
I'll toll the bell—I must go in';
I never passed a hail.

Stop her. Let her come in slow;
There! That will do—no more.
The lines are fast, and angels wait
To welcome me ashore.

Say, pilot, I am going with them
Up yonder through that gate;
I'll not come back—you ring the bell
And back her out—don't wait.

For I have made the trip—of life,
And found my landing place;
I'll take my soul and anchor that
Fast to the Throne of Grace.

Hays suffered a stroke and died in Louisville on July 23, 1907. Because of his many years writing the river columns in the Louisville newspapers, he was well known to the steamboat men throughout the entire Mississippi River system, and hundreds of steamboats flew their flags at half-mast to honor him.

At the time of his death, Hays was recognized as one of the great successful American ballad writers, editors, and composers. He wrote more than 500 songs and poems, and more than 350 of his songs were published during his lifetime. Currently, Hays seldom is given the credit he deserves as a songwriter, even though his songs were best sellers in the 1880s, and in the twentieth century his songs, or parts of them, were sung by many bluegrass and country musicians such as Emmylou Harris, Eddy Arnold, and the Carter Family.

Another individual who immortalized the steamboat era was Edna Ferber. After spending much time on showboats conducting research, Ferber wrote her novel *Show Boat* in the 1920s. Her story of showboating gained entertainment immortality when Jerome Kern and Oscar Hammerstein turned her novel into a Broadway musical. Likewise, singer Paul Robeson's rendition of the song "Old Man River" from the musical, especially in the 1936 film version, left an indelible impression on American music.

After the first three decades of the twentieth century, the number of steamboats diminished. The showboating band era came to an end; the excursions boats with their big-band sound were changing; and more modern songs were coming to radio. Even so, that did not stop the many pleasant memories of the steamboats and the river way of life from appearing in American popular music. "Walking to New Orleans" was written and performed by Antoine "Fats" Domino in the 1950s. The term "walking to New Orleans" was well known on big towboats in the coal trade on the Mississippi River. Its usage can be traced back to the *W. W. O'Neil* during the 1880s and on into the first decade of the twentieth century. A towboat, the *O'Neil* required so much fuel that her coal passers literally walked one mile moving coal from the fuel flats to the boiler room for every mile the *O'Neil* traveled as she moved big tows of wooden coal boats up and down the Ohio and Mississippi rivers between Louisville and New Orleans.

The song "Stagger Lee" was sung by Lloyd Price and his orchestra in late 1958, and most would not suspect that its origin can be traced back to a 1902 steamboat. The *Stacker Lee* was a stern-wheel packet of the Lee Line that ran between Memphis and Saint Louis. One of the steamboat's roustabouts was known for his strength, and over the years he became a folk hero in Saint Louis. Instead of the proper "Stacker Lee," the roustabout became known as "Stagger Lee."

John Fogerty wrote "Proud Mary," which was originally performed by his band, Creedence Clearwater Revival, in 1969. Ike and Tina Turner later performed it. What is most intriguing is that "Proud Mary" was not a big side-wheeler, such as one would assume from the line "big wheels keep on rolling." Fogerty's song was written about the steam tug *Mary Elizabeth,* originally built in Newburgh, New York, in 1905, as the *Ossining.* The *Mary Elizabeth* was rebuilt and converted to diesel power in Memphis, where she was owned by the Warner and Tamble Company.

John Hartford came to the contemporary music scene in the mid-1960s. He grew up in Saint Louis, and in 1947 he was fortunate to have Ruth Ferris as his fourth-grade teacher. Ferris was a devoted fan of steamboats. Her favorite in Saint Louis was the *Golden Eagle,* which sank at Grand Tower, Illinois, in 1947. Ferris was the guiding force behind the effort to preserve the *Golden Eagle*'s recovered pilothouse, which was brought to her school

and placed in the playground for a time before being moved elsewhere in Saint Louis for preservation.

Hartford fell under Ferris's influence and became most interested in steamboats. He followed in Hays's footsteps, combining his love of steamboats with music. Glen Campbell used Hartford's first big hit, "Gentle on My Mind," as the theme song of his 1968 television show. Studying the lines closely, one can hear Hartford thinking about steamboats: "upon some line that keeps you in the back roads by the rivers of my memory that keeps you ever gentle on my mind." Hartford's love of music and steamboats is evident in the titles of many of his songs: "Steamboat Whistle Blues," "Watchin the River Go By," "Where the Old Red River Flows," "White River," "Black River," "Down on the Levee," "Skippin' in the Mississippi Dew," "The *Julia Belle Swain*," "Old Time River Man," "When the *Guiding Star* Came to Tell City," "*Natchez* Whistle," "Natchez Under the Hill," and "Where Does an Old Time River Man Go."

The success of Hartford's first hit song gave him the freedom to write the kind of music he dearly loved. In the late 1970s he left California and made his way back to Nashville, where he spent the rest of his life devoted to bluegrass music, steamboats, and those Will S. Hays songs he remembered from his childhood. He wrote, recorded, and performed scores of incomparable steamboat songs. The songs and poems of John Hartford, Will S. Hays, and others continue to reveal that music, steamboats, and rivers are a timeless and artful combination.

*Sandra Miller Custer is the great-great-great-great granddaughter of Captain George "Old Natural" Miller, who took the first coal shipment down the Ohio and Mississippi rivers in 1829. Her specialty in steamboat research is prosopography and the women of steamboating. She is a coauthor of the Rock Island District of the Corps of Engineers' 1996 study,* Steamboat Wreck Sites on the Upper Mississippi and Illinois

Rivers *and a contributor to the* Louisville Encyclopedia *and the* British Museum Encyclopedia of Maritime and Underwater Archaeology. *Custer is the author of* Miller's Index to Gould's History of River Navigation. *She published the* Egregious Steamboat Journal *from 1991 to 1998. Her current project is research on and restoration of the K & I House, steamboat Captain James Irvin's former home, in the Portland section of Louisville.*

## SELECTED BIBLIOGRAPHY

Andrist, Ralph K. *Steamboats on the Mississippi*. New York: American Heritage Publishing, 1962.

Bates, Alan L. *The Western Rivers Steamboat Cyclopoedium*. Leonia, NJ: Hustle Press, 1971.

Chrisman, Martha Carol. "Will S. Hays: A Biography." Master's thesis, University of Minnesota, 1980.

Elder, C. W. "Music on the River." *S & D Reflector* (September 1965): 6–7.

Graham, Philip. *Showboats: The History of an American Institution*. Austin: University of Texas Press, 1951.

Grise, George C. "Will S. Hays: His Life and Work." Master's thesis, George Peabody College for Teachers, 1947.

Klein, Benjamin. *The Ohio River Handbook and Picture Album*. Cincinnati: Young and Klein, 1958.

Meyer, Dolores J. "Excursion Steamboating on the Mississippi with Streckfus Steamers, Inc." PhD diss., Saint Louis University, 1967.

Rosskam, Edwin, and Louis Rosskam. *Towboat River*. New York: Duell, Sloan & Pearce, 1948.

Samuel, Ray, Leonard V. Huber, and Warren C. Ogden. *Tales of the Mississippi*. New York: Hastings House, 1955.

Wheeler, Mary. *Steamboatin' Days*. Baton Rouge: Louisiana State University Press, 1944.

# 8

## The Steamboat *New Orleans* and Its Impact
## on Navigation on Ohio River Tributaries

GERALD W. SUTPHIN

When the *New Orleans*, the first steamboat on America's western rivers, left Pittsburgh in October 1811, those on board and those who would see their first steamboat could not imagine what an impact the event would have on the fledgling United States and on the Ohio and Mississippi rivers and their tributaries. Within a few years a steamboat would "poke its nose" up almost any stream deep enough to keep it afloat. This uniquely American invention would be the vessel of exploration, migration, and commerce, as well as the reason for technical evolution on rivers between the Appalachian Mountains and the foothills of the Rocky Mountains. State and federal governments would strive in every way possible to create and improve navigation on any stream that would enhance the economy, commerce, lifestyle, and culture of the citizens of these river valleys.

As the *New Orleans* steamed down the Ohio River, it passed numerous rivers that would be improved for its successors, extending into the twenty-first century. Because of the steamboat, locks and dams and many other navigation improvements would be made on the Ohio and Mississippi rivers and their countless tributaries. The impact of the invention and development of the western rivers steamboat on almost every aspect of the commerce and development of the American frontier would be unfathomable for more than seventy-five years. The steamboat would alter the face of America as no other mode of transportation before or since its invention.

In 1809 Nicholas Roosevelt, his pregnant wife Lydia, and their large black dog named Tiger arrived at Pittsburgh from New York City to oversee the construction of a custom-designed flatboat to carry them down the Ohio and Mississippi rivers. The reason for building the Roosevelt flatboat was to travel from Pittsburgh to New Orleans to explore, survey, and evaluate river conditions, as well as to locate sites for supplies and fuel for the planned 1811 voyage of the first steamboat on the western rivers. While the boat was being built, Roosevelt likely had numerous occasions to observe and discuss the river routes and commodities being carried by the never-ending parade of flatboats and keelboats moving in and out of the Pittsburgh harbor, on the Ohio River and on the two rivers that formed it, the Allegheny and Monongahela.

After the successful maiden voyage of the *North River Steamboat of Clermont*, better known as the *Clermont*, on the Hudson River in 1807, the New York City newspaper *American Citizen*

*The Steamboat* Allegheny, *the first stern-wheel steamboat on the western rivers*

clearly announced the intent for steamboats on the western rivers: "Mr. Fulton's ingenious steamboat, invented with a view to navigation of the Mississippi from New Orleans upward. . . . It is said it will make a progress of two miles per hour against the current of the Mississippi, and if so, it will certainly be a valuable acquisition to the commerce of Western States."

During the six months that it took the flatboat to travel the river, one can be sure that Roosevelt was making notes about the number of major tributaries that might be navigated by the steamboats built by Robert Fulton, Robert Livingston, and Roosevelt. Upon arrival at New Orleans on or about December 1, 1809, the Roosevelts took the first ship available back to New York City. Roosevelt and his partners began planning for the construction of the first steamboat to operate on the Mississippi River; it was to be named the *New Orleans*.

The Roosevelts returned to Pittsburgh in May 1810 with their daughter Rosetta, who had been born at New York upon the Roosevelts' return from their flatboat journey. For more than a year and a half, Nicholas would supervise the building of the *New Orleans* while his family became a part of the Pittsburgh community. During this time Roosevelt once again studied the growing river commerce on Pittsburgh's three rivers.

History does not record who the first European was to see or travel on the Allegheny, but some historians contend it was René-Robert Cavelier de La Salle who, in 1669, floated down the river on his way from Canada to "discover" the Mississippi River. The Allegheny's close vicinity to Lake Erie via French Creek, one of its major tributaries, would lead it to become a preferred route of exploration and conflict between the European powers vying for control and ownership of America. However, as its valley was settled, the Allegheny quickly grew into a river of

commerce because of its vast natural resources and the need for manufactured items from Pittsburgh.

At first this trade was maintained by flatboats and keelboats. Just five years after the *New Orleans* completed her historic voyage, the small steamboat named *Harriet* tested the currents of the Allegheny River. A decade later, in 1827, the steamboat *Albion* ascended upstream forty-five miles to Kittanning, Pennsylvania, to establish a regularly scheduled service. In 1828 the steamboat *Wm. D. Duncan* landed at Franklin, Pennsylvania. Two years later the steamboat *Allegheny* had expanded steamboat travel to Olean, New York, 250 miles from Pittsburgh. With the increasing development of the Allegheny River Valley came an increase of steamboats carrying passengers as well as farm and wood products and whiskey. By 1840 there were six steamboat packets, the *Eliza*, *Pulaski*, *Forrest*, *Beaver*, *Orphan Boy*, and *Pauline*, running regular service on the Allegheny River during boating season when there was sufficient water to permit navigation.

The discovery of oil in the basin and the first oil well near Titusville, Pennsylvania, in 1859 brought changes to commerce on the Allegheny and spurred the first call for navigation improvements on the river. The oil trade brought a new type of boat to the river, as well—the towboat pushing large fleets of petroleum barges. Unlike the steam packet boats, the towboat was built to tow barges filled with large quantities of raw material. It did not carry passengers or on-deck cargo.

With packet boats and towboats towing large fleets of barges filled with oil, any problems encountered with navigation conditions could be very costly for all concerned. However, it was not until 1878 that the first state appropriation was granted to survey the Allegheny for navigation improvements. This survey revealed the river's natural obstructions and thirty-two low bridges that would have to be raised or removed. In the years that followed, improvements on the river included the removal of boulders, snags, and wrecked boats, and, at major islands and ripples, the building of stone dikes or wing dams (dikes extending from the bank to near the river's center to deepen a navigable channel). In 1898 a 150-foot-wide channel with a minimum depth of one foot at low water was completed from Pittsburgh to the New York state border.

By the middle of the 1860s, steam packet commerce on the Allegheny had virtually disappeared because of the railroads. However, towboats continued to prosper. As navigation improvements were being made, some steam packets returned to the river. The *Nellie Hudson* and the *Florence Belle* provided regular packet service until 1898. These two boats would make occasional runs up the Allegheny until 1913. During this same period the wooden barge-building business along the river thrived.

The first lock and dam on the Allegheny was built at Herrs Island just a little more than one and a half miles above Pittsburgh. After numerous delays this project was started in 1893. It was dedicated in 1903, although many of the boats wishing to travel through the lock could not reach the project because the Union Bridge near Pittsburgh was too low to pass under. By 1903 Lock and Dam Numbers 2 and 3 were under construction on the Allegheny. Farther upstream, another lock and dam was authorized to extend slack-water navigation (controlled river flow with deeper pools) to Monterey, Pennsylvania, eighty and a half miles from Pittsburgh. However, low bridges on the Allegheny would continue to be an obstruction to navigation until 1923, when the Army Corps of Engineers would finally gain approval to raise or remove obstructing bridges on the river.

In 1927 Lock and Dam Numbers 4 and 5 were completed, extending slack-water navigation to thirty-six miles above Pittsburgh. By 1931 Lock and Dam Numbers 6, 7, and 8 had been completed, providing year-round navigation to Rimerton, Pennsylvania, more than sixty-one miles upstream. Lock and Dam Number 9 was finished in 1938, adding another twelve miles upstream to East Brady, Pennsylvania. (It should be noted that the original Lock and Dam Numbers 2 and 3 had been removed and replacement locks and dams built in the same general area of the original projects during this period.)

---

Roosevelt also became very familiar with the commerce and boatbuilding activities on the Monongahela River. On the banks of this river at Pittsburgh, his 1809 custom-built flatboat had been constructed, and the *New Orleans* was built there in 1811. The importance of the Monongahela River was not limited to boatbuilding but included the vast amount of coal and other raw products being shipped both upstream and downstream.

The Monongahela could correctly be called the birthplace of America's inland river industry. More than fifty miles of the river—to beyond California, Pennsylvania—became a hotbed of boat construction. Flatboats, keelboats, barges of several types, and even oceangoing sailing ships were built along this stretch of the river. This same area would become the center of the steamboat-building industry, but in the beginning steamboat traffic would develop very slowly because of problems navigating the Monongahela. The small steamer *Enterprise* would travel to Brownsville, Pennsylvania, in 1814, but it would be 1826 before the *Reindeer* would finally reach Morgantown, Virginia (now West Virginia), 101 miles upstream from Pittsburgh. By February 1850 the steamboat *Globe* would work her way 127 miles upstream to Fairmont, Virginia (West Virginia), at the head of the Monongahela. This feat would earn the captain a one-thousand-dollar prize for being the first boat to reach this city.

Within three years after the *New Orleans* had steamed out of the Monongahela, the Pennsylvania legislature directed the governor to appoint a commission to survey the river. The survey was finished by the end of the summer of 1815. The conclusion of the survey stated, "There is no way of making said river navigable at all seasons but by erecting dams and locks." Upon this recommendation the state chartered the Monongahela Navigation Company in 1817, setting aside funds to purchase stock in the company. Although locks and dams were recommended in 1817, 1822, and again in 1828, work was not started until 1836 when a new Monongahela Navigation Company was chartered with funding from private banks, individuals, and the commonwealth of Pennsylvania. W. Milnor Roberts, engineer in charge, recommended construction of ten eight-foot-high dams from Pittsburgh to the Virginia (now West Virginia) border.

In 1838 the company let contracts for the construction of Lock and Dam Numbers 1 and 2, followed by contracts for Lock and Dam Numbers 3 and 4 in late 1840. Lock and Dam Numbers 1 and 2 were completed and opened to navigation on October 18, 1841. Although the projects proved successful, many of the pilots on the boats resented having to pay tolls for passage and would often purposely damage the locks. Encountering numerous financial, natural, and man-made difficulties, repairs to Lock and Dam Numbers 1 and 2 and construction at Lock and Dam Numbers 3 and 4 were halted in 1842. But the perseverance of the company directors, principally General James K. Moorhead, was demonstrated as they completed construction of five locks and dams to Brownsville, Pennsylvania. On November 13, 1844, the steamboat *Consul* hosted dignitaries steaming to Brownsville to celebrate the completion of the Monongahela slack-water project.

The impact of the five locks and dams on the Monongahela was readily felt as the Pittsburgh and Brownsville Packet Company was established, with the steamboats *Consul*, *Josephine*, and *Louis McLane* providing service between the two cities. Not only did this project improve navigation for trade, but its impact on the Monongahela River coal business would also extend into the twenty-first century. Coal shipments on the river had occurred as early as the 1780s, with the first commercial shipment being made in 1814. The completion of the locks and dams on the Monongahela River meant that loaded coal barges could be fleeted together in the pool behind Lock and Dam Number 1 to wait for a rise on the Ohio River and then be shipped south.

The success of the Monongahela River locks and dams led to the building of two locks and dams on the Youghiogheny River. This river is a major tributary of the Monongahela, located fifteen and a half miles above Pittsburgh. Although Lock and Dam Number 2 on the Monongahela River provided a slack-water pool for seven miles up the lower Youghiogheny, the owners and operators in this region saw the need to extend year-round navigation nineteen miles up the river to export their high-quality coal and coke. Two locks and dams were completed and opened for navigation on October 31, 1850, extending slack-water navigation to West Newton, Pennsylvania. The steamboats *Atlantic*, *Shipper*, and *Youghiogheny* carried celebrating passengers to the dedication on November 15, 1850. Soon the steam packets *Genesee* and *Shriver* were carrying passengers from West Newton to Pittsburgh. But the success of the Youghiogheny River system was short lived. By 1858 the projects were in disrepair due to a lack of funding, and by 1867 the projects were abandoned after an ice gorge and a flood virtually destroyed the dams.

While the Youghiogheny River projects were experiencing problems, the locks and dams on the Monongahela proved to be a resounding success. In less than ten years, traffic was so heavy that the Monongahela Navigation Company built a second and larger lock at Dam Numbers 1 and 2 to keep up with the steady increase in traffic. Seeing the impact the locks and dams were having on the economy of the lower Monongahela, the people living along the middle and upper parts of the river petitioned the Monongahela Navigation Company to continue building locks and dams up the river. The Pennsylvania legislature directed the company to build Lock and Dam Numbers 5 and 6, extending slack-water conditions to Geneva, Pennsylvania. The two new locks were completed and opened in November 1856.

Now the citizens of Morgantown and Fairmont, Virginia (West Virginia), demanded that the Monongahela Navigation Company build locks and dams to the headwaters of the river near Clarksburg, Virginia (West Virginia), on the West Fork River. However, with the start of the Civil War all navigation improvements ceased.

Almost as soon as the Civil War ended, the government of the new state of West Virginia requested the U.S. Congress to initiate work on improving the rivers within its borders. The newly established state government was determined to extend Monongahela River navigation to Morgantown and on to Fairmont. By 1872 a small appropriation had been obtained, and a survey was conducted to locate Lock and Dam Numbers 8 and 9. Work was started in 1873 to build Lock and Dam Number 9 but was not completed until 1879 due to contractor problems. Lock and Dam Number 8 construction started in 1881, while four miles downstream construction began on Lock and Dam Number 7. Interesting is the fact that Lock and Dam Number 7 was being built by the Monongahela Navigation Company, while Lock and Dam Number 8 was being built by the federal government, which had also built Lock and Dam Number 9. Lock and Dam Number 7 was completed in 1883, but Lock and Dam Number 8 was halted temporarily due to a lack of funds from Congress. Funds were provided in 1887, and the lock work was continued. Thereafter, the steam packets *Adam Jacobs* and *James G. Blaine* began running a regular packet service between Pittsburgh and Morgantown.

At the end of the Civil War more and more states turned to the federal government to assist in the development of a national transportation system, and this included the waterways. When West Virginia asked the federal government to build a system of locks and dams on the Great Kanawha River, many other private and state-operated lock and dam systems were soon interested in having the government take control of the rivers in their states. One result was that the U.S. government purchased the Monongahela Navigation Company in 1897 for $3.7 million. With this acquisition, the U.S. Army Corps of Engineers began the required program of repairing and rebuilding projects on the river. Between 1897 and 1915 all nine of the Monongahela River locks and dams were extensively repaired or totally rebuilt.

During this same period construction of six locks and dams on the upper Monongahela River to Fairmont was under way. After the completion of Lock and Dam Numbers 10 through 15 in 1903, the tiny steamboat *Gazette* was the first to reach Fairmont on slack water on March 18, 1904. However, it was a few years before regular packet service along the entire length of the Monongahela was established after the railroad bridge one and a half miles below Fairmont was raised by court action. In 1907 the large side-wheel packet *Columbia* landed at Fairmont, inaugurating this service.

*Monongahela River steamboats* I. C. Woodward *and* Elizabeth *stuck in the lock chamber entrance after racing to be the first boat locked through*

Packet boats were not the only beneficiaries of the improvements to the Monongahela. This river has always been a towboat river, moving millions of tons of coal through the locks as it still does well into the twenty-first century. Between 1948 and the 1990s, improvements on the Monongahela resulted in three high-lift locks and dams being built to replace six older structures on the upper river above Morgantown. Of the remaining seven lock and dam projects, improvement or replacements came in periods controlled by the appropriations made by Congress from 1948 until the present.

———◆———

Roosevelt would have been astonished had he been able to see what impact the *New Orleans* would have, not only on the tributaries of the Ohio, but also on the Ohio River itself. When the *New Orleans* steamed past Marietta, Ohio, the first permanent settlement in the Northwest Territory, she was greeted by a waving crowd and saluted by a booming cannon.

With the settling of Marietta at the mouth of the Muskingum River in 1788 came the opening of the Muskingum Valley and its vast agricultural production potential. Within a few years the pioneers were building flatboats to transport large quantities of farm products down the Ohio and Mississippi rivers. Roosevelt, on both his 1809 flatboat trip and on his 1811 steamboat trip, had to have been impressed with the flatboat/keelboat trades in and around the Muskingum River, but it would be thirteen years before the first steamboat would challenge the upstream current of the Muskingum. On January 9, 1824, the little steamboat *Rufus Putnam* pulled away from the Marietta wharf on a Muskingum River flood tide attempting to reach Zanesville, Ohio, within two days. After reaching its destination and celebrating this historic event for two days, the *Rufus Putnam* returned to Marietta on the crest of the flood.

Soon other steamboats were venturing up the Muskingum to establish commercial trade between the Muskingum Valley, Pittsburgh, Pennsylvania, and Parkersburg, Virginia (West Virginia) on the Ohio. During the late 1820s the steamboats *Mary Han*, *Tuscarawas*, and *Zanesville–Dresden Packet* made trips upriver to Coshocton, Ohio, where the Walhonding and Tuscarawas rivers join to form the Muskingum. In 1827 the packet *Speedwell* steamed from Pittsburgh to Zanesville, Ohio, probably the first steamboat to travel that distance. This lengthy trip was duplicated a year later by the *Red River*, which made several trips between these ports. By 1838 the *Coquette* was making weekly trips between Pittsburgh and Zanesville, but when the Muskingum was low, the *Coquette* only ran between Pittsburgh and Marietta. Reliable steamboat service was not assured until the building of a lock and dam system on the river.

Because of the successful flatboat and keelboat trades and the developing steamboat commerce on the Muskingum, citizens of the river valley were looking to the state to construct a year-round slack-water system on the river. Federal funding was not available for the Muskingum River because it was wholly within the state of Ohio, and to get federal funding the river had to border several states. So the state of Ohio decided that the Muskingum was close enough to the Ohio and Erie Canal, then under construction, that the two waterways could be connected at Dresden, Ohio, and the Muskingum could be improved as part of the canal system. As early as 1816, a dam for water-power and a canal for navigation had been built around falls of the Muskingum River at Zanesville by the Zanesville Canal and Manufacturing Company. In 1834 another lock and dam was completed near Symmes Creek, four miles downstream from Dresden, which was the gateway to the Ohio and Erie Canal. It was learned later that this dam had been located too far upstream above the slack-water pool created by the dam around

*Steamboats* Lorena *and* Sonoma *in "hour-glass" Lock Number 1 at the mouth of the Muskingum River*

the falls at Zanesville, and during low-water periods boats could not navigate to Dresden and the canal.

Construction began in October 1836 on a system of twelve locks and dams from Marietta to Dresden, a distance of 91 of the 107-miles of the Muskingum. Completed in 1841, the dams were primarily built of wooden cribbing filled with stone, and the cut-stone locks were hand operated. Now the Muskingum had slack-water navigation from Marietta to Zanesville, and the lock and dam at Zanesville provided slack water sixteen miles to Dresden, where small boats could connect with Ohio's canal system. Although the canal connection proved to be successful, with canal boat trips from New York City to Zanesville taking fourteen days, there were continuing problems on the lower Muskingum. Due to the primitive construction methods used when building the lock and dam system as well as the changing river conditions, many of the projects developed serious structural problems. With the passage of time more and more of the locks and dams experienced severe deterioration and required more and more maintenance.

The building of railroads paralleling the Muskingum also had a negative impact on steamboat commerce. In 1887 the state of Ohio welcomed the opportunity to transfer the Muskingum River system to the federal government as the government continued its efforts to create a unified waterway system throughout the United States. The federal government did not pay the state of Ohio any money but assumed a heavy financial obligation to repair and update the entire Muskingum River system. As was true with all of the federal waterway programs, this work was carried out by the U.S. Army Corps of Engineers. During the next thirty-nine years steamboat traffic continued while improvements were made on the locks and dams, includ-

ing the building of Lock and Dam Number 11 at Ellis, Ohio, between Zanesville and Dresden. The state of Ohio was required to pay at least $200,000 to rejuvenate the Ohio Canal between Dresden and Lake Erie during this same period. However, the flood of 1913 was so destructive that traffic on the canal was never resumed.

By 1927 boat traffic had declined to the point that the Army Corps of Engineers was in favor of abandoning the Muskingum River. Twenty-five years later, on June 30, 1952, through traffic on the Muskingum River came to an end, and the Muskingum River projects were returned to the state of Ohio. Since that time, the state of Ohio has improved the locks and dams and placed the system under the jurisdiction of the Ohio Department of Natural Resources. In 1968 the river was designated as an Ohio state park, and in 2006 the Muskingum River lock system was designated as the first Navigation Historic District in the United States by the National Park Service.

———————

Twelve and a half miles down the Ohio River from Marietta, the *New Orleans* passed Parkersburg, Virginia (West Virginia), at the mouth of the Little Kanawha River. As with almost all of the major tributaries on the upper Ohio, the Little Kanawha was already a commercial avenue for logs and flatboats carrying agricultural products as well as salt from saltworks near Bulltown, Virginia (West Virginia).

In 1836 the steamboat *Paul Pry* ascended the Little Kanawha to the "wonder and terror" of the inhabitants along the river. Within five years the steamboat *Scioto Belle*, steaming on flood waters, managed to reach the community of Creston, Virginia (West Virginia), forty-eight miles upstream, before hurriedly

*Five stern-wheel gas boats on the Little Kanawha River near Big Root Shoals, eight miles below Grantsville, West Virginia*

returning downstream to the Ohio River before the Little Kanawha receded. By 1842 the steamboats *Lodi* and *Zanesville* had made trips up the Little Kanawha River, and over the next twenty years other steamboats would make occasional trips up the river. As traffic increased, the citizens of the Little Kanawha River Valley began working toward having locks and dams built on the river to improve commerce. The Little Kanawha Navigation Company was formed in 1847 to improve navigation from Parkersburg to Bulltown, a distance of more than 130 miles.

The discovery of natural gas and oil brought greater demand for the building of a slack-water system on the river. Oil production in the Little Kanawha Valley prior to the Civil War created boomtowns with names such as Burning Springs, Oil Springs, and Petroleum that used river barges to both store and ship petroleum products down the river. By the beginning of the Civil War there were several hundred wells drilled along the river and loaded petroleum barges awaiting shipment on a rise down the Little Kanawha River.

In 1863 Confederate General William E. Jones, with 1,500 troops, moved into the oil fields and set fire to the oil storage areas and the loaded oil barges awaiting shipment, destroying more than 300,000 barrels of oil. At the end of the conflict, the new state of West Virginia began efforts once more to reorganize the Little Kanawha Navigation Company and to establish unobstructed navigation on the river. The first step in this effort was to remove the numerous mill dams from Parkersburg to Burning Springs, West Virginia, a total of thirty-eight and a half miles. Meanwhile, efforts were under way to construct the river's first lock and dam. In 1867 work was started at Shacktown, West Virginia, three and a half miles up the river. Within a short time construction of the second lock and dam was started near Leachtown, West Virginia, fourteen miles upstream above the

mouth of the river. By 1869 work on two more locks and dams was started. One was located at Elizabeth, West Virginia, at river mile twenty-six, and the other at Palestine, West Virginia, at river mile twenty-nine.

As a result of the U.S. government's interest in a unified national water transportation system, the Army Corps of Engineers built Lock and Dam Number 5 in 1891 on the Little Kanawha. Although most of the oil trade had died off by this time, steamboat companies such as the Little Kanawha Transportation Company and the Parkersburg and Creston Packet Company ran regular packet trades. Some of the steamboats operating after the locks and dams were completed included the *George Thompson*, *Zebra*, *Naomi*, *Silver Hill*, and *Dorame*. At the turn of the century, steamboats began to be replaced by single-cylinder stern-wheel gas boats as the chief vessels of commerce on the river. These smaller boats were very efficient, particularly on the upper Little Kanawha above the five locks and dams between Creston and Glenville, West Virginia.

The Little Kanawha became characterized as the gas-boat river, although this type of boat was often operated on other streams as well as on the Ohio River. Gas boats such as the *Calhoun*, *Edith H.*, *Dove*, *Glenville*, and *Creston* became combination packet boat/towboats operating between Parkersburg and Glenville, 103 miles upstream.

In 1905 the federal government decided to add the Little Kanawha River locks and dams to its growing list of national waterways. In the next decade, more than ten thousand passengers are estimated to have traveled on Little Kanawha boats. River traffic continued to be strong for another twenty years, but eventually the Little Kanawha Railroad and improved highways negatively impacted boats. By the early 1950s the federal government turned the five locks and dams back to the state of West Virginia for operation and maintenance. Due to lack of funding and the complete lack of commercial possibilities, the locks and dams on the Little Kanawha River were abandoned.

———

Passing the mouth of the Little Kanawha River, the *New Orleans* steamed past Blennerhassett Island, the largest island on the Ohio River, with ruins of a once beautiful mansion. As the *New Orleans* continued downstream passing Letart Falls, a treacherous series of rapids considered to be the upper Ohio River's greatest challenge, she prepared for the planned stop at Point Pleasant, Virginia (West Virginia), to obtain fuel. Roosevelt once again had the opportunity to observe the commercial activities around the mouth of the Great Kanawha River.

Since the time of the earliest European settlements along this region of the Ohio River Valley, the Great Kanawha River had been the principal artery of commerce. As early as 1784 George Washington proposed internal improvements to create a road and waterway route from the headwaters of rivers flowing east to the Atlantic Ocean and those flowing west toward the Ohio River. Although the James River Company was started in 1786 to survey and make improvements on the James River, little was accomplished. On February 17, 1820, the commonwealth of Virginia assumed the operation of the James River Company in an effort to speed up and expand the work to complete a waterway connection to the Great Kanawha River. In 1832 a new company was incorporated, the James River and Kanawha Company. Private investors and commonwealth stockholders in the company worked to develop a waterway in the Great Kanawha Valley.

As can be expected, the most difficult part of the route was finding a way over the Appalachian Mountains. In 1836

the James River and Kanawha Company authorized the turnpike road from Covington, Virginia, to the Falls of the Great Kanawha. This turnpike then continued to the mouth of the Big Sandy River, at today's border between Kentucky and West Virginia on the Ohio River, a total distance of 208 miles. At the same time, minor improvements were being made on the Great Kanawha River, including building wing dams and cutting sluices through the many shoals, shallow areas with sandbars.

Long before the first steamboat appeared on the Great Kanawha, thousands of flatboats, keelboats, and other man-powered vessels were used to transport salt down the river. The salt springs, located about three miles above present-day Charleston, West Virginia, and extending several miles upstream, became the prime source for development and transportation in the valley.

Some of the primary improvements accomplished by Virginia were in place by 1819, when the *Robert Thompson* attempted to steam to Charleston. The steamboat was unable to get past the notorious Red House Shoals, thirty-two and a half miles above the mouth of the river. She would spend two days trying to best this major obstacle before returning back downstream.

In December 1820 the *Andrew Donnally* was the first steamboat to finally reach Charleston. In 1824 the *Fairy Queen* became the first steamboat to carry on a Charleston–Cincinnati packet trade. Between the mid-1820s and 1860, the Great Kanawha River Valley became a hotbed of steamboat construction and regular packet trades between Pittsburgh, Cincinnati, and all points in between as Virginia sought to connect the blue water of the Atlantic Ocean with the muddy waters of the Ohio River.

While the Great Kanawha River was being improved and commercial traffic on it was growing, one of its major tributaries was also being improved. The Coal River, named in 1742 for the large quantities of coal lining its banks, was also becoming a river of commercial activity. The coal along the banks was discovered to be cannel coal. Because of its high content of refinable oil, cannel coal could be used to replace the costly whale oil then used in wick-type lamps. The oil from cannel coal could also be refined into a high-grade lubricating oil for a nation moving into the Industrial Age. The fact that an oil refinery had been built near Charleston in the 1850s gave even more reason to develop mining of Coal River's cannel coal.

In 1849 William M. Peyton acquired a charter for the Coal River Navigation Company from the commonwealth of Virginia. Soon thereafter, others joined Peyton, who, with the assistance of the state, moved to build a series of eight locks and dams on the Coal River thirty-five miles upstream to Paytona, Virginia (West Virginia), and a single lock and dam on the Little Coal River about one and a half miles above its junction with the Coal River. This lock and dam system, completed by 1859, was constructed of stone-filled timber crib dams, consisting of timbers driven into the streambed with box-like cribs built on them, filled with stone. However, as early as 1857, heavy flooding damaged all nine of the structures.

With the onset of the Civil War in the Great Kanawha Valley, the Coal River locks and dams fell into disrepair, and in 1861 a record flood severely damaged all the structures. After the Civil War minor repairs were made to the locks and dams and mining was resumed. However, by 1882 the slack-water system was abandoned for other means of transportation.

Although the Great Kanawha River Valley continued to prosper during the 1850s, the outbreak of the Civil War brought an immediate change to activities on the river. Because of the strategic location of the valley as a route between Union and Confederate states, military operations were started within five days after Virginia seceded from the Union. Confederate units arrived at Charleston in June 1861 to secure and hold the valley. Meanwhile, Union forces were being amassed at Gallipolis, Ohio, to begin a combined land and river assault to drive all Confederate troops and supporters out of the valley. In early July a flotilla of twelve steamboats, including the *Economy*, *Mary Cook*, *Silver Lake No. 2*, and *Fanny McBurnie*, led by the flagship *Eunice*, steamed up the Great Kanawha carrying Union troops and supplies to occupy the valley. During one of these early operations on the Great Kanawha, the side-wheel steamboat *Moses McLellan* carried more than a thousand tons of supplies for federal troops to Camp Piatt, located ten miles above Charleston. The *Moses McLellan* was one of the largest boats ever to operate on the Great Kanawha River.

For most of the national conflict, the opposing sides continued operations along the Great Kanawha, with steamboats being captured and/or burned as late as 1864. Many packet-boat owners attempted to continue their commercial trade during the war. Boats such as *Annie Laurie*, *Victor*, *Kanawha Belle*, *T. J. Pickett*, and *Allen Collier* were among those that continued to carry passengers and freight.

Even before the Civil War ended, the legislature of the new state of West Virginia passed a joint resolution calling on Congress to improve the inland rivers. This 1863 resolution did not center on the rivers of West Virginia alone but addressed the need for "adequate and permanent" improvements on the Ohio River. Efforts to reunify the nation centered on improvements of waterways, and one of the oldest waterways became the new center of development. The James River and Kanawha Canal/Turnpike was once more viewed as the major connecting link between the Eastern Seaboard over and through the Appalachian

STEAMBOAT PHOTO COLLECTION OF GERALD W. "JERRY" SUTPHIN

*The steamboat* Kanawha Belle *locking through one of the ten original Great Kanawha River locks and dams*

Mountains to the Great Kanawha and Ohio River basins. This was planned as the first section in what would become known as the Great American Central Water Line. The route would follow the James River in Virginia to the Appalachian Mountains, traverse the mountains, and then connect with a tributary of the New River that emptied into the Great Kanawha River. The Great Kanawha emptied into the Ohio River that in turn flowed into the Mississippi River. On the Mississippi the traveler would go upstream to the Missouri and follow it to the Kansas River to the foothills of the Rocky Mountains. Although this "water route to the west" was never fully realized, it was the beginning of the effort to create slack-water navigation for the full length of the Great Kanawha River.

Between 1875 and 1898 Congress authorized the U.S. Army Corps of Engineers to construct a series of twelve locks with movable dams on the Great Kanawha. Lock and Dam Numbers 1 and 12 were never built. The dams for Lock and Dam Numbers 2 and 3 were fixed, with the remaining eight dams being movable wicket structures. The first series of Great Kanawha River locks and dams set a "series of firsts" for America. Dam Numbers 4 and 5 would be the first movable wicket dams completed in the United States, and in 1898 the Great Kanawha became the first river in the nation completely canalized with wicket dams. Wicket dams were constructed of a series of flat movable timbers, called wickets, that were attached to metal frames, allowing the wickets to be raised or lowered. For more than forty years the movable wicket dam system served the Great Kanawha Valley well, but by the late 1920s age and wear and tear were beginning to be reflected in the number of repairs required to keep the system working.

Beginning in 1931 construction of two new high-lift, non-navigable roller-gate dams with twin locks was started. These dams are constructed of movable metal control gates attached to concrete piers across a river. Locks must be used at all times with them because boats cannot pass over or through them. One of the new dams was located at Marmet, West Virginia, sixty-eight miles above the mouth of the Great Kanawha River, and the other was at London, West Virginia, eighty-three miles above the mouth of the river. Each of the new structures had a hydroelectric power plant included as a part of the dam to generate power for both operation of the project and to be sold to the public. In the fall of 1933 Marmet Locks and Dam was dedicated with a steamboat parade in honor of U.S. Vice President Charles Curtis, who was visiting the Great Kanawha River Valley. However, it would be May 1934 before Marmet was fully completed and June 1934 when London Locks and Dam was finished.

While these two projects were under construction, improvements for the lower Great Kanawha River were being addressed. The Army Corps of Engineers recommended that a third high-lift roller-gate dam with twin locks be built near Winfield, West Virginia, thirty-one miles above the mouth of the river. The corps also recommended that a much larger lock and dam project be built thirty-two miles down the Ohio River from Point Pleasant to provide slack-water navigation on the Great Kanawha to the Winfield project as well as to eliminate three wicket-style locks and dams on the Ohio River. This latter project was named Gallipolis Locks and Dam and was located near Hogsett, West Virginia. By the standards of the day this project was considered to be huge in size and scope. The nonnavigable dam, with eight 125-foot-wide roller-gates, stretched across the Ohio River. The project had one lock measuring 110 feet by 600 feet and another measuring 110 feet by 300 feet. Both projects were started in 1933, with Winfield being completed in 1937. Gallipolis was completed and dedicated on June 12, 1938, with

a large steamboat parade. The completion of these three locks and dams on the Great Kanawha and the one Ohio River lock and dam provided a nine-foot navigable channel for all of the Great Kanawha and forty-eight miles on the Ohio River. All of these projects proved to be worth their investment by providing year-round navigation for the Great Kanawha for more than half a century.

By the mid 1980s the Great Kanawha River locks and dams required improvements and modernization to accommodate larger barges towed by more powerful towboats. Rather than replace the present structures, the Army Corps of Engineers took an innovative approach to remodel three of the four structures. The Ohio River project, Gallipolis Locks and Dam, would be the first of these to be modernized. Beginning in 1987, a two-mile-long canal was dug adjacent to the old locks, and two new larger lock chambers were constructed in the canal. The two new lock chambers measured 110 feet by 800 feet and 110 feet by 600 feet, making this project more in line with the size of the newer locks and dams that had been built on the Ohio River. The old lock chambers were sealed off and became a part of the dam, which underwent a complete rehabilitation. Dedicated on September 10, 1992, the project's name was changed to Robert C. Byrd Locks and Dam in June 1993.

The next project to be modernized was Winfield Locks and Dam. Construction began in May 1990 with a canal being dug adjacent to the locks, similar to what was done at Gallipolis. A single 110-foot-by-800-foot lock chamber was constructed in the canal replacing the 56-foot-by-360-foot twin locks. The new lock was dedicated on November 21, 1997. Marmet Locks and Dam modernization began in May 2002. As was done at Winfield, a new lock chamber was dug beside the existing lock chambers. A new lock measuring 110 feet by 800 feet was constructed in the canal to replace the twin 360-foot-by-56-foot locks. This project was completed in January 2008.

———•◆•———

Leaving Point Pleasant, Virginia (West Virginia), after taking on fuel, the *New Orleans* passed the French colony of Gallipolis, Ohio. Soon the *New Orleans* was passing the mouth of the Big Sandy River. In 1811 this small stream marked the boundary between the commonwealths of Virginia and Kentucky.

Although the Big Sandy was a small river, it was the principal route of travel and commerce for the settlers living along its torturous, meandering, steep valleys and on its two major tributaries, the Tug Fork and the Levisa Fork. As early as the 1830s small steamboats were running short trips up the lower Big Sandy River. Steamboats such as the *Mountain Girl*, *Pillsbury*, and *Red Buck* were among the first to attempt to establish trade on this narrow mountainous stream, but these ran only for a short period of time.

This stream has the distinction of having the most unusual steamboats to operate on the western rivers. Although there is no record of who built the first of the unique Big Sandy River "bat-wing," side-wheel steamboats, they began to appear on the river after the Civil War. These lightly built vessels with exposed side-wheels, which apparently looked like the flapping of a bat's wings when running, drew about eighteen inches of water when fully loaded, making them ideal for service on this shallow river.

The navigation period on the Big Sandy was usually from December until March or April. The bat-wing boats and a few stern-wheel boats would travel up the Big Sandy River twenty-six miles to Louisa, Kentucky, where the Tug and Levisa Forks join to create the Big Sandy. At this point the boats would either travel up the Levisa Fork for eighty-six miles to Pikeville, Ken-

tucky, or steam up the Tug Fork thirty-five miles to Warfield, Virginia (West Virginia), or sixty miles to Williamson, Virginia (West Virginia). Because of their ability to operate during extreme low-water conditions, many of the bat-wing boats would also be contracted for work on the Ohio River when the river level was so low that all of the larger packet boats were tied up.

As early as the 1830s Kentucky attempted to improve navigation of the Big Sandy River by removing boulders and snags and blasting out channels. In 1874 the U.S. Congress authorized a survey of the Big Sandy and later funded open-channel improvements such as the building of dikes and wing dams to improve the more severely obstructed areas of the river. Construction on the first lock and dam on the Big Sandy began in 1883. Built just below the junction of the Tug and Levisa Forks, Lock and Dam Number 3 was an experimental Poiree needle dam that would allow the immense volume of sand that moved constantly down the river to pass the dam, which had a single lock chamber. Completed on New Year's Day of 1877, the success of this project led to the construction of two more locks and dams on the main stem of the Big Sandy. One lock and dam each also were built on the Levisa and Tug Forks. Lock and Dam Numbers 1 and 2, located at Catlettsburg, Kentucky, and Kavanaugh, Kentucky, respectively, were completed in 1905. The lock and dam on each of the two tributaries were operational by 1909.

During this same period railroads were being built on both sides of the Big Sandy River as well as on the Tug and Levisa Forks. Railroad competition and continuing problems with massive amounts of sand depositing against the dams and filling the lock chambers eventually led to the river being used less and less. In 1921 Captain John F. Davis attempted to revive the steamboat trade on the Big Sandy River by running the

*The steamboat* Thealka, *one of the unique "bat-wing" side-wheel boats that operated on the Big Sandy River as well as on the Tug and Levisa Forks*

steamboat *J. P. Davis* from Catlettsburg to Pikeville, but the service ended after five trips. In 1951 and 1952 the Army Corps of Engineers suspended locking services at all five locks and dams on the Big Sandy, and only nine miles of the river are used today to move coal and petroleum barges to and from the Ohio River.

———•◦•———

Continuing down the Ohio River, the *New Orleans* crew noticed that the river was getting broader with longer and smoother pools. They soon passed the small community of Portsmouth, Ohio, at the mouth of the Scioto River, then continued on downstream past Limestone (Maysville), Kentucky, before arriving at Cincinnati, Ohio. The *New Orleans* stopped at Cincinnati only to refuel and continued 133.5 miles downstream to Louisville, Kentucky. As was the practice of almost all boats traveling on the Ohio and Mississippi rivers at this time, the *New Orleans* crew was using a copy of the 1811 edition of Zadok Cramer's *The Navigator* to guide them down the river. As the boat passed the mouth of the Kentucky River, the crew may have consulted *The Navigator*'s lengthy discussion on Frankfort, Kentucky. Located about sixty miles up the Kentucky River, Frankfort was the seat of Kentucky's government.

As early as 1787 flatboats and barges were carrying the natural and agricultural abundance of the Kentucky River Valley down the Kentucky and Ohio rivers to Louisville and beyond. However, the first steamboat did not appear on the Kentucky River until 1816, when a group of Lexington shippers built the steamboat *Kentucky* at the mouth of Hickman Creek, a tributary of the Kentucky River. By 1820 the steamboat *Fayette* was advertising "New Orleans goods" for sale, illustrating that round-trip commerce had been established in the valley. Prior to the Civil War, riverboats were the major mode of transportation and

commerce for trans-Appalachian settlers. Because of the importance of river transportation, Kentucky soon realized the need to improve its rivers to insure its future growth and prosperity. In 1818 the Kentucky legislature provided $100,000 to insure safety and to make navigation improvements on the Kentucky River.

After several surveys, Kentucky awarded contracts in July 1836 to build five locks and dams. Lock Number 1 (Carrollton) was built at Horseshoe Bend, river mile four; Lock Number 2 (Lockport) at Six Mile Ripple, river mile thirty-one; Lock Number 3 (Gest) at Cedar Creek Ripple, river mile forty-two; Lock Number 4 (Frankfort) at Lee's Ripple, river mile sixty-five; and Lock Number 5 (Tyrone) at Steeles Ripple, river mile eighty-two. When completed in 1842, the lock and dam system created slack water for ninety-five miles upstream. However, only the lower sixty-six miles could be used year-round because steamboats could not pass under the low bridges at Frankfort. Nevertheless, the locks and dams provided for a high influx of steamboat traffic on the Kentucky River and served major ports on the Ohio and Mississippi rivers.

All of these projects were built by the standards of the 1830s, with the dams being stone-filled timber cribs and the lock chambers built of cut limestone. Because of the construction methods and the frequent flooding on the Kentucky, maintenance of these projects was a major financial burden from the beginning. As was true of all of the Ohio River's navigable tributaries, the Kentucky River experienced loss of commerce with the building of railroads and this, along with the onset of the Civil War, resulted in a major decline of navigation on the river until the end of the conflict.

The lack of maintenance, poor management, and a series of floods in 1873 resulted in even more deterioration of the five

*The steamboat* John Quill *locking through one of the lower Kentucky River locks*

Kentucky River projects. Once again individuals and organizations, both political and private, began to call for repairs to the existing projects and to extend slack-water navigation to the Three Forks Area, where the North Fork, Middle Fork, and South Fork joined at the headwaters of the main stem of the Kentucky River.

Development on the river entered a new phase with the passage of the federal Rivers and Harbors Act of 1879. The federal government acquired the five existing locks and dams and began a series of surveys of the Kentucky River from Lock and Dam Number 5 to the Three Forks Area near Beattyville, Kentucky. Although a contract was awarded for the building of Lock and Dam Number 6 (Salvisa Lock and Dam) in May 1887, it was not until May 1891 that actual construction began. The first contractor for the project was to provide the necessary stone for construction by August 1888 but failed to do so. Acceptable construction-quality stone was not delivered to the dam site near Oregon, Kentucky, until May 1890. One year later construction was started, and Lock and Dam Number 6 was opened for navigation on December 2, 1891.

The construction of Lock and Dam Number 7 (High Bridge Lock and Dam), began in 1896, and it was opened to navigation on December 11, 1897. While Lock and Dam Number 7 was being built, plans and specifications for Lock and Dam Number 8 (Little Hickman Lock and Dam) were being prepared. It was the first project on the Kentucky River to be constructed totally by contracted labor. The project was started in September 1898 and was completed and opened to navigation on October 15, 1900. With the completion of Lock and Dam Number 8 and because of increasing construction costs, the Army Corps of Engineers evaluated both its construction methods and the need to continue building locks and dams farther upstream.

However, Congress continued to fund additional projects and directed the corps to complete the work on the Kentucky River. While Lock and Dam Numbers 1 through 8 had all been built with stone masonry, timber-crib dams, and cut-stone locks, the corps now employed new construction methods. Lock and Dam Numbers 9, 10, 11, and 12 were built between 1901 and 1910 using concrete and steel. Although the new construction materials and methods reduced construction time, they caused problems with the logging and lumber industry on the upper river. No longer could loose logs and log booms be allowed to float freely down the river, often ramming into the locks and dams. Logs would have to be rafted together and towed to prevent blocking the river and harming the dams. The Army Corps of Engineers was also required to redesign Lock and Dam Numbers 11, 12, 13, and 14. The dams at each of these projects were built with a movable dam crest that would allow for a six-foot minimum depth to be maintained for slack-water navigation while helping secure the structures against damage from flooding and logjams.

Construction of Lock and Dam Number 9 (Valley View Lock and Dam) began in July 1901 and it was opened to navigation on December 3, 1903. At the same time, work was also started on Lock and Dam Numbers 10 and 11. After beginning construction on Lock and Dam Number 9, the contract was awarded for the building of Lock and Dam No. 10 (Boonesboro Lock and Dam). This project would be completed in 1906. In the meantime, construction began on Lock and Dam Number 11 (College Hill Lock and Dam). Once again, due to the uncontrollable nature of the Kentucky River, changes were made in the construction of this project. A movable extension (crest gate) had to be installed on the crest of the dam so minor adjustments could be made to the navigation pool and the extension/crest leaf could be lowered for the passage of floodwaters. Lock and Dam Number 11 was completed on December 26, 1906. Lock and Dam Number 12 (Ravenna Lock and Dam) was built in the same manner as Lock and Dam Number 11. It, too, would have movable crest gates on the dam. Work was started in June 1907 and completed on January 13, 1910.

As the federal government was continuing to build locks and dams upstream toward the Three Forks area to provide an outlet for coal and other minerals of the region, the railroads continued to expand their areas of operation. The packet-boat trade on the Kentucky River was gradually declining due to improved highways and the advent of automobiles and trucks. By 1910 many, including a growing number of Army Corps of Engineers officers, did not feel it would be worth the expense to continue building the last two planned projects on the Kentucky River. In May 1909 a contract to construct the lock for Lock and Dam Number 13 (Thirteen Lock and Dam) was awarded and progressed smoothly. However, when the contract was awarded for construction of the dam in October 1910, problems developed. The contractor moved very slowly in building the dam before the company went bankrupt in 1912.

The contractor for Lock and Dam Number 14 (Heidelberg Lock and Dam) began work in May 1911, but the developing problems at Lock and Dam Number 13 created problems for the construction efforts at Lock and Dam 14. Construction at both projects became even more complicated when the contractor at Lock and Dam Number 14 agreed to assume the construction of the dam at Lock and Dam Number 13 but soon ran into financial problems as well. Corps officials had planned that the construction of locks and dams on the Kentucky River would be complete by 1913. However, because of the contractors' financial problems, landowner difficulties, lack of congressional support, and

the flood of 1913, the Kentucky River system was not completed until January 20, 1917, when Lock Number 14 quietly opened to traffic.

Over the next sixty-plus years commercial traffic on the river diminished slowly, with the occasional peaks brought on by World War I and World War II, increased coal and petroleum shipments, and an influx of pleasure boaters. Recreational boating had its birth on the Kentucky River after World War I. Over the ensuing years, boating, fishing, and other water-related activities benefited from the pools on the river created by the dams. As early as 1951, the Army Corps of Engineers proposed closing navigation on the Kentucky River above Frankfort, but because of opposition they were not able to achieve this until 1981. By 1997 the corps entered into an agreement with the commonwealth of Kentucky to begin procedures to turn over all fourteen lock and dam projects to the state.

———— •-•-• ————

As the *New Orleans* moved swiftly down the Ohio, the crew prepared for the boat's stop at Louisville, Kentucky, and the challenge of passing over the Falls of the Ohio River. Upon their arrival at Louisville, Roosevelt and his crew discovered that because of low-water conditions, the *New Orleans* could not pass the Falls. Roosevelt used the delay at Louisville to renew friendships from the flatboat trip of 1809 and to give tours of the boat to the area residents. As the crew waited for the river to raise enough to allow passage over the Falls, Roosevelt decided to prove that the *New Orleans* could steam upstream against the current of a western river and return to Cincinnati. The *New Orleans* encountered no difficulties during the 133.5-mile return to Cincinnati. A week was spent at the Ohio city taking citizens on short cruises and allowing Roosevelt time to make as many

*The steamboat* Chaperon *approaching Mammoth Cave landing on the upper Green River*

*Stern view of the steamboat* Evansville *in Barren River Lock Number 1*

business contacts as possible. Roosevelt was proving to be an outstanding salesman for his partners and the Ohio Steamboat Navigation Company.

However, the time came to steam down the Ohio past the Falls, and the wait for higher water at the barrier began to generate a great deal of concern. A short period later, the river finally appeared to be ready for the *New Orleans* to attempt passage over the Falls. To the delight of all, the *New Orleans* made the perilous trip without incident. After a brief stop at Shippingport, Kentucky, just below the Falls, to take on supplies and hear the latest news and river conditions from the boatmen and woodsmen, the journey continued. As the boat progressed downstream, the crew began to encounter an increasing number of islands that required a great deal of attention to navigate around. After a brief stop at Yellowbanks (Owensboro), Kentucky, to take on fuel, the *New Orleans* was soon passing the mouth of the Green River on Kentucky's shore.

Navigation on the Green River began almost as soon as the first settlers arrived in its valley. Flatboats were used to transport products as far south as New Orleans. In 1818 Kentucky allocated funds to clear the state's rivers to improve navigation. In 1828 the *McLean* steamed 150 miles up the Green River, then thirty miles up the Barren River, one of Green River's major tributaries, to Bowling Green, Kentucky. Just five years later, Kentucky authorized the development of a slack-water system on the Green and Barren rivers. As was later done on the Kentucky River, the Kentucky Board of Internal Improvements had the rivers surveyed and provided funding for the construction of locks and dams.

The Green River and Barren River improvement projects were the first of their kind in the United States, with funding provided for Lock and Dam Numbers 1 and 2 in 1834. Lock and Dam Number 1 on Green River was completed in late 1835. While this was being accomplished, the dam site for Lock and Dam Numbers 3 and 4 on the Green River as well as the site to build Lock and Dam Number 1 on the Barren River were selected. As the system of five locks and dams neared completion in 1841, the steamboat *Sandusky* navigated the 175 miles from the mouth of the Green River up to Bowling Green on the Barren. With the slack-water system completed, regular steamboat commerce was active between Bowling Green, Kentucky, and Evansville, Indiana, on the Ohio River.

Between 1860 and 1865, as the Civil War raged, the Green and Barren rivers' locks and dams were neglected and/or damaged. Rather than assume the expense of the repair and operation of the system, after the war the state leased the locks and dams to the Green and Barren River Navigation Company, a private organization. The company began to charge tolls at each of the locks except for the company-owned steamboats *Evansville* and *Bowling Green*. Soon competition was driven off the Green and Barren rivers, leading to a series of court challenges in state legislation and eventually to the U.S. Congress before the situation was settled. The United States government purchased the locks and dams in 1888 and directed the U.S. Army Corps of Engineers to undertake their maintenance. Improvements were made to these and other navigational projects.

By 1890 commerce on the two rivers had improved to the point that there were as many as sixteen steamboats operating regularly in various commercial trades. This success led the U.S. government to authorize the construction of Lock and Dam Numbers 5 and 6 on the Green River. The steamboat *Chaperon* made the initial trip through the new locks in 1906, carrying passengers from Evansville, Indiana, on the Ohio River to Mammoth Cave, Kentucky. This particular trip would soon develop into a regular tourist and excursion trade on the river.

During the 1920s and 1930s traffic declined steadily, and by the 1950s Lock and Dam Numbers 5 and 6 discontinued operations. However, during this same period there was a resurgent need for Lock and Dam Numbers 1 and 2. With the construction of several giant steam-electric power plants on the Ohio River in the vicinity, the need for coal from the Green River Valley mines brought new life to the river. To meet the need, Congress authorized the reconstruction of Lock and Dam Number 2 as well as the enlargement of the locks at both Lock and Dam Numbers 1 and 2 between 1953 and 1956. Throughout the 1960s and 1970s tonnage shipped on the Green River continued to increase.

The success of the Green and Barren rivers projects led to improvements on another major tributary of the Green River. The Rough River had been surveyed in 1836, and a recommendation had been made to build locks and dams. In 1856 the Rough Creek Navigation and Manufacturing Company was established to improve navigation on the river. However, little was accomplished until after the Civil War, when a crude lock and dam was built about eight miles above the union of the Green and Rough rivers. Although this lock and dam did open slack-water navigation to Hartford, Kentucky, it only lasted a short period due to the Green River locks having tolls placed on them.

In 1890 the U.S. Congress directed the Army Corps of Engineers to reestablish navigation on the Rough River. The corps responded by removing the old lock and dam and building a new lock and dam near the site of the old project. Unfortunately, the traffic that was hoped for never developed on the river, with only a few smaller boats operating there. The only significant commerce was the logging industry, which used the lock for moving log rafts downstream. The Rough River Lock and Dam ceased operation in 1941. The project deteriorated slowly and was finally authorized for disposal by the federal government in 1959.

———

Leaving the Green River area, the *New Orleans* steamed past the community of Henderson, Kentucky. Now the boat and its crew would steam through the oxbow region of the Ohio River, with its numerous bends and increasing number of islands. The next major landmark was the mouth of the Wabash River, which formed the boundary between the Indiana and Illinois territories.

The Wabash River had long been used by Native Americans as well as early French traders as a connector route between the Great Lakes and the Ohio River Valley. During the 1830s and 1840s, thousands of flatboats floated down the Wabash and its tributaries carrying a multitude of natural and agricultural products to the Ohio and Mississippi rivers. Keelboats abounded on the Wabash as well, transporting passengers and commodities upstream until the appearance of the steamboat.

In 1823 the *Florence* steamed up the Wabash River 214 miles to Terre Haute, Indiana. This feat was followed two years later by a steamboat reaching Lafayette, Indiana, 312 miles above the mouth of the river. As had been done on all of the Ohio River tributaries, steamboat captains wanting to have their boat be the first to reach a certain point on a river would wait for high water to steam upstream as far as the flood tide permitted. This was done on the Wabash River and its tributaries. The *Republican* landed at Logansport, Indiana, in 1834, 355 miles from the

*Steamboat* City of Idaho *at a Wabash River landing*

*The steamboat* Governor Morton *on White River at Indianapolis*

Ohio River. In 1831 the *General Hanna* steamed up the Wabash River 96 miles to the White River and then went up the White River 232 miles to Indianapolis.

The Wabash Navigation Company was chartered in 1844 and began construction on a lock and dam at Grand Rapids Shoals, 97 miles above the mouth of the Wabash and the river's main obstacle. The 1,030-foot-long, timber-crib dam with its 210-foot-by-52-foot lock was completed in 1849. However, the U.S. Congress did not authorize a survey of the Wabash and its tributaries until after the Civil War. The 1870 survey led Congress to appropriate funds for snag removal, channel clearing, and other minor navigation improvements during 1872 and 1879. Not until 1885 would the Army Corps of Engineers begin construction on a new lock and dam at Grand Rapids Shoals to replace the poorly built 1849 structure. When it was completed in 1894, commerce on the Wabash River and its tributaries had already begun to decline to such a level that the new lock and dam did little to improve business development on the river. Over the next half century, repeated recommendations for navigation improvement projects for the Wabash River basin were made, but funding was never forthcoming, and no slack-water project was constructed.

———— ◆ ————

Continuing down the Ohio, past the Wabash River, the Roosevelts anticipated passing the notoriously famous Cave-In-Rock they had seen on their flatboat trip two years earlier. From this unique natural rock formation, river pirates enticed travelers to enter the cave and robbed and sometimes killed them. After passing Cave-In-Rock, the *New Orleans* crew and passengers were nearing the point where the Ohio and Mississippi rivers join.

The *New Orleans* would pass two more major tributaries before moving onto the Mississippi River. The first of these was the Cumberland or Shawnee River. From the time of the earliest explorers, hunters, and settlers, the Cumberland River served as a trade route for pirogues, flatboats, and keelboats. In 1780 a fleet of 30 boats carrying about 150 settlers floated down the Holston River from Fort Patrick Henry (Kingsport, Tennessee) to the Tennessee River. From here the flotilla floated down the Tennessee River to the Ohio River, then worked its way up the Ohio and Cumberland rivers to the present site of Nashville, Tennessee. A lucrative flatboat and keelboat trade would soon be developed from this settlement along the Cumberland to the Ohio and Mississippi rivers. By 1818 the *General Jackson* steamed 191 miles up the Cumberland from the Ohio River to establish a Nashville–Louisville commercial connection. Steamboats with names such as *Rifleman*, *General Robertson*, *Cumberland*, *Nashville*, and *Red Rover* soon began making Nashville a major port of call. By 1828 other steamboats were venturing up the Cumberland 309 miles to Caney Fork River in Tennessee and beyond. In 1833 the *Jefferson* steamed upstream 516 miles to Point Isabel (Burnside), Kentucky, and opened the upper Cumberland River Valley to steamboat travel. The Cumberland remained the major route of commerce until 1880 when the railroads were built.

Although navigation on the lower Cumberland was considered to be relatively unimpeded, one major obstacle located just thirty-eight miles below Nashville was a major challenge during low-water periods. Harpeth Shoals extended along a five-mile stretch of rapids on the Cumberland and was considered to be one of the worst natural impediments along the 516-mile navigable course of the river. During the spring and fall of the year there was usually sufficient water to allow boats to make their

*Cumberland River steamboats* Bob Dudley *and* Henry Harley *at the Nashville, Tennessee, public landing*

way through the shoals with little difficulty. However, passing over or through the shoals was often impossible during low-water periods. Harpeth Shoals would be the reason the state of Tennessee would petition Congress to survey the Cumberland River in 1825.

As early as 1832, the Army Corps of Engineers improved the channel of the Cumberland River through clearing and snagging. The improvements on the lower Cumberland soon had the citizens on the upper river above Nashville seeking funding from Congress to improve that part of the river as well. In 1834 the corps began the survey of the upper Cumberland River from Nashville to Cumberland Falls, 371 miles. The survey revealed the abundant mineral resources, timber, and agricultural potential of the upper river and projected how navigation improvements would benefit commerce. Congress appropriated funds in 1837 for improvements on the upper Cumberland River that included snagging, clearing, and the building of wing dams or dikes. These efforts made a significant improvement to navigation on the entire length of the Cumberland and revealed that the building of a lock and dam slack-water system on the river would insure year-round navigation.

Between 1839 and the beginning of the Civil War, little was accomplished on the Cumberland due to a lack of funding. In 1871 interest in improving the Cumberland with locks and dams was again explored. After numerous delays the first lock and dam on this river was started in 1888. Located at river mile 188.4, just three miles below Nashville, the completion of Lock and Dam Number 1 set into motion efforts to create a slack-water system for the entire length of the river. In 1892 Congress appropriated funding for the building of Lock and Dam "A" below Harpeth Shoals.

Breaking from the usual method of numbering locks and dams on other streams, the six locks and dams on the lower Cumberland River would be identified by letters A through F, extending downstream. The first lock and dam above the mouth of the river was letter F at river mile forty-four. The locks and dams constructed above Nashville would be numbered in the normal manner with the exception of Lock and Dam Number 1, built just below Nashville to create a pool for the city, the river's busiest port. Lock and Dam A was built to inundate Harpeth Shoals, the lower Cumberland River's greatest obstacle.

The original plan for the Cumberland River lock and dam system was to build twenty-one structures from the Ohio River to Burnside, Kentucky. The locks and dams would be numbered from one to twenty-one beginning with the first project just above the mouth of the Ohio River. However, with the passage of time, numerous changes were made in the number of locks and dams built as well as how they were named or numbered.

Construction was underway on locks and dams on the upper and lower Cumberland River during the same period of time. Lock and Dam Number 2, located ten miles above Nashville, was completed in 1907, and Lock and Dam Number 7 was completed in 1910. When all fourteen locks and dams on the upper Cumberland were completed, slack-water navigation extended upriver 331.4 miles to Niagara Shoals, Tennessee.

Although Lock and Dam Number 21 had been part of the original plan to build a complete system of locks and dams on the Cumberland River, not all of the proposed projects were constructed because of a decline in commercial traffic over time. This decline in commerce led to the decision not to build any more locks and dams above Lock and Dam Number 7. However, Lock and Dam Number 21, located at Burnside, Kentucky, was the exception and was authorized in 1905 to provide a navigation pool behind the dam to load and fleet barges for shipment downstream during high-water periods. Lock and Dam Number 21 was completed in 1911 and retained its original number although there would not be any other projects built between Lock and Dam Numbers 7 and 21.

There was still strong public support for construction of the remainder of the proposed locks and dams along the upper Cumberland River. In 1913 the Cumberland River Improvement Association with the support of local, state, and federal elected officials pushed to complete the entire Cumberland River slack-water system. A compromise was agreed upon concerning flowage damages along the part of the river where the Lock and Dam Number 8 pool would be. Construction began in 1920. This would be the last piece of the Cumberland River Canalization Project because by the time Lock and Dam Number 8 was completed in 1924, commerce on the upper river was almost nonexistent. Whereas hundreds of steamboats had been competing for business on the river, by 1933 only three packets remained, the *Burnside*, *Rowena*, and *Celina*, and these soon relinquished the river to towboats and their multiple barge tows.

In the early 1920s Congress directed that the nation's rivers be surveyed to develop multipurpose-use programs that included navigation, flood control, hydroelectric power generation, and low-flow augmentation. This legislation would eventually lead to the creation of the Tennessee Valley Authority and the building of a series of multipurpose projects on the Tennessee River. It would also have an impact on the development of projects on the Cumberland River. The need to increase the navigable depth on the Cumberland led to the existing locks and dams being modified to impound a higher slack-water pool.

Federal legislation dealing with the disastrous floods of 1927 on the Mississippi River and 1937 on the Ohio River changed the Cumberland River as well. The Flood Control Act of 1938 resulted in Wolf Creek Dam construction beginning in 1941. This flood control and hydroelectric power generation project with no locks was constructed on the main stem of the Cumberland 475 miles above the mouth of the river. When completed in 1951, the project created a lake, named Lake Cumberland, that extended 101 miles up the river. This project was followed with the construction of Cheatham Lock and Dam on the lower Cumberland River between 1950 and 1954. Cheatham Lock and Dam was a multipurpose project in that it not only had locks for navigation but also hydroelectric power production units. In 1952 construction was started on Old Hickory Lock and Dam on the upper Cumberland. Put into operation in 1957, Old Hickory was also a multipurpose project with navigation and hydroelectric power production capabilities.

All of these projects had a significant impact on the lower Cumberland River. Since the early 1950s there had been ongoing controversy between proponents of a single high, multipurpose dam with locks and those in favor of two medium-height, multipurpose dams with locks similar to those of the Cheatham Lock and Dam project. In 1956 construction was started on the high, multipurpose dam with locks, which was named Barkley Lock and Dam for Alban Barkley, Kentucky senator and vice president. When completed in 1966, the new lake created by Barkley Lock and Dam extended upstream to Cheatham Lock and Dam. The most unusual aspect of the Barkley Lock and Dam project was that Congress required the Army Corps of Engineers to create a navigation channel between the Cumberland River's Lake Barkley and the Tennessee River's Kentucky Lake.

Located just over two miles above Barkley Dam, this canal created a narrow finger of land that was named the "Land Between the Lakes." The canal also provided a shorter route between the Cumberland, Tennessee, and Ohio rivers. Now, the Cumberland and Tennessee rivers, referred to as "twin rivers" because they paralleled each other for several miles as they approached the Ohio River, were connected by the canal.

———◆———

The Tennessee, or Cherokee, River would be the last major Ohio River tributary the *New Orleans* would pass before it steamed into the larger Mississippi River. The Tennessee River flows 652 miles through parts of Tennessee, Alabama, and Kentucky before emptying into the Ohio River at Paducah, Kentucky. It is the Ohio River's largest tributary and from the earliest days of settlement was navigable 250 miles upstream to the river's greatest obstruction, Muscle Shoals.

As early as 1817 steamboats were ascending the Tennessee River, but it was 1821 before the steamer *Osage* landed at Florence, Alabama, near the foot of Muscle Shoals. The *Osage* was soon followed by the *Courier* and *Velocipede*, and within a short period the steamboat *Rocket* started regularly scheduled runs between Florence and Trinity, Illinois (near Cairo), on the Ohio River.

While steamboat traffic was increasing on the lower Tennessee River, it was 1828 before the *Atlas* steamed upstream to Muscle Shoals and spent several days attempting to work its way over the shoals to finally arrive at Knoxville. Although the citizens of Knoxville believed the arrival of the *Atlas* was a sign that more steamboats would soon be coming to their city, this would not be the case. The *Atlas* returned back downstream

never to return, and it would not be until the 1890s that regular steamboat service would be available on the upper river. Small steamboats were built to operate on the upper Tennessee River but were very limited in their trade, normally operating between Decatur, Alabama, and Knoxville, Tennessee, a distance of 342 miles.

The state of Tennessee established internal improvement programs in 1829, with one of its major goals to open up the Tennessee River Valley to navigation. The major priority was to unify the upper and lower parts of the Tennessee River by finding a way to bypass Muscle Shoals. Located 250 miles upstream from the Ohio River and approximately 400 miles below the head of the Tennessee River near Knoxville, this obstruction all but insured limited navigation throughout the Tennessee River Valley. In *Steamboats on the Western Rivers* (1949), Louis Hunter describes Muscle Shoals:

> A series of rapids extending from Brown's Ferry thirty-five miles above Florence to Waterloo thirty miles below. The three main rapids—Elk River, Muscle, and Colbert's shoals—had an aggregate fall of some 134 feet in a distance of twenty-nine miles, with Muscle Shoals accounting for an eighty-five foot fall in half of the distance. . . . Ascending navigation was out of the question almost all the time, and descent of the rapids was possible only for about one month of the year during the highest freshets.

Between 1824 and 1837 various methods were recommended and attempts made to pass Muscle Shoals. In 1830 the Army Corps of Engineers proposed a thirty-five-mile canal to be constructed around the shoals. Plans were presented to the state of Alabama, which turned the construction of the canal over to its Board of Tennessee Canal commissioners. The commissioners decided to follow their own plans for building the canal rather than those prepared by the Army Corps of Engineers. Due to a shortage of funding and unsound construction methods, the twelve-mile section of the canal experienced problems from its opening in 1837. Because of a growing national financial depression, no future funds were appropriated for the project, and the canal was abandoned. Work would not be renewed on the Muscle Shoals obstruction until after the Civil War.

In 1853 efforts were made to eliminate another series of major navigation obstructions referred to as "Narrows" or "Sucks" below Chattanooga, Tennessee, on the upper Tennessee River. The obstructions consisted of a series of dangerous, fast-flowing, natural narrow chutes. Wing dams were constructed at numerous shoals on the river, and channels were blasted through others. However, the infamous Sucks were not eliminated due to a disagreement about the method to correct the problem and the potential consequences of blasting the channel's rocky river bottom. After the Civil War, improvements on the Tennessee River were again a priority, and in 1867 the river was surveyed from Chattanooga to Paducah, with the purpose of creating year-round navigation on the Tennessee River. This survey led to open-channel work being done to eliminate the Sucks.

In 1882 seventeen rivers were being improved for navigation in the Cumberland and Tennessee river basins. They were the Cumberland, Tennessee, Hiwassel, French Broad, Clinch, Duck, Obeys, Caney Fork, Coosa, Oostanaula, Coosawattee, Ocmulgee, Etowah, Oconee, Red River, Big South Fork, and Little Tennessee. Additional improvements at Muscle Shoals were renewed in 1871. Work started with rebuilding and enlarging the old structure that had been built in 1837. Also, new

canals were to be built around Elk River Shoals and Little Muscle Shoals. At Muscle Shoals twelve miles of rock were excavated, and a sixteen-mile lateral canal was built, along with twelve miles of wing-dam construction. On November 10, 1890, the Muscle Shoals Canal was opened to traffic when a steamboat from Saint Louis passed through to Chattanooga. A steamboat company was organized at Chattanooga in 1891, and two steamboats were put into regular service between Saint Louis and Chattanooga. The steamboats *Herbert* and *City of Chattanooga* ran in trade for several years and even expanded the trade to include trips to Joppa, Illinois, and Evansville, Indiana. The success of the Muscle Shoals canal system encouraged the construction of a lateral canal around the Colbert and Bee-Tree shoals. In addition, the Colbert Canal and Riverton Locks were opened to commercial traffic in 1911.

While these projects were being built and placed into operation, plans for new multipurpose projects were being developed for the Tennessee, as on the Cumberland River. In 1905 Hales Bar Lock and Dam construction was started. Located thirty-three miles downstream from Chattanooga, this project was a navigation and multipurpose hydroelectric power production dam. The first boat locked through the project on November 1, 1913. While Hales Bar Lock and Dam were being constructed, other multipurpose projects were being planned. Among these were Dam Number 2, which was later named Wilson Dam for President Woodrow Wilson; Dam Number 1, which was a navigation dam just below Wilson Dam; and Dam Number 3, later named Wheeler Dam. These projects and others like them would soon change the face of the Tennessee River Valley. Dam Number 1 was completed in 1925, and Dam Number 2 was opened to navigation in 1927. Construction began on Dam Number 3 in

*The steamboat* City of Charleston *navigating through the Tennessee River's Shoals Creek Aqueduct near Florence, Alabama*

1933 and was completed in 1934. Another navigation dam was completed in 1924 at Windows Bar between Wilson Dam and Hales Bar Dam.

When the Tennessee Valley Authority was created in 1933, the U.S. Army Corps of Engineers' responsibility for the operation and maintenance of all navigable inland waterways of the United States remained in effect on the Tennessee River. Since that time the Tennessee Valley Authority and the Army Corps of Engineers have jointly shared the management of the Tennessee River. In the ensuing years ten multipurpose dams with locks were constructed on the Tennessee River. Some of these projects replaced older projects, while others were built new, providing slack-water navigation from the Ohio River to the junction of the five rivers that create the Tennessee River: the Powell, Clinch, Holston, French Broad, and Little Tennessee rivers. Improvements on the Tennessee River were begun to insure safe and reliable navigation. Through the years, twenty-eight multipurpose dams were built on the Tennessee and its tributaries for a multitude of purposes, including navigation, power generation, low-flow augmentation, recreation, and environmental enhancement.

———— •◦• ————

As the *New Orleans* steamed toward the Mississippi River, it left an indelible mark on the Ohio River Valley. The next two hundred years would see rapid settlement of the western lands, the development of America's western navigation system, and increased trade and commerce across the nation and internationally. Modern diesel-powered towboats pushing half-mile-long multiple barge tows through giant 1,200-foot-by-110-foot lock chambers at modern high-lift gated dams reflect the heritage of the intrepid little *New Orleans*.

*Gerald W. Sutphin, better known as Jerry, is a native West Virginian and a graduate of Marshall University. He was an employee of the U.S. Army Corps of Engineers, Huntington District for twenty years before resigning to establish his own company. In 1982 Sutphin was project consultant for the Ohio River Odyssey, a major Ohio River exhibition at the Huntington Museum of Art. He was contracted by the Smithsonian Institute to write and coproduce a series of films used in the M/V Herman T. Pott Pilothouse permanent exhibit and served as consulting creator/designer for the Always A River exhibition barge. Sutphin was the principal author of* Sternwheelers on the Great Kanawha River; *he wrote and produced the visual history of the Steamboat* Delta Queen; *and he researched, wrote, and produced a DVD of the history of the first steamboats. Sutphin is presently researching and writing an illustrated history of the life of Captain Jesse P. Hughes.*

## SELECTED BIBLIOGRAPHY

Ambler, Charles Henry. *A History of Transportation in the Ohio Valley: With Special Reference to its Waterways, Trade, and Commerce from the Earliest Period to the Present Time.* Glendale, CA: Arthur H. Clark, 1932.

Clark, Thomas D. *The Kentucky.* The Rivers of America. New York: Farrar and Rinehart, 1942.

Crowe-Carraco, Carol. *The Big Sandy.* Lexington: University Press of Kentucky, 1979.

Dean, William H. *Coal, Steamboats, Timber, and Trains: The Early Industrial History of St. Albans, West Virginia & the Coal River, 1850–1925.* Charleston, WV: Pictorial Histories Publishing, 2007.

Dick, David, and Eulalie C. Dick. *Rivers of Kentucky.* North Middletown, KY: Plum Lick Publishing, 2001.

Dohan, Mary Helen. *Mr. Roosevelt's Steamboat: The First Steamboat to Travel the Mississippi.* New York: Dodd, Mead and Co., 1981.

Gamble, Jay Mack. *Steamboats on the Muskingum.* Staten Island, NY: Steamship Historical Society of America, 1971.

Grier, William F. *The Five Lives of the Kentucky River.* Ashland, KY: Jesse Stuart Foundation, 2001.

Harralson, Agnes S. *Steamboats on the Green and the Colorful Men Who Operated Them*. Berea: Kentucky Imprints, 1981.

Hunter, Louis C. *Steamboats on the Western Rivers: An Economic and Technological History*. Cambridge, MA: Harvard University Press, 1949.

Johnson, Leland R. *Engineers on the Twin Rivers: A History of the Nashville District, Corps of Engineers, United States Army*. Washington, DC: U.S. Government Printing Office, 1978.

———. *The Falls City Engineers: A History of the Louisville District, Corps of Engineers, United States Army, Louisville, Kentucky*. Washington, DC: U.S. Government Printing Office, 1974.

———. *The Headwaters District: A History of the Pittsburgh District, U.S. Army Corps of Engineers*. Washington, DC: U.S. Government Printing Office, 1979.

———. *Men, Mountains, and Rivers: An Illustrated History of the Huntington District, U.S. Army Corps of Engineers, 1754–1974*. Washington, DC: U.S. Government Printing Office, 1977.

Johnson, Leland R., and Charles E. Parrish. *Kentucky River Development: The Commonwealth's Waterway, Louisville, Kentucky*. Washington, DC: U.S. Government Printing Office, 1999.

Jones, Robert Ralston. *The Ohio River: Charts, Drawings, and Description of Features Affecting Navigation*. Washington, DC: U.S. Government Printing Office, 1916, 1920, 1922, 1929.

Kane, Adam I. *The Western River Steamboat*. College Station: Texas A & M University Press, 2004.

Kemp, Emory L. "Benjamin Franklin Thomas and Introduction of the French Needle Dam into the United States." In *Canal History and Technology Proceedings,* vol. 24. Edited by Lance E. Metz. Easton, PA: Canal History and Technology Press, [2005].

———. *The Great Kanawha Navigation*. Pittsburgh: University of Pittsburgh Press, 2000.

Kemp, Emory, and Larry Sypolt. "The Little Kanawha Navigation." In *Canal History and Technology Proceedings*, vol. 10. Edited by Lance E. Metz. Easton, PA: Canal History and Technology Press, 1991.

Kirkwood, James J. *Waterway to the West*. Interpretive Series, No. 1. Philadelphia, PA: Eastern National Park and Monument Association in cooperation with Blue Ridge Parkway, National Park Service, and U.S. Department of the Interior, 1963.

Leahy, Ethel C. *Who's Who on the Ohio River and Its Tributaries: An Ohio River Anthology*. Cincinnati: E. C. Leahy Publishing, 1931.

*Muskingum River Water Trail*. Columbus: Ohio Department of Natural Resources, 2006.

Schafer, Jim, and Mike Sajna. *The Allegheny River: Watershed of the Nation*. University Park: Pennsylvania State University Press, 1992.

Sutphin, Gerald W. "Steamboat Navigation on the Big Sandy River, Kentucky." Unpublished manuscript, 2004.

Sutphin, Gerald W., and Richard A. Andre. *Sternwheelers on the Great Kanawha River*. Charleston, WV: Pictorial Histories Publishing, 1991.

Tennessee Valley Authority Information Office. *A History of the Tennessee Valley Authority*. Knoxville: Tennessee Valley Authority, 1982, 1983, 1986.

Way, Frederick Jr. *The Allegheny*. Rivers of America. New York: Farrar and Rinehart, 1942.

# 9

## The Ohio River: A World-Class Inland Waterway

ROBERT WILLIS

Could Nicholas Roosevelt have imagined what the Ohio River would become two hundred years into the future? He certainly knew there was tremendous potential, as evidenced by his extraordinary initiative, but he would be amazed if he could see the Ohio today.

The Ohio River today is the highest commercial-tonnage, fully canalized inland river in the world. Tows, which carry the commercial cargo, are uniquely American in design and have been efficiently adapted for passage through typical main-lock chambers on the Ohio River. These main chambers, measuring 1,200 feet by 110 feet, are the largest in the world for an inland waterway system. The Ohio River navigation system operates 365 days a year and only rarely shuts down because of extreme high water, navigation accidents, or major equipment failures. The system maintains a project operating depth of nine feet, and a typical 1,200-foot tow can carry approximately 22,500 tons. Fifteen barges, arranged three barges wide and five barges long, are aligned at the bow of the towboat. To fully appreciate how much cargo this is, a comparison of rail and truck equaling one 1,200 tow follows in Figure 1.

So how does a river that in 1811 could be crossed by foot during low-water periods and had a tremendous obstacle, the Falls of the Ohio at Louisville, Kentucky, which drops approximately twenty-six feet during low water, become such a great commercial waterway? The best place to begin describing this transformation is with Nicholas Roosevelt beginning his famous trip on the *New Orleans,* departing Pittsburgh, Pennsylvania, on October 20, 1811.

Starting at Pittsburgh, where the Ohio River is formed by the Monongahela and the Allegheny, the "Beautiful River," as the French called the Ohio, flows in a west-southwesterly direction for approximately 981 miles to where it empties into the Mississippi River at Cairo, Illinois, 168 miles below Saint Louis, Missouri. The Ohio River portion of Roosevelt's famous trip took about four days from Pittsburgh to Louisville. Once at Louisville he could not continue because of low-water conditions that made the Falls impassable. During his stay at Louisville waiting for river conditions to improve, Roosevelt accomplished an amazing feat—he took on passengers and steamed upriver to Cincinnati.

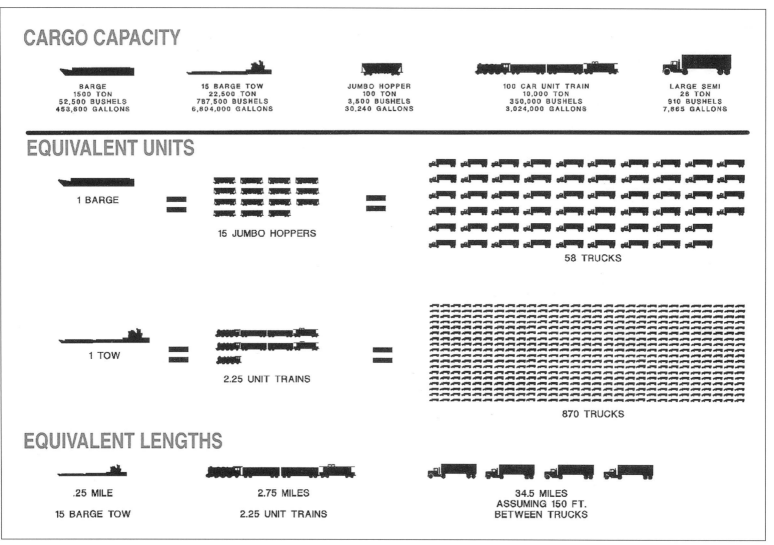

**Figure 1.** *Comparison of rail and truck equaling one 1,200-foot tow*

One can only imagine what it felt like for those passengers to move upstream against the currents of the mighty river in such an efficient, effortless way. Passengers of that era could only relate to moving upriver in a boat powered by the arduous, labor-intensive efforts typical of the keelboat men, who either poled or pulled the vessels against the current. Although Roosevelt was reasonably sure he could replicate an upriver trip (as he had demonstrated during low flows on the Monongahela before starting his trip downriver), he must have savored the moment—showing that his *New Orleans* was truly an

**Figure 2.** *Typical low water on the Ohio River, late 1800s*

engineering marvel. Finally, after approximately one month of waiting for the river to rise, there was adequate depth of water to make passage through the turbulent Falls with the help of a local pilot.

The steamboat *New Orleans* was only the first attempt at what would turn out to be a rapidly developing technology. Steam engines and riverboat design would evolve quickly. In 1815 the *Washington*, a side-wheel steamboat designed and built by Henry Shreve, would set the standard for inland river steamboats. The *Washington* was designed with a wide, shallow hull to ride over the shallows of the rivers, and by using a higher pres-

sure steam engine, it had enough power to make the trip upriver by steam power from New Orleans to Louisville (Shippingport) in twenty-four days.

Navigation improvements to the Ohio River, however, would not come so quickly as the evolution of the steamboat. The delay at Louisville due to river conditions—that is, the obstruction at the Falls and the unpredictable flows of the Ohio River—demonstrated the two main obstacles to efficient year-round navigation on the river.

The first, the Falls of the Ohio, represented the single greatest obstacle to efficient navigation on the Ohio in 1811. Vessels

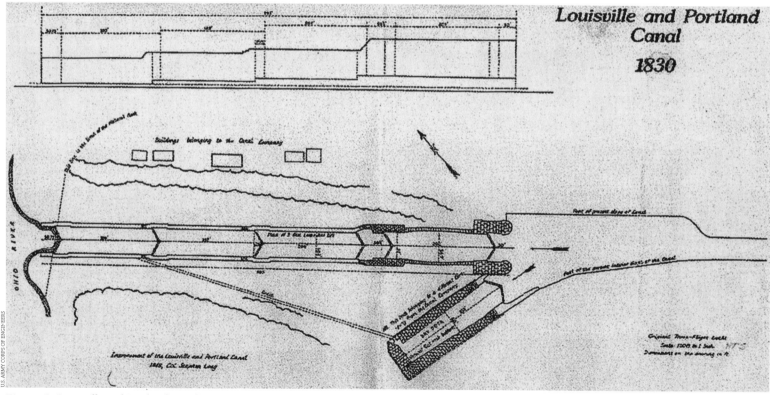

**Figure 3.** *Louisville and Portland Canal, 1830*

would have to wait for enough flow and then take the hazardous passage through the Falls with the help of a licensed Falls pilot. It was to alleviate this problem that the first major application of waterways engineering on the Ohio was begun in 1825. The construction of a canal and three lift locks, called the Louisville and Portland Canal and built by the Commonwealth of Kentucky, was completed in 1830. The locks were 50 by 185 feet, and the canal was 50 feet wide. These locks were the largest in the world when completed. This monumental undertaking was the first major step to making the Ohio River one of the greatest commercial inland rivers in the world.

Although the locks and canal provided passage around the Falls, navigation on the river was only possible when river flows produced sufficient water depth. Until the beginning of canalization, navigation can best be understood by the following description taken from the historical preface of *The Ohio River*, issued by the Chief of Engineers of the U.S. Army in June 1934:

> In its original condition, the Ohio River was much obstructed throughout its entire length by snags, rocks, and gravel and sand bars, rendering navigation difficult and hazardous. The width of channel was exceedingly variable. The depth available for navigation over the worst shoals at extreme low water varied from a minimum of 1 foot between Pittsburgh, Pa. and Cincinnati, Ohio (470 miles) to 2 feet between Cincinnati and the mouth of the river (511 miles). When the depth over the worst shoals was 3 feet or more, the river was navigable throughout its entire length for steamboats and other craft, except as its use was affected by floods or ice.

Until the first dam was completed at Davis Island in 1885, traffic along the Ohio was greatly constrained by the seasonal whims of the river. A further challenge to profitable shipping was the need for commercial vessels to be designed with relatively low drafts, thus limiting tonnage.

By 1885 a number of major inland waterway improvements had been accomplished in North America that had profound effects on the development of the United States and Canada and set the stage for further development of the Ohio River. A few of the most important included the Erie Canal, the Welland Canal, and the Soo Locks, which connected the Great Lakes to each other, to the Saint Lawrence Seaway, and to the northeast coast of North America.

While these early canal and lock projects helped connect North America's riverways and eased some transportation challenges, a final solution to unpredictable river flows and depths on the Ohio River was needed. Managing commercial traffic around somewhat predictable seasonal flows did not make for

**Figure 4.** *Chanoine Wicket*

**Figure 5.** *Wicket dam and locks*

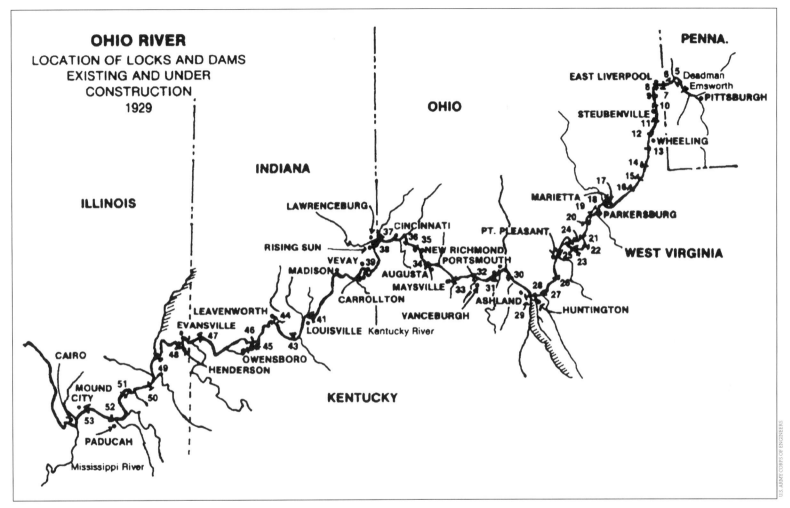

**Figure 6.** *Graphical representation of the first canalization of the Ohio River*

efficient operations. The Rivers and Harbors Act of 1875 appropriated $100,000 toward building a movable dam at Davis Island, located 4.7 miles below Pittsburgh. The Davis Island Lock and Dam, begun in 1877 and completed on October 7, 1885, had a dam 1,222 feet in length with a Chanoine-wicket navigable pass of 559 feet. The lock was 600 feet long by 110 feet wide.

This wicket-type dam and large lock size was to become the prototype for a series of navigation projects numbered 1 to 53 that would effectively canalize the Ohio River from Pittsburgh to the Mississippi.

The wicket dam was invented in 1852 by Chief Jacques Chanoine of the French Corps of Engineers. The Chanoine

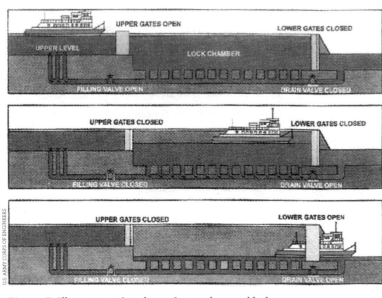

**Figure 7.** *Illustration of working of a simple pound lock*

wicket could be raised during low flows to create a pool or impoundment of deep water behind it to allow for navigation. With the wicket dam in the up position, vessels could pass through the dam by locking through a "pound" lock. During high flows the wickets could be lowered to rest on the river bottom to allow unconstrained traffic over the dam.

By canalizing a river through a series of lock and dam projects, navigable water is maintained by creating slack-water pools between the dams. In a waterway like this there may be periods of high flows or extreme drought that impede navigation, but overall the waterway becomes vastly more efficient.

Interestingly, it was the Chinese who created the first pound locks (960–1279 CE), which is the type of lock used almost exclusively today on canals and rivers. This lock is used today on the Ohio and was used on the first navigation projects with the wicket dams.

Before the Davis Island project was finished in 1875, a board of three engineer officers appointed pursuant to the Rivers and Harbors Act of 1881 recommended the construction of four dams below Davis Island. Appropriations for Locks 2 through 6, inclusive, were made by various Rivers and Harbors acts beginning in 1890. These five additional projects (numbered 2 through 6), downstream of Davis Island, were completed in 1908. Before their completion a board of engineer officers, designated under the Rivers and Harbors Act of 1902, advised that a navigable depth of nine feet be provided for the upper portion of the river. The Rivers and Harbors Act of 1905 appropriated funds for securing a nine-foot stage in the pools made by Dams 2, 3, 4, 5, and 6 by modifications of these locks and dams. A nine-foot navigable depth marked a major departure from existing slack-pool development of tributaries to the Ohio, which were typically six feet. The lock size of 600 feet by 110 feet was also significantly larger than existing tributary locks at that time. The development of the Ohio as the "main stem" of the developing system of rivers was under way.

On December 15, 1906, a special board designated as the Lockwood Board recommended the development of a nine-foot navigable depth for the rest of the Ohio. After reviewing this report, the Board of Engineers for Rivers and Harbors supported the recommendation "without qualification" with its own report dated October 18, 1907. Subsequently, the Rivers and Harbors Act of 1910 provided for a minimum navigable depth of nine feet for the entire Ohio River. The full canalization of the Ohio was to be completed in twelve years (1922). Actual final canalization to nine feet was accomplished in 1929 with fifty fully operational lock and dam projects. Of these, all but two were wicket dams, with all projects having one 600-foot by 110-foot lock. The two exceptions were Emsworth Locks and Dams, which replaced Locks and Dams 1 and 2, and Dashields, which replaced

U.S. ARMY CORPS OF ENGINEERS

**Figure 8.** *Emsworth Locks and Dams*

Lock and Dam 3. Emsworth, with its steel vertical lift gates, would become the prototype for the next generation of "mechanized" dams on the Ohio.

Because Emsworth and Dashields did not have wicket dams, they could not alleviate traffic delays by allowing traffic to pass over the lowered wickets. Instead, when the locks were out of operation, auxiliary lock chambers were used for the first time, to calm the fears of shippers who had confidence in the reliability of the wicket dam projects. The necessity for reliability of the system was becoming entrenched as the importance of the river to trade increased throughout the region.

If there was any doubt about the importance of the Ohio River to the nation or justification for the investments made for canalization, World War II vindicated all of those people who worked so hard to make the project a reality. The building of military vessels at inland shipyards along the Ohio River and its tributaries offered a key supplement to shipbuilding by the larger coastal yards. Of the 1,058 landing ship tanks (LSTs) built

**Figure 9.** *LST 157, the Evansville Shipyard's first ship, descending the launching ramp, October 31, 1942*

during the war, 724 came from inland river ports. The number of military craft built on the Ohio and its tributaries during the war added up to more than a thousand submarine chasers, minelayers, tugboats, destroyer escorts, LSTs, and naval dry docks. A typical example of those inland shipyards is the Evansville Shipyard, which was the largest producer of LSTs in the nation. The Ohio River could not have served the country in so strategically important a way without the canalization project.

Today LST 325, which is moored just upriver of the Evansville waterfront, serves as a museum and is listed on the National Register of Historic Places. Typical of the LSTs built on the inland waters, the vessel, approximately 345 feet by 55 feet, had a displacement or weight of approximately 5,000 tons when fully loaded.

Raw material and commodities supporting the war effort were shipped on the Ohio, and the river allowed for a "protected route" for petroleum products to reach the East Coast ports. Although forgotten today by most Americans, German submarines were devastating American shipping off the Atlantic and Gulf coasts in the early years of World War II. The sinking of oil tankers caused a shortage of 175,000 barrels of oil a day. The Mississippi and Ohio, along with the intracoastal waterways, solved this problem by providing a protected waterway to move this vital commodity.

Operation Pastorius further emphasized the importance of the Ohio River to the war effort. This Nazi plot, now mostly forgotten, to destroy strategic economic targets in the United States points out in a unique but profound way how very important our enemies saw the Ohio River system to the war effort. Eight German saboteurs landed on American soil via submarine—four at Ponte Vedra, Florida, and four at Long Island, New York. The saboteurs had eight high-priority targets that included

a lock on the Ohio River near Cincinnati. The saboteurs were captured and their plot failed.

In 1942, 38 million tons of cargo were moving on the Ohio River on a system that was built to handle 13 million tons. By 1950 total cargo moved was approaching 49 million tons and 1,000-foot tows that had to be broken apart to lock through the existing 600-foot-long lock chambers were becoming common. It was also becoming evident that greater efficiency could be gained by lengthening the navigation pools. In March 1953 a detailed plan of modernization for the system was approved.

The existing wicket dams, which could not be designed to hold pools much higher than approximately twelve feet, would be replaced by nonnavigable dams of higher lifts, thus eliminating the number of required dams while still maintaining a nine-foot system. The new dams would have lifts ranging from 16 to 37 feet and would provide navigation pools with average lengths of fifty-nine miles. By comparison, the existing wicket dams had an average pool length of less than twenty miles. The new projects would have a main lock chamber 1,200 feet by 110 feet and an auxiliary chamber 600 feet by 110 feet. The new lock arrangement would allow for tows up to 1,200 feet to efficiently lock through without having to break up as before. Auxiliary chambers the size of the old main chambers would provide reliability to the system when the main chamber was out of service.

Today, this intended modernization of the Ohio River navigation system is almost complete. The system has vastly increased capacity for commercial tonnage and has essentially delivered on its promise to increase both the efficiency and capacity for commercial traffic on the Ohio River. Compared to the original canalization of more than fifty projects, today's system is comprised of twenty navigation projects. With the completion of the Olmsted Lock and Dam project in 2015,

**Figure 10.** *Aerial photo of the Markland Lock and Dam, a typical modern era project on the Ohio River*

which will replace the last two wicket-type projects (Locks and Dams 52 and 53), the Ohio River navigation system will be comprised of nineteen navigation projects, of which sixteen will be of the "modern" variety as envisioned in 1953. These projects utilize large steel radial or Tainter gates in the dam (named for their inventor Jeremiah B. Tainter) to control the river flow and thus the navigation pool. The concrete structure utilizes a low concrete sill and a series of piers connected by bridge decks. The gates are typically actuated by a mechanical electrical system using reduction gearing and cable drums from which the gates (up to five hundred tons each) are suspended. Although during high flows the gates may be raised clear of the river, the typical 100-foot or 110-foot openings between the piers are not navigable. Actual cessation of navigation due to high water is only experienced rarely, when river levels make the lock chambers inoperable. The typical navigation locks at these projects consist of one 1,200 by 110-foot main chamber and a 600 by 110-foot auxiliary chamber.

Increasing commercial tonnages since 1953 led to building double 1,200-foot lock projects. This next evolution of project design was initiated with the construction of Smithland Locks and Dam. At Smithland (approximately sixteen miles upriver from Paducah, Kentucky) two 1,200-foot chambers were built to accommodate tonnage levels nearing 90 million tons per year. Essentially, at tonnage levels this high, the typical 600-foot auxiliary chamber can no longer do its job when the main chamber is down for maintenance or unscheduled events. With the main chamber closed a queue of tows builds, threatening the reliability of the system. As tonnage levels dictate, additional 1,200-foot chambers will have to be built throughout the system if it is to remain efficient and reliable.

As of this writing, projects are authorized and awaiting funding to extend to 1,200 feet existing auxiliary chambers at Greenup Locks and Dam (approximately fifteen miles upstream from Portsmouth, Ohio) and at John T. Myers Locks and Dam (approximately fifty-three miles downstream from Evansville, Indiana). The Olmsted project will have two 1,200-foot chambers, and a new 1,200-foot chamber was recently put in operation at McAlpine Locks and Dam at Louisville, Kentucky, making it the second navigation project on the Ohio River with double 1,200-foot chambers. To put the right perspective on double 1,200-foot chambers, one needs to realize they exist on no other inland river system in the world. By comparison, the Panama Canal, although a ship canal and not an inland river system, uses double 1,000 by 110-foot locks.

Today, the Ohio plays an important role for the region by providing cost-effective movement of bulk commodities both into and out of the area. Coal, petroleum, chemicals, grain, iron ore, steel, and aggregates are all moved at ton-to-mile rates that are lower than rail or truck. With the abundance of coal in the region, along with the efficiency of the Ohio River navigation system, the Ohio Valley enjoys some of the lowest electric utility rates in the nation. Taken together, the economic benefits to the region and to the nation are measured in billions of dollars. Factors such as energy costs and others including clean air, safety, and environmental considerations associated with spills are receiving more attention in America as social issues increase in importance.

At the same time, the European Union (EU) is mandating that more cargo move along its inland navigation system. There is a broad EU policy to incentivize cargos to move on waterways, which is intended to alleviate some highway congestion. Under

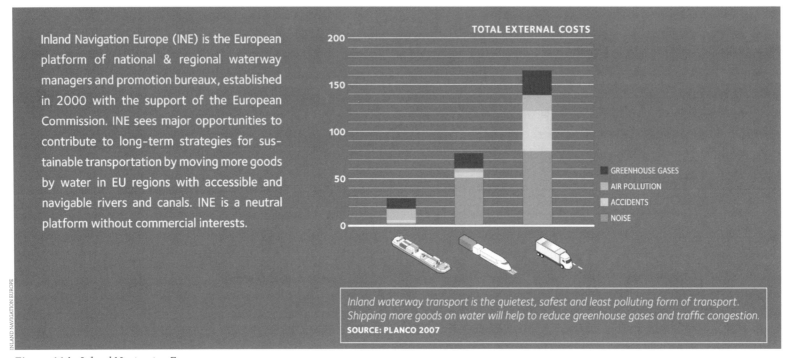

Inland Navigation Europe (INE) is the European platform of national & regional waterway managers and promotion bureaux, established in 2000 with the support of the European Commission. INE sees major opportunities to contribute to long-term strategies for sustainable transportation by moving more goods by water in EU regions with accessible and navigable rivers and canals. INE is a neutral platform without commercial interests.

**TOTAL EXTERNAL COSTS**

- GREENHOUSE GASES
- AIR POLLUTION
- ACCIDENTS
- NOISE

*Inland waterway transport is the quietest, safest and least polluting form of transport. Shipping more goods on water will help to reduce greenhouse gases and traffic congestion.*
**SOURCE: PLANCO 2007**

**Figure 11A.** *Inland Navigation Europe*

the title "Clean, Safe and Eco-Efficient," the charts in Figures 11A and 11B can be found in Inland Navigation Europe (INE) literature.

Although direct comparisons between the European inland river system and the American system are difficult to make because of inherent differences between the systems and waterways, the shift in the EU to social issues as reasons to promote waterway transportation may be where America is headed as well. Information that would promote waterway use, such as the charts in Figures 12A, 12B, and 12C, produced by the Texas Transportation Institute, are beginning to raise public awareness in this country.

In conclusion, it would be interesting to imagine what Roosevelt would experience if he made the same trip down the Ohio River on his vessel, the *New Orleans*, today. First, there would be no delay for a month or more at the Falls, awaiting a river rise. The nine-foot minimum water depth passes boats through a canal around the Falls. The *New Orleans* would pass through twenty locks, most of them 110 feet by 1,200 feet. Each lock is capable of passing at the same time forty boats the size

# TODAY'S ACTIONS MAKE TOMORROW'S DIFFERENCE

## INNOVATION FOR A GREEN ECONOMY

Forecasts predict that, despite the current slump, the demand for transport will pick up again and increase until 2020. Financial priorities should be innovation, clean propulsion, sustainable infrastructure, integration of smart networks and information systems. **Today's new inland shipping engines already save up to 30% on energy and CO$_2$.** It is clear that inland waterway transport is already an asset against global warming. By 2020, savings will have gone up significantly thanks to new propulsion solutions with the ambition to achieve zero emissions. That's the agenda of waterway transport and that's why it's a worthwhile investment.

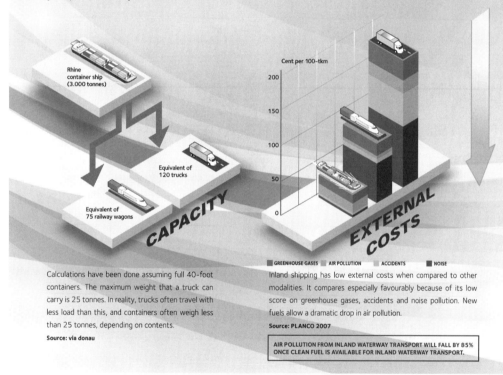

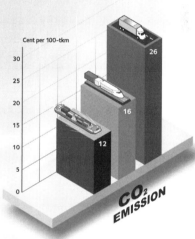

Calculations have been done assuming full 40-foot containers. The maximum weight that a truck can carry is 25 tonnes. In reality, trucks often travel with less load than this, and containers often weigh less than 25 tonnes, depending on contents.

**Source: via donau**

Inland shipping has low external costs when compared to other modalities. It compares especially favourably because of its low score on greenhouse gases, accidents and noise pollution. New fuels allow a dramatic drop in air pollution.

**Source: PLANCO 2007**

AIR POLLUTION FROM INLAND WATERWAY TRANSPORT WILL FALL BY 85% ONCE CLEAN FUEL IS AVAILABLE FOR INLAND WATERWAY TRANSPORT.

Carbon dioxide is the principal greenhouse gas. Because of its high capacity, inland shipping compares very favourably to other modalities.

**Source: PLANCO 2007**

**Figure 11B.** *The charts in Figures 11A and 11B compare greenhouse gases, air pollution, accidents, noise, carbon dioxide emissions, as well as tonnage capacity and costs for truck, rail, and inland navigation in Europe.*

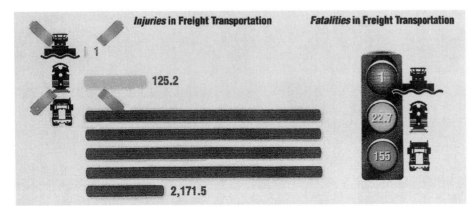

Figure 12A.

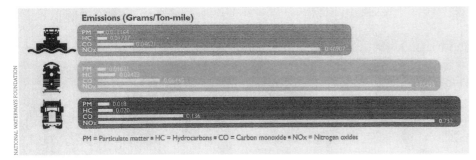

Figure 12B.

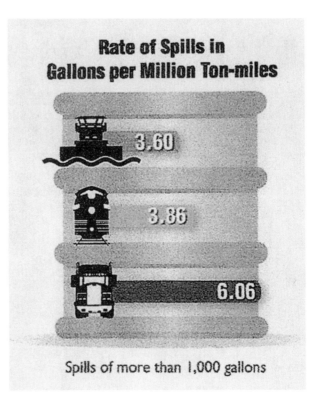

Figure 12C.

*Figures 12A through 12C compare injury and fatality rates, clean air emissions, and spill rates between road, rail, and waterways in the United States.*

of the *New Orleans* (148 feet by 20 feet) or eight rows of boats, five abreast.

The locks and dams on the Ohio should withstand an earthquake even the size of the 1811 New Madrid quake because the new projects are designed to withstand such quake stresses. Likewise, Roosevelt probably would encounter no hostile natives, although he should be aware that the greatest threats in today's world would come from terrorists.

Roosevelt would find abundant coal fuel at every port and would not have to stop and wait while his crew cut driftwood. Indeed, if he equipped the *New Orleans* with radio he could arrange for supply vessels to meet his boat in midstream to supply any provision he needed without stopping his boat. Perhaps the only reason he would need to put into port along the Ohio would be to find a physician to deliver a baby—his son.

If history is any indicator of the future, the river will continue to present challenges, but with the help of forward-looking Americans, the Ohio River will continue to make huge contributions to our society.

*Robert Willis graduated from SUNY Maritime College (Marine Engineering). He served in the United States Army from 1971 to 1975, after which he began a career with the Army Corps of Engineers, where he was employed from 1975 to 2009, retiring as Chief of Operations for the Great Lakes and Ohio River Division. Willis has a working knowledge of the commercial inland waterways of the United States as well as the Panama Canal, the Saint Lawrence Seaway, and the Great Lakes system.*

## SELECTED BIBLIOGRAPHY

Chaitkin, Anton. "The Chinese Model for America's Canals." *American Almanac* (December 1989). http://american_almanac.tripod.com/canal.htm.

Cheung, Sui-wai. "Construction of the Grand Canal and Improvement in Transportation in Late Imperial China." *Asian Social Science* 4, no. 6 (June 2008): 11–22.

Chief of Engineers, United States Army. *The Ohio River: Charts, Drawings, and Description of Features Affecting Navigation; War Department Rules and Regulations for the River and Its Tributaries; Navigable Depths and Tables of Distances for Tributaries.* Fifth ed. Revised to June 30, 1934. Washington, DC: U.S. Government Printing Office, 1935.

Inland Navigation Europe. "Facts and Figures." http://www.inlandnavigation.org/en/factsandfigures.html.

Johnson, Leland R. *The Ohio River Division U.S. Army Corps of Engineers: The History of a Central Command.* Cincinnati, OH: U.S. Army Corps of Engineers, Ohio River Division, 1992.

Johnson, Leland R., and Charles E. Parrish. *Triumph at the Falls: The Louisville and Portland Canal.* Louisville, KY: U.S. Army Corps of Engineers, 2007.

McCall, Edith. *Conquering the Rivers: Henry Miller Shreve and the Navigation of America's Inland Waterways.* Baton Rouge: Louisiana State University Press, 1984.

Ryder, F. Van Loon. "The 'New Orleans': The First Steamboat on Our Western Waters." *Filson Club History Quarterly* 37 (1963): 29–37.

U.S. Army Corps of Engineers, Great Lakes and Ohio River Division. *Great Lakes and Ohio River Navigation Systems Commerce Report, 2004.*

U.S. Army Corps of Engineers, Ohio River Division. *Ohio River Navigation, Past—Present—Future.* Cincinnati, OH, 1979.

U.S. Coast Guard, Western Rivers Sector. *Proceedings of the Marine Safety and Security Council* 64, no. 4 (Winter 2007–8): 1–96.

United States Inland Waterways Commission. *Preliminary Report of the Inland Waterways Commission.* Washington, DC: Government Printing Office, 1908.

*Waterways: Working for America.* Highlights of *A Modal Comparison of Freight Transportation Effects on the General Public*, conducted by the Texas Transportation Institute, Center for Ports & Waterways, Texas A&M University. National Waterways Foundation with the U.S. Department of Transportation and Maritime Administration, 2008.

# Afterword
# The River Today and Tomorrow

KENNETH A. WHEELER

Most of the content of this collection of essays is devoted to topics related to the development of the steamboat and its successor, the diesel towboat, since the initial voyage of the *New Orleans* from Pittsburgh to New Orleans in 1811. The collection would not be complete, however, without some discussion of the significance of America's rivers to the United States that we know today, together with some views "'round the bend" of the opportunities and challenges that face the river in the twenty-first century. The 1811 voyage marked the beginning of the Industrial Revolution in America west of the Allegheny Mountains and stimulated the development of our inland river system as well as the economic development of the entire country.

Flying from coast-to-coast today at forty thousand feet, the casual observer might notice little change in the landscape along the Ohio and Mississippi rivers from a similar view, had it been possible, in 1811. The general course and shape of the rivers are essentially unchanged, and much of the adjacent river bank is as forested as it was then, when only a few small settlements existed along the entire route from Pittsburgh to New Orleans. Descending in altitude, however, there emerges a whole civilization of cities, towns, and industries that have developed over

the past two hundred years. All manner of industry, including steel mills, electric generating stations, grain facilities, petroleum distribution centers, and a multitude of other industries have found it beneficial to locate along the riverbank. Most of these industries have been drawn to their sites by the presence of two things that the river affords: an adequate supply of water for industrial processes and access to low-cost transportation. Without the ready availability of these two assets afforded by the rivers, the economic growth of the United States over the last two centuries would have been drastically different.

By the same token, cities along the riverbank generally developed as a result of this manufacturing activity. While many of the larger river cities today, such as Pittsburgh, Cincinnati, Saint Louis, and Memphis, have developed along other lines, so that river-related commerce is no longer their primary activity, they continue to benefit from the river as a component of their industrial base, as well as from the recreation that the river provides.

Industrial development along the riverbank continues to this day. For example, the largest single industrial development project announced in 2008 in the entire country was a new steel mill located on the Tombigbee River, which is directly connected to the Ohio-Mississippi river system. This facility will make use of both the readily available process water and the low-cost water transportation the river supplies. These attributes are in such demand that sites for large developments are becoming scarce. The Tennessee Valley Authority, in a study conducted in 2008, identified only a handful of large sites in the southeast that provide both water transportation and abundant process water for industrial uses and are available for development.

At this point, it may be appropriate to interject some thoughts about the environmental condition of the rivers. Two hundred years ago, few, if any, people were concerned about the impact upon water quality of industrial development along the rivers. While the deterioration of river water quality has been the subject of much discussion over the past few decades, the good news is that the pendulum is swinging the other way. The development of much stricter permitting regulations, coupled with the recognition by industrial users as well as riverbank communities that the river's ability to provide water for all its users is finite, have resulted in significant improvements in water quality in many areas. For example, the Cuyahoga River near Cleveland, Ohio, was so polluted in the 1950s that it caught fire and burned for several days. However, with a concerted effort between public and private users, water quality has been significantly improved on the Cuyahoga over recent years. Another example is the cooperative effort by the Sierra Club and the American Waterways Operators to promote increased use of the rivers, while improving water quality at the same time. While many rivers still remain polluted, these cooperative efforts continue to reap benefits.

Economic development enhanced by the river system also includes the vessels on the rivers, which are also concerned with their environmental impact. Alas, these vessels are now limited to transporting cargo and not passengers. The last passenger-carrying vessels on the inland waterways ceased operation in 2009. While there is a thriving demand for river tours in Europe, operators in the United States have been unable to develop an adequate market. Movement of freight on the rivers, however, continues to grow. Today, about 14 percent of all freight in the United States is moved by water. Cargoes include a wide variety of both raw materials and finished products. Coal, steel, rock, grain, petroleum, and chemicals are common cargoes, but unique structures such as rocket engines also find their way to the river because of their size. Tonnage is expected to increase by 43 percent between 2010 and 2020.

More than four thousand line-haul towboats, assisted by several thousand smaller harbor vessels, were in service on the rivers in 2009, moving a fleet of eighteen thousand barges. Well more than one hundred thousand operators and support personnel man these vessels. The cargoes are moved by water in a remarkably efficient manner as water transport is significantly less expensive than any other form of surface transportation. For example, the 14 percent of total tonnage moved by water in the United States is transported for only 2 percent of the nation's total freight costs. At the same time, shippers pay an economic penalty for the slower transit time by water, so that waterborne cargoes tend to be predominantly commodities that do not have a high unit value.

Water transport represents the most environmentally friendly and beneficial means of transport. For example, the airborne emissions of greenhouse gases generated by moving a ton of cargo one mile are approximately one-fourth of that generated by a truck carrying the same cargo. Water transport is also the safest form of transportation, resulting in far fewer accidents and injuries per ton of cargo transported than other forms of surface transportation.

The towboats and barges that move cargo in the early twenty-first century look at first glance much as they did fifty years ago. In fact, since river towboats are built quite sturdily in order to deal with the stresses induced by operation in shallow water, many of the towboats in service today are several decades old. Nevertheless, in many other ways these vessels represent the latest innovations in electronics, navigation, and safety equipment, due to constant upgrading and replacement. Some of the examples of equipment and features to be found on the fleet currently in service include satellite communications systems that allow constant communication between the vessel and shoreside facilities, electronic navigation aids that precisely locate the vessel on the river at all times, fuel monitoring and speed control systems that determine the most economical operating speed for the vessel, and even systems that monitor the pilot's activities and alert other crew members if the pilot becomes incapacitated. Pilots of modern towboats have at their disposal many of the navigation and information tools provided to aircraft pilots.

Apart from electronic system improvements, many other safety and crew support features have been introduced into towboats in recent years. Examples include the use of flexible high-strength rope in place of bulkier steel towlines, improved vessel lighting for nighttime service, exercise rooms for off-duty crew members, and sound-deadening and vibration-isolation features that minimize background noise and crew fatigue while under

*View from the pilothouse of a modern diesel-powered towboat, the M/V (Motor Vessel)* Chuck Zebula, *showing some of the navigation and communication equipment that aids the pilot in safe and efficient operation of the vessel. Note the loaded barges in front of the vessel, amounting to more than twenty thousand tons of cargo.*

*Exterior of the M/V* Chuck Zebula

*Exterior of a modern diesel-powered towboat, the M/V Hoosier State. The vessel includes many modern features, including air-conditioning, soundproofing, individual crew quarters, a full kitchen and dining room, and an exercise facility.*

way. Some improvements in environmental controls include upgraded propulsion engines that reduce atmospheric emissions, low-volume waste-oil filters, storage for later shore disposal of shipboard-generated waste, and strict adherence to underway discharge regulations. All have been employed to reduce the environmental impact of towboats and barges upon the rivers.

Taken as a whole, the line-haul towboat of today continues to evolve as a modern transportation mode, equal to or ahead of other forms of surface transportation. The changes have been, in the main, developed by cooperative efforts between the towing industry trade groups, the U.S. Coast Guard, the U.S. Army Corps of Engineers, and Congress, and represent a continuing effort to improve the safety and efficiency afforded by water transport, as well as to benefit from the environmental advantages they afford.

*View inside the pilothouse of the modern diesel-powered towboat, the M/V* James H. Hunter

Looking to the future of inland water transport, it would be rash to attempt to predict all of the factors that may influence its development over the next several decades. Nevertheless, several factors stand out as being of major significance and are outlined below.

**Development of a National Marine Transportation Policy**: Despite its obvious economic and environmental advantages, inland marine transportation in the United States has usually been treated as one of several individual means of moving goods, often on a regional scale. Europe, on the other hand, has established economic incentives and environmental regulations that encourage the use of marine transport as part of an international network that also reduces the demand for other forms of surface transportation. Recognizing the disparity between the American and European approaches, the Maritime Administration has initiated a program to develop "marine highways" that can reduce congestion and improve traffic flow in key areas of the country. Together with other efforts undertaken by the Maritime Administration, this program has the potential to develop a national transportation policy that includes water transport as a key element, rather than as an afterthought. Although similar initiatives have been started in the past with limited success, the increasing need for such a policy should make it a higher national priority as traffic continues to increase.

**Funding of Navigation Infrastructure Improvements**: Construction of new navigation projects on the inland rivers has become an extraordinarily expensive task, with projects running into the hundreds of millions, or even billions, of dollars. Currently, construction is financed by a cost-sharing agreement between the inland river towing industry and the federal government, with each entity contributing one half of the project cost. As project costs have continued to rise, the available funding from both sources has become inadequate to keep pace with the need for new projects. With the shipment of goods by river projected to increase significantly by 2020, this situation will only be exacerbated without new sources of revenue. Industry and the federal government are currently engaged in a debate over how to best resolve this thorny issue.

Regardless of the source of increased funding, river projects have demonstrated time and again a return several times their original cost to the U.S. economy over the life of the project. Much as the construction of the interstate highway system revolutionized domestic transport in the second half of the twentieth century, development of an integrated national transportation system, including river transport, can have a similar impact in the twenty-first century.

**Global Transportation Impacts**: With the opening of the expanded Panama Canal in 2014, which will double the canal's capacity, a major shift in domestic transportation routes may occur. Ocean-borne freight from both the Near East and Europe can be redirected from America's overloaded East and West Coast seaports into the Gulf of Mexico and into the heartland via the Mississippi and Ohio river systems. By the same token, global warming of the oceans may signal the availability of ice-free ocean routes through the Arctic, further modifying trading patterns. Entirely new uses for river transport, such as moving containers by barge, are being tested, as the economic benefits of shipping by water continually evolve.

**Environmental regulations**: As concern for the environment, with regard to both air and water, continues to increase, efforts to control the effects of water transport on the environment will become a more significant factor in establishing the cost of shipping goods. Transportation costs, which often equal the cost of the goods being transported, will be directly impacted by the way in which regulators seek to limit environmental impacts. Some examples of the new limits currently being implemented include the control of vessel discharges to limit the spread of invasive species and the promulgation of stricter standards for engine emissions. If these regulations are designed in a stand-alone environment, whereby regulations for water transport are made separate from regulations for other surface transportation industries, without recognizing the entire transportation system implications they generate, they may well have the unintended consequence of increasing pollution by forcing cargo traffic away from the rivers.

**Scarcity of water resources**: Freshwater has been called the oil of the twenty-first century. As the demand for freshwater continues to grow, its value will likewise increase and pressure will mount to restrain or limit the amount of water used for transportation purposes. Currently, U.S. law mandates that the U.S. Army Corps of Engineers maintains much of the inland river system at a minimum navigable depth of nine feet. As communities and industries along the river continue to require more water, they will compete for the available amounts, which in some cases are already inadequate. Again, the only way to successfully address this issue is via a long-range, comprehensive, regional and national planning effort.

In spite of all the uncertainties regarding the future of "the river"—all rivers in the inland river system—one thing remains true. In the words of Oscar Hammerstein, "Ol' man river, he just keeps rollin' along." Likewise, just as it has for the past two hundred years, "the river" will continue to be a vital component of our nation's transportation system for centuries to come.

*Kenneth A. Wheeler is a retired maritime executive who spent his career in a wide variety of fields within the maritime industry, ranging from construction of nuclear submarines to operation of river transportation companies. Wheeler served as founding chairman of the River Discovery Center in Paducah, Kentucky, and has been active in many trade and civic groups. He has received lifetime achievement awards from the Seaman's Church Institute and the National Rivers Hall of Fame. Wheeler is a graduate of Southern Methodist University and the Oak Ridge School of Reactor Technology.*

## SELECTED BIBLIOGRAPHY

Tennessee Valley Authority internal study (restricted distribution), 2008.

U.S. Chamber of Commerce, "Statement on Marine Transportation," September 2009. Appended to "Statement of the U.S. Chamber of Commerce on Water Resources Development Act of 2010: Jobs and Economic Opportunities," delivered to the U.S. Senate Committee on Environment and Public Works, May 6, 2010, pdf available at http://epw.senate.gov/public/index.cfm?FuseAction=Files.View&FileStore_id=30606d5b-648f-4977-86f5-4f979f466c49.

*Waterways: Working for America.* Highlights of *A Modal Comparison of Freight Transportation Effects on the General Public*, conducted by the Texas Transportation Institute, Center for Ports & Waterways, Texas A&M University. National Waterways Foundation with the U.S. Department of Transportation and Maritime Administration, 2008, amended 2009.

# Appendix 1

## *Belle of Louisville*: Sole Survivor of the Pioneering *New Orleans*

LINDA HARRIS AND KADIE ENGSTROM

To research the founding of river cities is to learn the impact vessels such as the steamboat had on America. Following in the wake of the *New Orleans*, steamboats were directly responsible for a period of unprecedented progress in the growth of river cities in the nineteenth and early twentieth centuries. Steamboats were the workhorses of the rivers. They accelerated the settlement of the American frontier.

When rail, highways, and air replaced the need for steamboats, the riverboat excursion business began. Hundreds of people lined the shores as the few remaining riverboats plied inland waterways tramping from town to town, picking up paying passengers for cruises. The *Belle of Louisville* inherited that history from the *Idlewild* (1914–47) and the *Avalon* (1948–62), giving her the distinction of being the most-known and most-traveled excursion boat on the inland waters of America.

The *Belle of Louisville* was built in 1914 by James Rees and Sons at Pittsburgh for the West Memphis Packet Company. Her original name was the *Idlewild*, and her sturdy, well-built frame sat atop a steel hull that needed only five feet of water to float.

Such a shallow draft allowed her passage on practically every navigable waterway in the eastern half of the United States. The *Idlewild* first operated as a ferry between Memphis, Tennessee, and West Memphis, Arkansas. Built for packet trade, she hauled cargo such as cotton, lumber, and grain, but she was outfitted for excursion work also. During the 1920s she took on a vagabond's life, traveling from town to town and offering cruises to the public. For most of the next two decades the *Idlewild* tramped the Ohio, Illinois, Mississippi, and Missouri river systems.

In the 1920s an excursion steamer called the *America* operated in Louisville. When the *America* burned in 1930, the *Idlewild* was brought in to replace her. In 1931 she was chartered to run trips between two area amusement parks, Fontaine Ferry, near downtown, and Rose Island, about fourteen miles upriver from Louisville. In 1934, after tramping for three years, she returned to Louisville and operated a regular excursion schedule until World War II. During World War II the *Idlewild* did her part for the American effort. She was outfitted with special equipment to push oil barges in the off season. She also served as a floating USO nightclub for troops stationed at military bases along the Mississippi River.

In 1947 the *Idlewild* was sold. Due to a deathbed wish of the boat's master, Captain Ben Winters, whose career had started aboard a different steamboat of the same name, she became the *Avalon* the following year. A group of Cincinnati-based investors bought the *Avalon* in 1949, and during the next thirteen years she became the most widely traveled river steamer in the country. The *Avalon* pulled into many ports including those along the Mississippi, Missouri, Saint Croix, Illinois, Kanawha, Ohio, and Cumberland rivers.

By 1962 the *Avalon* was in desperate need of major repairs and improvements and was literally days away from the scrap yard. When the boat was put up on the auction block instead, Judge Executive Marlow Cook of Jefferson County, Kentucky, with assistance from Louisville Mayor Charles Farnsley, bought the boat with $34,000 of county funds. Along with her new life

on the Louisville waterfront came a new name, the *Belle of Louisville*. Many hours went into repairing and restoring the boat. On April 30, 1963, the *Belle* made her first cruise in a race against the steamboat *Delta Queen* as one of that year's Derby Festival events. It was the beginning of an unparalleled river tradition known as the Great Steamboat Race, which took place every year on the Wednesday before the world-famous horse race, the Kentucky Derby. The last traditional steamboat race was in May 2008. The following October, the *Delta Queen* lost her battle with Congress to continue river operations.

The *Belle* is recognized as the oldest continuously operating Mississippi River-style steamboat in the world. She was designated a National Historic Landmark in 1989 and is on the National Register of Historic Places. She will celebrate her one hundredth birthday in 2014. The *Belle* continues to be owned by the Louisville Metro government and is operated by the Waterfront Development Corporation. Preservation will continue annually, as professional architects have noted that she may have

The Idlewild, 1914–48

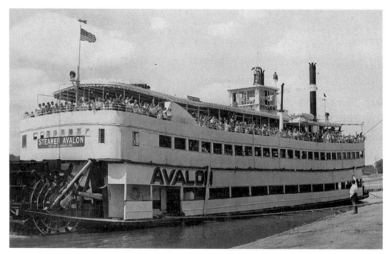

The Avalon, 1948–63

*The Belle of Louisville, 1963–present*

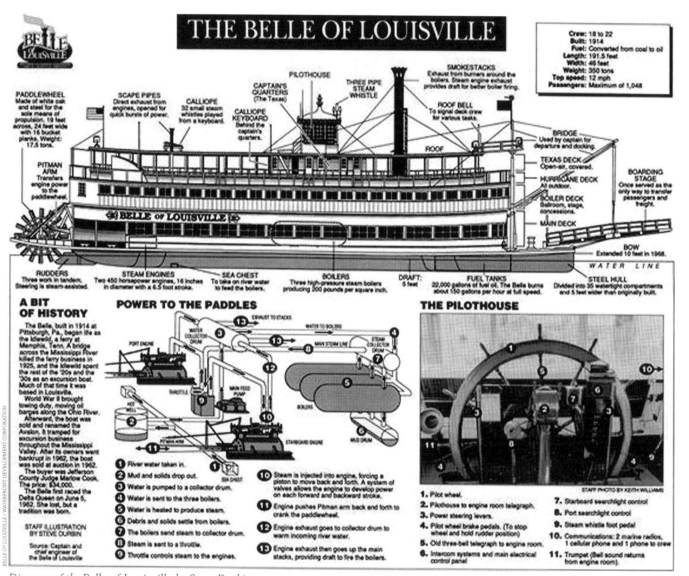

*Diagram of the* Belle of Louisville *by Steve Durbin*

another seventy-five years of operation if properly cared for. The intention is to do just that. Heating, ventilation, and air-conditioning systems installed in 2010 will extend the *Belle*'s market capabilities and her season and will be a major enhancement for passengers. As years pass her boilers will have to be addressed, as will other historic equipment. The engines installed in 1914 date back to 1890, having previously been used in another steamboat. They are showing no signs of wear and are amazing in their operation, a statement of the quality workmanship of the James Reese Company.

No other river steamboat in American history has lasted as long, been to as many places, or traveled as many miles as the *Belle of Louisville*. Her name and outward appearance have changed over the years, but her steam-powered soul and structure are pure turn-of-the-century paddle wheeler. She is the only remaining vessel of an era that contributed dramatically to the economic, social, and cultural development of our country. When she is gone, there will be no others.

*Linda Harris, CEO,* Belle of Louisville, *manages the daily operations of the historic steamboat (and its sister riverboat, the* Spirit of Jefferson). *Kadie Engstrom is education coordinator for the* Belle.

# Appendix 2

## The Rivers Institute at Hanover College: A List of Materials on River People, Steamboats, and the Ohio–Mississippi River System in the Agnes Brown Duggan Library

DOUGLAS DENNÉ AND KATHERINE MCCARDWELL

## River People

### Firsthand Accounts and Analyses: Boatmen, Settlers, and Travelers

Abdy, Harry Bennett. *On the Ohio*. New York: Dodd, Mead, and Co., 1919.

*On the Ohio* is a travelogue of a voyage east from Kansas to Pennsylvania, including the entire length of the Ohio River. The author took some liberties in terms of collapsing multiple individuals and events into one, or in changing names, for "artistic or romantic effect."

The narrative is liberally illustrated by Rowena Meeks Abdy from sketches and other depictions she made during the voyage.

Albach, James R. *Annals of the West: Embracing a Concise Account of Principal Events Which Have Occurred in the Western States and Territories, from the Discovery of the Mississippi Valley to the Year Eighteen Hundred and Fifty-Six*. Pittsburgh: W. S. Haven, 1856.

The first edition (Cincinnati, 1846) was compiled by James H. Perkins, based on a general plan by James R. Albach. The second edition (Saint Louis, 1850) was revised and enlarged by John Mason Peck, again based on Albach's general plan. Albach himself revised and substantially enlarged this third edition.

Allen, Michael. *Western Rivermen, 1763–1861: Ohio and Mississippi Boatmen and the Myth of the Alligator Horse*. Baton Rouge: Louisiana State University Press, 1990.

This work purports to trace "a social and cultural portrait of the western boatmen" and to examine the "myth of the alligator horse" with reference to the lives of actual boatmen and changes in the patterns of shipping and economic development.

Beste, J. Richard. *The Wabash; or, Adventures of an English Gentleman's Family in the Interior of America*, 2 vols. Freeport, NY: Books for Libraries Press, 1970.

This two-volume account relates the voyage of Beste and his family from Bordeaux, France, through their travels to America and temporary settlement in Terre Haute, Indiana. Part of the travels were made by steamboat, including on the Hudson and Ohio rivers. The narrative is written in part by Beste and in part by his children, who he required to keep diaries from which he later gleaned the information compiled in this work.

Buchanan, Thomas C. *Black Life on the Mississippi: Slaves, Free Blacks, and the Western Steamboat World*. Chapel Hill: University of North Carolina Press, 2004.

This volume is a long-overdue treatise on African American river men—both slave and free—and their experiences traversing the river that became synonymous with slavery.

Collins, Thomas C. *Adventures of T. C. Collins, Boatman: Twenty-Four Years on the Western Waters, 1849–1873*. Edited by Herbert L. Roush. Baltimore: Gateway Press, 1985.

According to the book's jacket, "Collins' curiosity took him far beyond his home in the small village of Little Hocking, Washington County, Ohio. He travelled and explored the length of the Ohio, Mississippi, and Missouri rivers and watched his country go to work and war."

Coomer, James. *Life on the Ohio*. Ohio River Valley. Lexington: University Press of Kentucky, 1997.

While not directly related to the *New Orleans* and steamboating, this memoir of a river man working primarily in tugboating and towboating is likely to be of interest for its portrayal of the human side of river transportation.

Curry, Jane. *The River's in My Blood: Riverboat Pilots Tell Their Stories*. Lincoln: University of Nebraska Press, 1983.

Based largely on oral histories conducted with riverboat pilots in the 1970s, this book deals with both historic and current themes related to river travel, such as the work, technology, and social lives of river boats. Also featured are a number of sketches of individuals ranging from quasi-mythic Mike Fink (d. 1822) to river pilots active in the 1970s.

Fordham, Elias Pym, and Frederic Austin Ogg. *Personal Narrative of Travels in Virginia, Maryland, Pennsylvania, Ohio, Indiana, Kentucky, and of a Residence in the Illinois Territory, 1817–1818*. Whitefish, MT: Kessinger Publishing, 2008.

This work was composed of transcripts from Fordham's letters back to England and from his journal, made while living in Illinois. Like many such primary documents, it is part travelogue, part natural history log, and part persuasive writing to induce new immigrants from among the author's acquaintances.

Foster, Emily, ed. *American Grit: A Woman's Letters from the Ohio Frontier*. Ohio River Valley. Lexington: University Press of Kentucky, 2002.

An edited series of letters written by Anna Briggs Bentley, resident of Columbiana County, Ohio, from 1826 to 1881. The letters are of interest as primary documents relating to the settler experience and also speak to a variety of social topics, including slavery and temperance.

———. *Ohio Frontier: An Anthology of Early Writings*. Ohio River Valley. Lexington: University Press of Kentucky, 1996.

A delightful anthology of primary source documents from and about the Ohio River Valley, the work is divided chronologically into three periods: 1750–1782, 1782–1815, and 1816–1843.

Grayson, Frank Y. *Thrills of the Historic Ohio River*. Florence, IN: Spancil Hill, 2000.

Originally published serially in the *Cincinnati Times-Star* and then in book form in 1929, this work is essentially a thematic compendium of brief articles based on firsthand accounts and anecdotes from river men. A fun and engaging read with a number of attractive photographs.

The Harlan Hubbard Papers, MSS 148. The Joseph Wood Evans Memorial Special Collections and Archives Center, Duggan Library, Hanover College.

Harlan Hubbard was an American artist and author who favored a simple, pastoral style. This collection includes newspaper articles, correspondence, documents related to his lectures at Hanover College, and other materials.

Havighurst, Walter. *Voices on the River: The Story of the Mississippi Waterways*. Minneapolis: University of Minnesota Press, 2003.

Havighurst grew up in Wisconsin and was a prolific and passionate writer of regional history and fiction. A longtime professor of English at Miami University, he relates in *Voices* two centuries of tales of famous steamboats and the men who piloted them, from the renowned Mark Twain to the trailblazing Captain Henry Shreve.

Haygood, Wil. *Two on the River*. Boston: The Atlantic Monthly Press, 1986.

Haygood and photographer Stan Grossfeld spent six weeks traveling 2,550 miles, from the headwaters of the Mississippi on Lake Itasca in northern Minnesota to the Gulf of Mexico.

Heckewelder, John Gottlieb Ernestus. *The First Description of Cincinnati and Other Ohio Settlements: The Travel Report of Johann Heckewelder*. Edited by Don Heinrich Tolzmann. Lanham, MD: University Press of America, 1988.

In 1792–93 Heckewelder, a former Moravian missionary, wrote this report as he traveled down the Ohio River Valley, accompanying General Rufus Putnam on an expedition to "pacify" the Native Americans then living north of the river.

Hesse-Wartegg, Ernst von. *Travels on the Lower Mississippi, 1879–1880: A Memoir*. Edited and translated by Frederic Trautmann. Columbia: University of Missouri Press, 1990.

Trautmann translated and edited the travels of Ernst von Hesse-Wartegg (1854–1918) who, during the crucial time between Reconstruction and the rise of the New South, followed the Mississippi River from Saint Louis to the Gulf of Mexico and witnessed the agonized transformation of that region.

Hubbard, Harlan. *Harlan Hubbard Journals, 1929–1944*. Edited by Vincent Kohler and David F. Ward. Lexington: University Press of Kentucky, 1987.
*Harlan Hubbard Journals* is the first of three volumes of journals written by Harlan Hubbard. This volume begins in 1929. Artist, author, and wilderness homesteader, Hubbard (1900–1988) is an enduring legend along the Ohio River. The volume includes illustrations by Hubbard.

———. *Payne Hollow Journal*. Edited by Don Wallis. Lexington: University Press of Kentucky, 1996.
*Payne Hollow Journal* is the third and final volume of the journals of Harlan Hubbard. This one begins in March 1955. The volume includes illustrations by Hubbard.

———. *Payne Hollow: Life on the Fringe of Society*. New York: Eakins Press, 1974.
Through word and art, Hubbard shares his life and observations with his readers.

———. *Payne Hollow: Life on the Fringe of Society*. New York: Thomas Y. Crowell, 1974.
A short-lived edition of the original.

———. *Payne Hollow: Life on the Fringe of Society*. Frankfort, KY: Gnomon Press, 1997.
This reprint is by Gnomon Press, which became the book's publisher in 1974. It is edited by Don Wallis.

———. *Shanty Boat: An Artist and His Wife Find Contentment and Simple Living Drifting Down the Mississippi*. New York: Dodd, Mead, and Co., 1954.
Harlan and Anna Hubbard were midwesterners, who had always lived on the Ohio River. Realizing the river was their way to freedom, they built a small but comfortable shanty boat and slowly drifted on it down the Ohio and Mississippi rivers to their eventual destination of New Orleans. This is their story.

———. *Shanty Boat Journal*. Edited by Don Wallis. Lexington: University Press of Kentucky, 1994.
*Shanty Boat Journal* is the second of three volumes of journals written by Harlan Hubbard. This one begins in September 1944. The volume includes illustrations by Hubbard.

Hutchins, Thomas. *The Courses of the Ohio River Taken by Lt. T. Hutchins, Anno 1766, and Two Accompanying Maps*. Edited by Beverley W. Bond Jr. Cincinnati: Historical and Philosophical Society of Ohio, 1942.
Hutchins's *Courses of the Ohio River* and his map are reproduced from the originals in the Huntington Library, San Marino, California. Also included is Captain Harry Gordon's map of the Ohio River, from the original in the Library of Congress.

Imbarrato, Susan Clair. *Traveling Women: Narrative Visions of Early America*. Athens: Ohio University Press, 2006.
Women's voices from early time periods are often less accessible than men's voices. Imbarrato analyzes women's travel writing from early America. Of particular interest is chapter 4, "Writing into the Ohio Frontier: Genteel Expectations and Rustic Realities."

James, Edwin. *Account of an Expedition from Pittsburgh to the Rocky Mountains, Performed in the Years 1819, 1820 by Order of the Hon. J. C. Calhoun, Secretary of War, under the Command of Maj. S. H. Long, of the U.S. Top. Engineers*. London: Longman, Hurst, Rees, Orme, and Brown, 1823. Repr., March of America Facsimile 65, Ann Arbor, MI: University Microfilms, 1966.
This work primarily includes travelogue and natural history observations taken during the authors' travels down the Mississippi and its western tributaries. The facsimile does not include the map for the Mississippi western section.

McDermott, John Francis. *Before Mark Twain: A Sampler of Old, Old Times on the Mississippi*. Shawnee Classics. Carbondale: Southern Illinois University Press, 1998.
This anthology contains unannotated sketches published before the 1874 publication of Mark Twain's "Old Times on the Mississippi." This work can be used by both the general reader and the scholar. The compiler of this volume generally does not comment on the texts, but the volume is indexed.

Owen, Robert Dale. *Robert Dale Owen's Travel Journal, 1827*. Edited by Josephine M. Elliott. Indianapolis: Indiana Historical Society, 1977.
Owen immigrated to the United States in 1825 from Scotland and helped his father Robert Owen found the utopian colony of New Harmony along the Wabash River in Indiana. In his *Journal* he describes his travels down both the Ohio and Mississippi rivers by steamboat: "I am sitting on one of the finest steamboats of these Western waters, moving down the Mississippi at the rate of 15 miles an hour, yet without any unpleasant motion whatever."

Rosskam, Edwin, and Louise Rosskam. *Towboat River*. New York: Duell, Sloan and Pearce, 1948.

This is several books in one. First, it is a magnificent picture record of the towboats of the Mississippi, Ohio, and tributary rivers by a pair of prize-winning photographers. Second, it is a story of a world and a way of life that stands apart. Third, the author-artists lived on the towboats for months and made notes about river life while recording the talk and life of river men.

Smith, Dwight L., and Ray Swick. *A Journey through the West: Thomas Rodney's 1803 Journal from Delaware to the Mississippi Territory*. Athens: Ohio University Press, 1997.

This edited journal, written before the advent of the steamboat, brings to the foreground the river travel experience from Pennsylvania to the territory of Mississippi, where Thomas Rodney, an acquaintance of Meriwether Lewis and William Clark, was to serve as a judge and land commissioner.

Thwaites, Reuben Gold. *Afloat on the Ohio: An Historical Pilgrimage of a Thousand Miles in a Skiff, from Redstone to Cairo*. Whitefish, MT: Kessinger Publishing, 2008.

Thwaites's travelogue originally was published in 1897 and dedicated to Frederick Jackson Turner, historian of the frontier. It includes sections on "house boat life," "the decadence of steamboat traffic," and "Cave-in-Rock."

———. *On the Storied Ohio: An Historical Pilgrimage of a Thousand Miles in a Skiff, from Redstone to Cairo*. Chicago: A. C. McClurg and Co., 1903.

This revised edition of *Afloat on the Ohio* contains a new preface and photographs.

Young, Jacob. *Autobiography of a Pioneer; or, The Nativity, Experience, Travels, and Ministerial Labors of Rev. Jacob Young, with Incidents, Observations, and Reflections*. Cincinnati: Cranston and Curts, 1857.

Though Jacob Young was in the vicinity of the Ohio during the transition from flatboats to steamboats, he unfortunately has very little to say on the transition, and nothing on the *New Orleans* itself. He does, however, mention undertaking travels by steamboat as early as 1812.

## The Ohio River Valley

Banta, R. E. *The Ohio*. Rivers of America. New York: Rinehart and Co., 1949.

Though more concerned with the Ohio River Valley as a whole than with the river itself, this volume admirably captures the dynamic of the people of the region and their relationship to this place. Part of the classic Rivers of America series, it features an extensive bibliography.

Bigham, Darrel E. *On Jordan's Banks: Emancipation and Its Aftermath in the Ohio River Valley*. Ohio River Valley. Lexington: University Press of Kentucky, 2006.

Through meticulous scholarship, Bigham illuminates the emergent African American experience just before, during, and immediately following the Civil War by contrasting and comparing settlements in counties along the southern and northern banks of the Ohio River.

———. *Towns and Villages of the Lower Ohio*. Ohio River Valley. Lexington: University Press of Kentucky, 1998.

There has been very little study of the lower Ohio River Valley, in large part because there are no great metropolises in the region. Bigham corrects this oversight and reveals the complex forces that shape the little places in America.

Burnet, Jacob. *Notes on the Early Settlement of the North-Western Territory*. Cincinnati: Derby, Bradley, and Co., 1847.

An autobiographical sketch of the author, the work includes facts and incidents of early settlement in the Ohio River Valley. The author settled in Cincinnati in 1796, helped shape the Ohio legal code, was an Ohio Supreme Court judge, and nominated William Henry Harrison for the presidency in 1839. This is one of the most important sources for the early period of the Northwest Territory and the states carved from it.

Butler, Mann. *A History of the Commonwealth of Kentucky*. Louisville, KY: Wilcox, Dickerman, and Co., 1834.

The author obtained his information from firsthand sources, including early settlers, military leaders, and Indian fighters, such as generals George Rogers Clark and William Henry Harrison.

———. *Valley of the Ohio*. Frankfort: Kentucky Historical Society, 1971.

This work was serialized in thirty issues of the *Western Journal and Civilization* between 1835 and 1855. Due to Butler's death in 1855 in a train accident, these writings, his contribution to American history, made their next appearance 116 years later. There is excellent material on early Kentucky history and the surrounding area along the Ohio River.

Downes, Randolph. *Council Fires on the Upper Ohio: A Narrative of Indian Affairs in the Upper Ohio Valley until 1795*. Pittsburgh: University of Pittsburgh Press, 1969.

This volume is about the coming of Native Americans to the upper Ohio Valley and of their struggle with the whites for control of the region from 1755 to 1795.

Eckert, Allan W. *That Dark and Bloody River: Chronicles of the Ohio River Valley*. New York: Bantam Books, 1996.

Six-time Pulitzer Prize nominee Eckert writes a history of the Ohio River and the struggle for dominance in the Ohio River Valley. It is the author's aim in this massive work to present as much fresh material as possible; that is, accounts of the people and events heretofore bypassed or only lightly touched upon in his other historical works in which the Ohio River played a significant role.

Hinderaker, Eric. *Elusive Empires: Constructing Colonialism in the Ohio Valley, 1673–1800*. New York: Cambridge University Press, 1997.

This volume examines the efforts of France, Great Britain, and the United States to extend imperial dominion over the Ohio Valley, focusing on relations between Europeans, Euro-Americans, and Native Americans to tell the story.

Hulbert, Archer Butler. *The Ohio River: A Course of Empire*. New York: G. P. Putnam's Sons, 1906.

This work is occupied with the history of the settlement of the Ohio River Valley, with great emphasis on so-called great events. It deals with the region from its occupation and use by the French to the turn of the twentieth century. Of particular interest vis-à-vis steamboating are chapters 10 ("From Keelboat to Schooner"), 11 ("From Pittsburg to Louisville in 1806"), and 14 ("When the Steamboat Was King").

Klauprecht, Emil. *German Chronicle in the History of the Ohio Valley and its Capital City, Cincinnati, in Particular*. Bowie, MD: Heritage Books, 1992.

The purpose of this work is to make available for the first time a translated edition of Klauprecht's pioneer history, originally published in 1864. His history focuses on the German American families and culture of the Ohio Valley.

McConnell, Michael N. *A Country Between: The Upper Ohio Valley and Its Peoples, 1724–1774*. Lincoln: University of Nebraska Press, 1992.

Identified by historian Lawrence Henry Gipson as a "zone of international friction," the Ohio country provided the spark that ignited the last of the Anglo-French wars for empire. But the upper Ohio Valley was more than this. It was also a cultural frontier, a region whose history was shaped not so much by the convergence of rivers, trails, or royal claims as by the Native Americans who lived there. This volume focuses on these peoples.

Perkins, Elizabeth. *Border Life: Experience and Memory in the Revolutionary Ohio Valley*. Chapel Hill: University of North Carolina Press, 1998.

In this original and sensitive ethnography of frontier life, Perkins recovers the rhythms of warfare, subsistence, and cultural encounter that governed existence on the margins of British America. Richly detailed, *Border Life* captures the intimate perceptive universe of the men and women who colonized Kentucky and southern Ohio during the Revolutionary era.

Reid, Robert L. *Always a River: The Ohio River and the American Experience*. Bloomington: Indiana University Press, 1991.

An interdisciplinary series of essays addressing a variety of aspects of the human experience of the Ohio River.

Shevitz, Amy Hill. *Jewish Communities on the Ohio River: A History*. Ohio River Valley. Lexington: University Press of Kentucky, 2007.

This book offers an analysis of Jewish immigration to the Ohio River Valley and the creation of Jewish communities within a number of towns supported by the riverine economy. This is a timely work on an often overlooked segment of Ohio River Valley society.

## Biographies of Individuals

Berry, Wendell. *Harlan Hubbard: Life and Work*. Lexington: University Press of Kentucky, 1990.

Written by novelist, poet, essayist, and environmentalist Berry, this volume pays homage to his friend Harlan Hubbard, whose life continues to be a source of inspiration. Berry shares Hubbard's life with his readers through both word and art.

Finley, James B. *Autobiography of Rev. James B. Finley; or, Pioneer Life in the West*. Edited by W. P. Strickland. Ann Arbor, MI: Scholarly Publishing Office, University of Michigan, University Library, 2007.

This volume is a reprint of the 1853 publication by Finley, a Methodist clergyman who was licensed to preach in the Western Conference of the Methodist Church, which then included all of Ohio as well as neighboring states and territories. Over the next fifty years, he served the Methodist cause in the West, traveling thousands of miles as a circuit rider, missionary, and presiding elder of frontier districts. There are numerous references to the Ohio River in this book.

*Memoirs of the Lower Ohio Valley: Personal and Genealogical with Portraits*. Evansville, IN: Unigraphic, 1971.

Originally published in 1905, this encyclopedic account of notable personages living in the Ohio River Valley includes a number of river men.

Prager, Frank D. *The Autobiography of John Fitch*. Philadelphia: American Philosophical Society, 1976.

This volume includes transcriptions of Fitch's *Life*, Fitch's *Steamboat History*, and introductory material on the Fitch Papers and his invention.

Shrader, Dorothy H. *Steamboat Treasures: The Inadvertent Autobiography of a Steamboatman*. Hermann, MO: Wein Press, 1997.

According to the book's acknowledgments, "This collection of short stories has been compiled with the intention to make a flowing historical narrative, using the life of William L. Heckmann, 'Steamboat Bill,' as the glue to hold the stories in an even flow. These stories tell the tale of the passing of steamboats on the Missouri and the struggle it took to keep them running as long as they did."

Sparks, Jared, ed. *The Library of American Biography*, 2nd ser., vol. 6. Boston: Charles C. Little and James Brown, 1847.

Sparks's series includes a biography of John Fitch written by Charles Whittlesey as well as a contemporary assessment of the steam engine and its impact on society at that time.

Sutcliffe, Alice Crary. *Robert Fulton and the "Clermont."* New York: Century, 1909.

A biography of Fulton, notable for its reliance on and publication of new primary documents.

Thurston, Robert H. *Robert Fulton: His Life and Its Results*. Makers of America. New York: Dodd, Mead, and Co., 1891.

An early biography of Robert Fulton, this work also contains some discussion of the idea of steam power apart from Fulton's contributions.

Virginskii, V. S. *Robert Fulton, 1765–1815*. Academy of Sciences of the USSR Science Biography. Washington, DC: Smithsonian Institution and the National Science Foundation by Amerind Publishing, 1976.

In 1965 the Soviet Union celebrated the 150th anniversary of the introduction of steam navigation into Russia, which also coincided with the bicentennial of Fulton's birth. This work covers ground already found in other treatments of Fulton, but it also devotes a whole chapter to Fulton's impact in Russia and the history of steamboats in that country.

Westcott, Thompson. *Life of John Fitch: The Inventor of the Steamboat*. Whitefish, MT: Kessinger Publishing, 2007.

Originally published in 1857, this work traces the life of Fitch, who by 1785 began working on his ideas for a steam-powered ship. He built several successful models and then with the help of a watchmaker, Henry Voight, he constructed a 45-foot steamboat.

Zimmerman, Donald J. *Reflections of a River Rat: An Ohio History and Memoir*. New Richmond, OH: CreateSpace, 2009.

This memoir begins in Blairville, Clermont County, Ohio, during the year of the great flood of 1937, but it really chronicles the very beginnings of Clermont County along the Ohio River as communities begin to spring up. The narrative runs to 1955.

## Biographies of Organizations

Carroll, Jane Lamm. *Engineering the Falls: The Corps of Engineers' Role at St. Anthony Falls*. Saint Paul, MN: U.S. Army Corps of Engineers, Saint Paul District, [1992–2004].

With numerous images, Carroll chronicles the history and geology surrounding Saint Anthony Falls and the Corps' work to allow vessels to navigate around it.

Hilton, George W. *The Night Boat*. Berkeley, CA: Howell–North Books, 1968.

A "vessels history" organized by company and chronology, this work largely emphasizes the New England steam lines, but does include a chapter on the Louisville and Cincinnati Packet Company.

Johnson, Leland R. *The Ohio River Division, U.S. Army Corps of Engineers: The History of a Central Command*. Cincinnati: U.S. Army Corps of Engineers, Ohio River Division, 1992.

This excellent history begins with the Channel Clearance Project, 1824–74, and ends with a treatment of the division through 1990. It is well researched, provides images on almost every page, and includes extensive notes.

Johnson, Leland R., and Charles E. Parrish. *The Falls City Engineers: A History of the Louisville District Corps of Engineers, United States Army, 1984–2004*. Louisville: U.S. Army Corps of Engineers, Louisville District, 2008.

The history of the Louisville Engineer District began in 1886 with its focus on managing the canal at the Falls of the Ohio. But its civil works mission quickly expanded to include many programs: open channel, canalization, flood control, and modernization. This concise and well-written history covers all of these facets and more.

Ringwald, Donald C. *Hudson River Day Line: The Story of a Great American Steamboat Company*. Berkeley, CA: Howell–North Books, 1965.

A corporate history of the Hudson River Day Line from 1863, when it was founded, until the 1960s, when this work was published. Abundantly illustrated in black and white.

Swift, James V. *Backing Hard into River History, Including Materials Autobiographical in Nature and a History of* The Waterways Journal. A Little River Book 1. Florissant, MO: J. R. Simpson and Associates, 2000.

Reviewer Charles Lehman states that this is "a memorable reading experience for anyone connected with mid-continent rivers. Swift takes the reader from the beginnings of the 'Riverman's Bible' (*The Waterways Journal*) in 1891 up to the present day. The book is a full speed ahead . . . must-read book for whoever loves seeing a flotilla of barges pushed by a powerful towboat along the Mississippi or Ohio River."

United States Army Corps of Engineers, Saint Paul District. *The Boatyard: History of the Fountain City Service Base*. Saint Paul, MN: U.S. Army Corps of Engineers, Saint Paul District, 1994.

For one hundred years, the Fountain City Boatyard has played an essential role in supporting the Corps' efforts to improve navigation on the upper Mississippi River. This pamphlet tells that story and includes many images.

## Steamboats

### Navigation and History: The Transition to the Steamboat

Dayton, Fred Erving. *Steamboat Days*. New York: Frederick A. Stokes, 1925.

Dayton's book is about the history of steamboats. The chapters describe the early developments of steamboats and the history of steamboats in New York and on the Hudson River.

Donovan, Frank. *River Boats of America*. New York: Thomas Y. Crowell, 1966.

With wonderful illustrations, this volume traces the history of the steamboat. Donovan takes the reader to life on the river before the steamboat, the invention and development of steam technology, the transformation of both the steamboat and culture as they relied more and more upon one another, and the eventual decline of riverboats.

Gillespie, Michael. *Come Hell or High Water: A Lively History of Steamboating on the Mississippi and Ohio Rivers*. Stoddard, WI: Heritage Press, 2001.

Intended as more of a popular than a scholarly history, this work covers a variety of steamboat-related topics, including the boats themselves, river men, boat races, and the hazards of river navigation.

Gould, E. W. *Fifty Years on the Mississippi; or, Gould's History of River Navigation*. Saint Louis: Nixon-Jones Printing, 1889.

Gould's *History* is an extensive study of steamboat development and navigation with an emphasis on the Mississippi River steamboating culture of the 1800s. Chapters include the various modes of early river navigation, inventors Robert Fulton and John Fitch, mail boats on the Ohio River, the first vessel to enter the Mississippi from the sea, and the boat wreckers of the Ohio.

Kane, Adam I. *The Western River Steamboat*. College Station: Texas A&M University Press, 2004.

Kane describes the importance and impact of the steamboat in American history and complements his historical analysis with clear, concise technical explanations of the construction and evolution of western river steamboats. Using photographs, drawings, and charts to help readers visualize the early steamboats and the study of their remains by archaeologists, Kane explains how the rivers dictated the design of the hull, why stern wheels replaced side wheels, how hogging chains kept hulls from buckling, and why safety valves were of little use when engineers regularly overloaded them.

Latrobe, John H. B., and Carl R. Bogardus. *First Steamboat Voyage on the Western Waters*. Austin, IN: Muscatatuck Press, 1961.

Bogardus republished Latrobe's 1871 book, which tells the story of the historic maiden voyage of the *New Orleans* in 1811.

Morrison, John H. *History of American Steam Navigation*. New York: Stephen Daye Press, 1958.

The library owns a reprint of the 1903 edition, which was published the same year as Winthrop Marvin's history, *The American Merchant Marine*, but is far more detailed and vastly richer than Marvin's work. It is a mine of material concerning steamships and steamboats of the ninety-five years following Fulton's famous *North River Steamboat*, commonly known as the *Clermont*.

Preble, George Henry. *A Chronological History of the Origin and Development of Steam Navigation*. Whitefish, MT: Kessinger Publishing, 2008.

Rear Admiral Preble takes the reader from 1543 with the very earliest experiments in steam navigation up through 1882 with descriptions of contemporary vessels known by the author at the time the book was published originally.

Roland, Alex. *The Way of the Ship: America's Maritime History Reenvisioned, 1600–2000*. Hoboken, NJ: John Wiley and Sons, 2008.

Part 2 of this survey of American maritime history is devoted to "The Golden Age and the Rise of Inland Shipping, 1783–1861." It chronicles the emergence of the steamboat along with figures such as Robert Livingston, Robert Fulton, and Henry Shreve.

Trotter, Joe William. *River Jordan: African American Urban Life in the Ohio Valley*. Ohio River Valley. Lexington: University Press of Kentucky, 1998.

This book builds upon the recent explosion of scholarship in African American urban history. It is conceived and presented as a partial contribution to a larger synthesis. The Ohio Valley is an excellent place to start because it holds great symbolic significance in African American history. The volume examines African American life in four Ohio Valley cities—Pittsburgh, Cincinnati, Louisville, and

Evansville—from the American Revolution to the mid-twentieth century.

## Material Culture of Steamboats

Corbin, Annalies. *The Material Culture of Steamboat Passengers: Archaeological Evidence from the Missouri River*. The Plenum Series in Underwater Archaeology. New York: Kluwer Academic/Plenum Publishers, 2000.

Through statistical analysis of the objects of material culture excavated from the *Bertrand* and *Arabia* steamboats, both of which sank in the Missouri River, Corbin draws out information about the gender and socioeconomic conditions of steamboat passengers during the mid-nineteenth century. The work includes a number of useful appendixes, including lists and counts of artifacts and an annotated list of steamboats on the Missouri River.

Petsche, Jerome E. *The Steamboat* Bertrand: *History, Excavation, and Architecture*. Publications in Archeology 11. Washington, DC: National Park Service, U.S. Department of the Interior, 1974.

This work chronicles the initial salvage archaeology undertaken on the *Bertrand* and deals with the material culture of the passengers as well as the form and construction of the ship itself. Both the superstructure of the boat and its machinery have been lost or were salvaged immediately after the *Bertrand*'s sinking, but the hull is well preserved, and the book's textual and photographic documentation of it yields much information about the design and construction of river steamboats of this type.

Switzer, Ronald R. *The* Bertrand *Bottles: A Study of 19th-Century Glass and Ceramic Containers*. Publications in Archeology 12. Washington, DC: National Park Service, U.S. Department of the Interior, 1974.

Another work looking at the cargo of the *Bertrand* steamboat, this monograph examines the different types of bottles recovered in the 1968–69 salvage archaeology of the historic site. The goal of the survey is to examine this cargo as an indicator of the lifestyle of their intended market—settlers and miners in the Montana Territory—as well as of economic and technological trends of shipping and mass distribution during the mid-nineteenth century. Lavishly illustrated in black and white.

## Biographies of Vessels, Past and Present

Barkhau, Roy L. *The Great Steamboat Race Between the* Natchez *and the* Rob't E. Lee. Cincinnati: Cincinnati Chapter, Steamship Historical Society of America, 1962.

In this booklet Barkhau chronicles perhaps the most famous steamboat race of all time, which occurred in June 1870 from New Orleans to Saint Louis between the *Natchez VI* and the *Robert E. Lee*. After much intrigue, the *Robert E. Lee* won the race by several hours.

Bates, Alan L. Belle of Louisville: *Ohio River Steamboat*. Berkeley, CA: Howell–North Books, 1965.

This volume documents the transformation of the steamboat *Avalon* into the *Belle of Louisville* with numerous diagrams and photographs throughout.

Cole, Phil. *Steamboat Echoes: With Over 160 Antique Photos of History's Greatest Steamboats*. League City, TX: RBT Communications, 1996.

*Steamboat Echoes* is a nostalgic illustrated compendium of America's steamboat age written by an author who was born and raised in Madison, Indiana, and graduated from Hanover College.

Davis, William C. *Portraits of the Riverboats*. London: Salamander Books, 2001.

According to the book's dust jacket, "All the adventure, drama, danger, sheer luxury, excitement, and nostalgia of the magnificent steamboat era on America's rivers are captured in this superb collection of contemporary images, with fascinating essays written with poignancy and wit by one of the most authoritative authors on the subject, William C. Davis."

Eifert, Virginia S. *Delta Queen: The Story of a Steamboat*. New York: Dodd, Mead, and Co., 1960.

Known for her many books about the Mississippi, Eifert traces the story of the *Delta Queen* from her beginnings in Scotland to her days plying the waters of the Ohio and Mississippi. Eifert traveled some 7,500 miles, talking with river men and poring over river journals to capture long-forgotten tales for this volume.

———. *Log of the S.S.* Delta Queen: *Cincinnati to Kentucky Lake and Kentucky Lake to Chattanooga*. Cincinnati: Greene Line Steamers, 1961.

Passengers received this booklet when they boarded the *SS Delta Queen*. Copious notes, photographs, and maps are included so the passengers are given an informed understanding of their trip.

Greene, Letha C. *Long Live the* Delta Queen. New York: Hastings House, 1973.

This book was written by the wife of Captain Gordon Greene, whose family owned the *Delta Queen*. After the captain's premature death in 1950, Greene inherited the duties of managing the steamboat. This is her story and the story of a great riverboat.

Jewell, Anne, with Captain Kevin Mullen. *Legendary Lady: The Story of the* Belle of Louisville. Louisville: Belle of Louisville Operating Board, 1999.

This book captures the history of the *Belle of Louisville* through the use of photographs, vivid illustrations, and slick graphics. Much of the text is pulled from personal interviews with passengers and crew and from the pages of the *Louisville Courier Journal*.

Way, Frederick. *The Saga of the* Delta Queen. Cincinnati: Picture Marine Publishing, 1951.

Way writes, "When I signed on as captain in the New Orleans Custom House I harbored a curious feeling of becoming a custodian or a curator rather than a river master." Way recounts the voyage of 5,261 miles the *Delta Queen* took from San Francisco Bay down the Pacific Ocean, through the Panama Canal, across the Caribbean Sea and Gulf of Mexico, into the Mississippi, and up the Ohio River to Cincinnati. The volume is copiously illustrated with black-and-white diagrams and photographs.

## Boat Directories

Lloyd, James T. *Lloyd's Steamboat Directory and Disasters on the Western Waters*. Ohio River Collection. Cincinnati: James T. Lloyd and Co., 1856.

Reprinted in 1979 by Young and Klein, this directory is the first general reference available on the subject of American riverboats. In fact, few histories on steamboating have given as deep and as broad a treatment of the subject. By his own admission, Lloyd's work was the first to detail the "full accounts of all the steamboat disasters since the first application of steam down to the present date."

Owen, Dan, ed. *Inland River Record, 1999*. Saint Louis: Waterways Journal, 1999.

This volume lists and briefly describes all diesel and steam vessels of the Mississippi River System and Gulf Intracoastal Waterway and Tributaries in operation as of April 30, 1998. It also includes a color-stack identification guide of 145 fleets.

Way, Frederick. *Way's Packet Directory, 1848–1983: Passenger Steamboats of the Mississippi River System since the Advent of Photography in Mid-Continent America*. Athens: Ohio University, 1983.

Frederick Way's directories have become the standard resource for researchers in steamboat—or other river-related—research.

———. *Way's Steam Towboat Directory*. Athens: Ohio University Press, 1990.

This is a companion volume to *Way's Packet Directory* published in 1983.

## Invention, Technology, and Construction of Steamboats

Bray, Stan. *Making Simple Model Steam Engines*. Ramsbury, Marlborough, UK: Crowood Press, 2005.

This book details the construction of a range of simple miniature steam engines and boilers. The projects, each of which can be completed with only a basic workshop, range from a single-acting oscillator to more sophisticated twin-cylinder, double-acting engines and a variety of boilers. A final project brings together engine and boiler for a simple steam railway locomotive.

Clark, B. E. G. *Steamboat Evolution: A Short History*. London: Lulu Enterprises, 2007.

This work is a short introductory history of the origins of powered vessels in America, the United Kingdom, and France from early thoughts to the successes of Robert Fulton in 1807 and Henry Bell of Scotland in 1812. It covers the boats, machinery, propulsive methods used, and people and places involved. The text with illustrations and appendixes of source material provide a sound basis for further study of any single aspect of the subject area.

Dayton, Fred Erving. *Steamboat Days*. New York: Tudor Publishing, 1939.

This work provides a global overview of the history of steam navigation, ranging from proto-steam engines from a number of ancient civilizations to modern implementations in a variety of aquatic transport systems. It contains a chapter on western rivers steamboats that includes a discussion of the *New Orleans* and of subsequent river transportation on the Ohio–Mississippi river system.

Flexner, James Thomas. *Steamboats Come True: American Inventors in Action*. Boston: Little, Brown, and Co., 1978.

First published in 1944, this volume outlines the major players in the development of steamboat technology and the intellectual climate of America during the time of these developers. Generally well received for its contributions on the invention of the steamboat, oddly for a technological history, it leaves something to be desired in terms of diagrams of the actual machinery.

Gillmer, Thomas C., and Bruce Johnson. *Introduction to Naval Architecture*. Annapolis, MD: Naval Institute Press, 1982.

With the possible exception of the Society of Naval Architects and Marine Engineers' *Principles of Naval Architecture*, there is currently no better introductory text for the naval architecture/marine engineering student. Chapters include "Engineering Fundamentals in Ship Design," "Ship Geometry and Hydrostatics," "Properties of Shipbuilding Materials," and the "Strength and Structure of Ships."

King, William H., and James W. King. *Lessons and Practical Notes on Steam, the Steam Engine, Propellers, etc., etc., for Young Engineers, Students, and Others.* New York: D. Van Nostrand, 1870.
> The Kings' work is a comprehensive and practical treatment of steam and its direct application to steamboats. It includes mathematical formulas and diagrams and charts designed to give the reader an in-depth understanding of the boat's workings and potential problems.

Latrobe, John H. B. *A Lost Chapter in the History of the Steamboat.* Fund-Publication, No. 5. Baltimore: John Murphy, 1871.
> Included in this work are the 1798 correspondence of Nicholas Roosevelt to Robert Livingston, the granting of the patent to Nicholas J. Roosevelt by President James Madison for his invention relating to propelling boats by steam, and other related material.

Sutcliffe, Andrea. *Steam: The Untold Story of America's First Great Invention.* New York: Palgrave Macmillan, 2004.
> In highly readable fashion, Sutcliffe argues that Robert Fulton, who is credited with inventing the steamboat in 1807, was actually a relative latecomer to the effort to build the first commercially viable steamboat. A full two decades before the *Clermont*, James Rumsey and John Fitch vied to be the first and to control potentially lucrative waterway monopolies. This is one of the many stories that Sutcliffe shares with her readers about the development and use of steam power.

Wing, Charlie. *How Boat Things Work: An Illustrated Guide.* Camden, ME: International Marine/McGraw-Hill, 2007.
> While not specific to steamboats, this work provides two-color cutaway drawings of eighty different marine systems and devices, as well as detailed explanations of how they are assembled, how they work, and how they can go wrong. This book covers every primary component of a boat's inner workings.

# Rivers

## River Culture

Botkin, B. A. *A Treasury of Mississippi River Folklore: Stories, Ballads, and Traditions of the Mid-American River Country.* New York: Crown Publishers, 1955.
> A popular rather than scholarly collection of folktales, songs, and related narratives, what this work lacks in method it makes up for in enthusiasm. Local color prevails over analysis; the area under consideration is vaguely defined as the Mississippi River and its tributaries. Contemporaneous reviewers suggested that it be "dipped into" rather than consumed at one sitting.

Cass, Kathleen. *Our River: An Architectural and Historical Study.* Indianapolis: Indiana Junior Historical Society, 1970.
> This large pamphlet is part of a series of publications of the Indiana Junior Historical Society's study of nineteenth-century regional architecture. It claims to be the first cooperative interstate effort of its kind in the nation. Attention, both in the study and in the publication, has been equally divided between the Indiana and Kentucky sides of the Ohio River.

Havighurst, Walter. *Upper Mississippi: A Wilderness Saga.* Rivers of America. New York: Farrar and Rinehart, 1937.
> This second volume in the Rivers of America series seeks to capture the local color of the upper Mississippi through a Scandinavian-American folk story. As in the other works in the series, this volume does not give much attention to the river directly, focusing instead on the society—in this case, including fictionalized characters—that live along its banks. It includes an essay by Constance Lindsay Skinner entitled "Rivers and American Folk."

Jakle, John A. *Images of the Ohio Valley: A Historical Geography of Travel, 1740 to 1860.* The Andrew H. Clark Series in Historical Geography of North America. New York: Oxford University Press, 1977.
> According to the book's back cover, "Using the documented impressions of early travelers to follow the evolution of the early Ohio Valley landscape between 1740 and 1860, this book focuses on place images, and deals with the landscape not so much as it was but as it was thought to be."

Lorentz, Pare. *The River.* New York: Stackpole Sons, 1938.
> Based on his brilliant motion picture of the Mississippi River, Lorentz's work is brought to life through striking black-and-white photography. It features both the river and the Depression-era people who lived along its banks.

Lund, Jens. *Flatheads and Spooneys: Fishing for a Living in the Ohio River Valley.* Ohio River Valley. Lexington: University Press of Kentucky, 1995.
> Though primarily concerned with recent history and fishing's place in it, the deeper history of the settling of the Ohio River is discussed in this work. Steamboats do not feature prominently; however, this resource would be of use to those interested in understanding the Ohio River system as the context for a variety of boat types and river activities.

Wallis, Don, ed. *Oyo: An Ohio River Anthology.* Yellow Springs, OH: OYO, 1987.

OYO is an anthology of river experience—of the Ohio River and the streams of its valley. Chapters are divided into three thematic sections: movement, voices of the river, and place. River art throughout the volume is by Harlan Hubbard.

Wheeler, Mary. *Steamboatin' Days: Folk Songs of the River Packet Era*. Freeport, NY: Books for Libraries Press, 1969.
Initial reviewers in 1944 raved that Wheeler's collection was one of the best books about American folksongs that had ever been published. The work includes lyrics, printed music, and, when appropriate, background notes on steamboat culture or the stories and events that inspired the music. Though clearly a period piece in terms of its perspective on "race music," for instance, it is nevertheless a valuable compendium of primary folk texts of its day.

## Navigation: Guides, Maps, and Atlases

Ball, William J. *Canal around the Falls of the Ohio*. Cincinnati: E. Shepard's Steam Press, 1850.
Authored by the chief engineer of the project to build a canal around the Falls of the Ohio River, this pamphlet publishes the *Charter and Organizations of the Indiana Canal Company* and a report that gives a survey and cost estimates for constructing the canal.

Brown, Lloyd Arnold. *Early Maps of the Ohio Valley: A Selection of Maps, Plans, and Views Made by Indians and Colonials from 1673 to 1783*. Mansfield Centre, CT: Martino Publishing, 2001.
This work is the culmination of years of research first begun by Pittsburgh industrialist Howard N. Eavenson, who loved the Ohio River. For pragmatic reasons, Eavenson narrowed his focus to early cartography on the upper Ohio River. According to its author, "This book is primarily a picture book containing a brief review and summary of the cartographic record left by the men who first explored the region of the Ohio." This is a modest statement by Brown. The reproductions of each map—while black and white—are vivid in their detail, and the treatments of each map are excellent.

Cramer, Zadok. *The Navigator: Containing Directions for Navigating the Monongahela, Allegheny, Ohio, and Mississippi Rivers*. Pittsburgh: Cramer, Spear, and Eichbaum, 1811.
This, the seventh edition of *The Navigator*, includes a map of Pittsburgh and twenty-seven woodcut sectional charts of the Ohio and Mississippi Rivers. In addition, there is an early notice of the Lewis and Clark expedition in the appendix. Demand for navigational aids of the inland waterways prompted Cramer, who was located in Pittsburgh, to first publish this work in 1801.

———. *The Navigator, Containing Directions for Navigating the Monongahela, Allegheny, Ohio, and Mississippi Rivers*. March of America Facsimile 61. Ann Arbor, MI: University Microfilms, 1966.
This is a facsimile copy of the 1814 edition.

Cumings, Samuel. *The Western Pilot*. Cincinnati: N. and G. Guilford and Co., 1832.
Cumings navigated the Ohio, Mississippi, and Missouri rivers, taking notes and readings. The subsequent charts he created illustrate all the bars and currents, necessarily revised yearly for the ever-shifting Mississippi. Cumings's *Western Pilot*s, first published in 1822, were the most important river guides for steamboating in the antebellum period.

———. *The Western Pilot*. Ohio River Collection. Cincinnati: Young and Klein, 1978.
This is a reprint of the 1847 publication. Based on Zadok Cramer's *The Navigator*, *The Western Pilot* provides detailed descriptions of how to navigate the rivers. Sandbars, islands, hazards, and falls, as well as towns are described along the route from the mouth of the Missouri to the Gulf of Mexico.

Hayes, E. L. *Illustrated Atlas of the Upper Ohio River and Valley from Pittsburgh, Pa., to Cincinnati, Ohio: From United States Official and Special Surveys*. Philadelphia, PA: Titus, Simmons, and Titus, 1877.
In its description of this atlas, Bauman Rare Books of Philadelphia and New York states, "This is perhaps the most extraordinary 'county atlas' produced in the 19th century. Although it is a regional atlas in scope, covering both sides of the Ohio River from Pittsburgh to Cincinnati, in format it is [a] county atlas with views, maps, and advertising directories of the local towns, cities, residences, and businesses along the river. There are twenty-six double page maps of the Ohio River plus an index sheet that are beautifully drawn and colored, as well as numerous maps of towns and cities on the river."

Rumer, Thomas. *Indiana*. Checklist of Printed Maps of the Middle West to 1900, edited by Robert W. Karrow, vol. 3. Boston: G. K. Hall and Co., 1981.
The *Checklist* was a fourteen-volume project of the Newberry Library's Hermon Dunlap Smith Center for the History of Cartography. It includes images of cards from the card catalog. The General Introduction outlines the information on each card. This is an extremely important resource for the study of maps that includes the Ohio and Mississippi rivers.

United States Army Corps of Engineers. *Ohio River Navigation Charts (Lower): Cairo, IL, to Foster, KY (Louisville District)*. Louisville: U.S. Army Corps of Engineers, Louisville District, 2008.

This atlas contains 122 charts as well as tables of river terminals, small boat harbors, ramps, and landings.

United States War Department Corps of Engineers. *List of Bridges Over the Navigable Waters of the United States*. Washington, DC: United States Government Printing Office, 1942.

This volume provides detailed lists of every bridge over navigable waters in the United States, including the Ohio and Mississippi rivers. Data includes miles above each river's mouth, nearest town, owner, type of bridge, number of spans, channel spans, authorization, date of completion, and purpose for which bridge is used.

———. *Middle and Upper Mississippi River: Ohio River to Minneapolis*. Washington, DC: United States Government Printing Office, 1940.

This volume provides detailed charts and diagrams of the river system from Cairo, Illinois, to Minneapolis, Minnesota. Details include the 9-foot channel project of locks and dams along the upper Mississippi River between 1930 and 1940. The design and construction of these locks and dams reflect the continuing evolution of river engineering and navigation on the upper Mississippi.

———. *The Ohio River: Charts, Drawings, and Descriptions of Features Affecting Navigation*. Washington, DC: United States Government Printing Office, 1935.

This volume provides detailed charts and diagrams of the full length of the Ohio River, including miles above the river's mouth, right or left of its channel, and miles below Pittsburgh. The volume also includes high- and low-water marks and detailed descriptions of every lock, dam, and bridge.

Young, James H. *Mitchell's Tourist Pocket Map of the State of Indiana Exhibiting Its Internal Improvements, Roads, Distances, &c*. Philadelphia: S. Augustus Mitchell, 1835.

First published in 1833, this lovely map is hand colored and folded down into a convenient and (relatively) sturdy pocket-size case. The map also shows the counties of Indiana and various towns and connecting roads, and gives information about population and steamboat routes.

## River Navigation, Commerce, and Urbanization

Ambler, Charles Henry. *A History of Transportation in the Ohio Valley, with Special Reference to its Waterways, Trade, and Commerce from the Earliest Period to the Present Time*. Glendale, CA: Arthur H. Clark, 1932.

Despite the broader title, the real emphasis of this book is on river travel, particularly on the age of the steamboat. Of particular note is the section on construction of seagoing vessels on the Ohio. Note that some "facts" cited in this work have been modified or tempered in light of continuing research and new evidence.

Bigham, Darrel E. *Towns and Villages of the Lower Ohio*. Lexington: University Press of Kentucky, 1998.

A treatment of the growth of population and development of towns along the Ohio River from the Falls of the Ohio to the confluence of the Ohio and Mississippi rivers, ca. 1792–1920. Part 1 deals with the time period 1792–1818 and part 2 with 1815–1850. Though the *New Orleans* is not discussed, her legacy underlies the entire discussion of the economic and demographic changes for this region.

Bramlett, Gene A., and Wilburn J. Pratt. *Economic Development in the Ohio River Valley Region*. Lexington, KY: Spindletop Research Center, 1964.

This report for the Kentucky Department of Commerce outlines the economy and industrial development of the Ohio River Valley region during the 1960s.

Brant, Warren E. *A Log to the Ohio River*. Saint Paul, MN: American Motor Logs, 1978.

This is the third of Brant's regional travel guides. After extensive research, Brant traveled along the river repeatedly over a three-year period and wrote the *Log* in the manner of the European travel guides. He places particular emphasis on the Ohio River as an industrial transit artery of mid-America.

Fishbaugh, Charles Preston. *From Paddle Wheels to Propellers*. Indianapolis: Indiana Historical Society, 1970.

This volume is based on the papers of the Howard Ship Yards and Dock Company of Jeffersonville, Indiana, housed in the Lilly Library of Indiana University. The papers include an almost complete listing of the boats and barges manufactured at the yard between 1834 and 1942, along with correspondence, ledgers, and other records of the Howard family enterprise. This is a very important contribution to the economic history of steam navigation on the western rivers.

Haites, Erik F., James Mak, and Gary M. Walton. *Western River Transportation: The Era of Early Internal Development, 1810–1860*. Johns Hopkins University Studies in Historical and Political Science, 93rd ser. Baltimore: Johns Hopkins University Press, 1975.

This monograph offers an analysis of transportation between the years 1810 and 1860 as an indicator of and contributor to economic development of the frontier region west of the Appalachians. Of particular interest are the numerous appendixes, which present, among other things, quantitative analysis of costs and revenues of flatboats and steamboats on the Louisville–New Orleans trade route.

Hall, James. *The West: Its Commerce and Navigation*. Burt Franklin Research and Source Works 531, American Classics in History and Social Science 141. New York: Burt Franklin, 1970.

Originally published in 1848, this work attempts to cover all topics related to the commercial use and navigation of the western rivers, specifically the Ohio and Mississippi. Chapters deal with flooding, sandbars, "some account of the first boats," and discussion of various ports, manufacturing centers, and products.

*History of the Ohio Falls Cities and Their Counties, with Illustrations and Bibliographical Sketches*, vol. 1. Cleveland: L. A. Williams and Co., 1882.

This work provides a useful overview of a number of river communities surrounding the Falls of the Ohio, including Louisville, New Albany, and Jeffersonville.

Hulbert, Archer Butler. *The Paths of Inland Commerce: A Chronicle of Trail, Road, and Waterway*. Chronicles of America 21. New Haven: Yale University Press, 1921.

Written in 1920, this is very much a period piece exploring the oppositional development of transportation in the interior of the United States. Of particular interest are chapters 3 ("The Mastery of the Rivers"), 5 ("The Flatboat Age"), 7 ("The Birth of the Steamboat"), and 11 ("The Steamboat and the West").

Hunter, Louis C. *Steamboats on the Western Rivers: An Economic and Technological History*. Studies in Economic History. Cambridge, MA: Harvard University Press, 1949.

This classic of the scholarly literature on river transportation and steamboats covers the introduction of the steamboat to the western waters through its decline with the ascendancy of railroad transportation. It may be the most comprehensive, though not most theoretically modern, treatise on the topic.

Lippincott, Isaac. *History of Manufactures in the Ohio Valley to the Year 1860*. New York: Arno Press, 1973.

As the title implies, this work strives to be a history of business in the Ohio River Valley. It discusses variously the impact of river transportation and, particularly, the introduction of the steamboat on the development of the local economy and settlements. It also includes a section on shipbuilding on the Ohio River.

Petersen, William J. *Steamboating on the Upper Mississippi*. Iowa City: State Historical Society of Iowa, 1968.

This work comprises forty-eight episodic chapters and, despite the broad title, focuses primarily on the immediate antebellum years. Though crafted with a relatively heavy use of primary sources, it has been criticized for its poor organization. It features an extensive bibliography.

Ringwalt, J. L. *Development of Transportation Systems in the United States: Comprising a Comprehensive Description of the Leading Features of Advancement, from the Colonial Era to the Present Time*. New York: Johnson Reprint Corp., 1966.

Originally published in 1888 by the author, this work is mostly devoted to the railroad, but there are significant sections on the navigation of interior water routes and steamboat operations.

## Biographies of the Rivers

Carter, Hodding. *Lower Mississippi*. Rivers of America. New York: Farrar and Rinehart, 1942.

This volume from the classic Rivers of America series gives special attention geographically to the region between Memphis and New Orleans and temporally from the time of Spanish explorer Hernando de Soto, who died near the Mississippi River in 1542, to Huey Long, Louisiana politician from 1928 through his assassination in 1935. It is very much in the "great men doing great works" school of history and does not include much on steamboats. It remains, however, a worthwhile volume for those interested in the region.

Childs, Marquis W. *Mighty Mississippi: Biography of a River*. New Haven: Ticknor and Fields, 1982.

Originally published in 1935, this "literary essay" might be best described as a tribute to the Mississippi River and as such is not footnoted or indexed. It was not published until the 1980s because of Childs's outspoken criticism of the timber industry and river engineering that he felt undermined the historic integrity of the river. Childs later received a Pulitzer Prize for his work with the *Saint Louis Post-Dispatch*.

Clark, C. M. *The Picturesque Ohio: A Historical Monograph*. Cincinnati: Cranston and Curtis, 1887.

This work is organized in three parts. The first deals with the deeper history of the river, the second with the European settlement of the river, and the third with transportation on and around the river, focusing on steamboats and railroads.

Dick, David, and Eulalie C. Dick. *Rivers of Kentucky*. North Middletown, KY: Plum Lick, 2001.

In its organization *Rivers* follows the contours of Kentucky's geography, beginning with the Ohio River, which forms Kentucky's northern border. The first section takes the reader on a leisurely journey

on a working towboat up the Ohio River from Louisville to Cattletts-
burg at the Ohio's confluence with the Big Sandy River.

Findlay, James A. *The Rivers of America: A Selected Exhibition of Books
from the Collection of Carol Fitzgerald, September 26–December 5, 1997*.
Fort Lauderdale, FL: Bienes Center for the Literary Arts, 1997.
This is a checklist from the Bienes Center for the Literary Arts for a
1997 exhibition of books compiled by Carol Fitzgerald, who would
author *The Rivers of America: A Descriptive Bibliography* in 2001.

Fitzgerald, Carol. *The Rivers of America: A Descriptive Bibliography*. New
Castle, DE: Oak Knoll Press, 2001.
This well-researched bibliography is the most comprehensive work
ever published on the historical series of books, Rivers of America,
that appeared between 1937 and 1974.

Fowke, Gerard. *The Evolution of the Ohio River*. Indianapolis: Hollenbeck
Press, 1933.
Fowke outlines his theories on the geological origins and evolution
of the Ohio River.

Havighurst, Walter. *River to the West: Three Centuries of the Ohio*. New
York: G. P. Putnam's Sons, 1970.
The work includes an extensive bibliography and numerous plates of
photography and period artwork. Havighurst provides a vivid and
compelling historical treatment of the Ohio River and its people
from prehistory up to the 1960s as the area begins to come to terms
with the impact of industrialization on its environment.

Hulbert, Archer Butler. *Waterways of Westward Expansion: The Ohio
River and Its Tributaries*. Historic Highways of America 9. Whitefish,
MT: Kessinger Publishing, 2007.
This monograph could perhaps be best described as a history of the
human-river interface within the Ohio River system. It traces this
interface from the earliest European awareness of the river through
the multiple "ages" of travel on the river, culminating, in Hulbert's
view, with the steamboat.

Keating, Bern. *The Mighty Mississippi*. Washington, DC: National Geographic Society, 1971.
This work is best characterized as a popular travelogue with photographs by National Geographic photographer James L. Stanfield. Its
text, including chapters "By Lock and Lake from the Twin Cities to
Dubuque" and "St. Louis to New Madrid: 'Old Man River' Begins,"
was only moderately well received and is marred by a number of
factual errors. Its photographs, however, were highly praised and are
the real strength of this volume.

Klein, Benjamin F., and Eleanor Klein. *The Ohio River Handbook: Consisting of Pictorial Incidents, with Random Notes and Comment Relating
to the Ohio River and Cincinnati, Ohio*. Cincinnati: Young and Klein,
1949.

With photographs, diagrams, and limited text, the Kleins tell the
story of the Ohio River from its beginnings to the Motorboat Act of
1940. The volume covers everything from Cincinnati's waterfront to
river sanitation.

———. *The Ohio River Handbook and Picture Album: Consisting of Picto-
rial Incidents, with Random Notes and Comment Relating to the Ohio
River and Its Environs, and Statistics, Charts, and Information on the
Ohio River and Its Tributaries*. Cincinnati: Young and Klein, 1950.
This is a revision of the 1949 edition in which errors in the material
have been corrected.

———. *The Ohio River Handbook and Picture Album*. 4th ed. Cincinnati:
Young and Klein, 1958.
The *Handbook* had been out of print for two years and requests for
a fourth edition were so numerous that the publishers decided to
publish it once again.

———. *The Ohio River Handbook and Picture Album*. Rev. ed., Cincinnati: Young and Klein, 1969.
This is the last edition of the *Handbook*.

Leahy, Ethel C. *Who's Who on the Ohio River and Its Tributaries: The Ohio
River from the Ice Age to the Future, History—Biography—Statistics*.
Cincinnati: E. C. Leahy, 1931.
This huge volume by compiler, editor, and publisher Leahy covers
two hundred pages before it gets to navigation and steam. It is divided into three sections, historical, biographical, and statistical, and
includes a list of seven hundred steamboats that operated between
1812 and 1836.

## River Dangers and Disasters

Bell, Rick. *The Great Flood of 1937: Rising Waters, Soaring Spirits, Louisville, Kentucky*. Louisville: Butler Books, 2007.
Published on the seventieth anniversary of the 1937 flood and
compiled from photographs in the University of Louisville Photographic Archives, this is an excellent look at how the flood impacted
Louisville.

Brockmann, R. John. *Exploding Steamboats, Senate Debates, and Technical Reports: The Convergence of Technology, Politics, and Rhetoric in the
Steamboat Bill of 1838*. Amityville, NY: Baywood Publishing, 2002.
A member of the English Department at the University of Delaware,
Brockmann documents the development of the Steamboat Bill of
1838. The bill was prompted by presidential calls for reform after
more than two thousand Americans were killed and many hundreds
injured in explosions on steamboats. However, explosions and
deaths would continue unabated for another fourteen years until
proper legislative reform was enacted.

———. *Twisted Rails, Sunken Ships: The Rhetoric of Nineteenth Century Steamboat and Railroad Accident Investigation Reports, 1833–1879.* Amityville, NY: Baywood Publishing, 2005.

This book is dedicated to the memory of those thousands who lost their lives on steamboats and railroads in the nineteenth century and whose lives allow us in the twenty-first century to travel more safely. As Brockmann writes, "The power of the steamboat beginning in the 1820s and the locomotive in the 1830s introduced the world to more than technology; it changed the very definition of causation and accident." This work explores that transformation.

The History Channel. "River Pirates." In Search of History. DVD. New York: A&E Television Networks, 1999.

A sometimes over-the-top recounting of the history of river piracy along the Ohio River. While decidedly not a scholarly resource, it provides an interesting overview of the topic for a general audience.

O'Donnell, Edward T. *Ship Ablaze: The Tragedy of the Steamboat* General Slocum. New York: Broadway Books, 2003.

The description on the front jacket of the book begins, "On a beautiful spring morning in June 1904, 1,300 New Yorkers boarded the steamer *General Slocum* for a pleasant daylong excursion. But in thirty minutes, disaster would strike and more than one thousand would perish." This was the greatest loss of life in New York City history until 9/11.

Rothert, Otto A. *The Outlaws of Cave-in-Rock: Historical Accounts of the Famous Highwaymen and River Pirates Who Operated in the Pioneer Days upon the Ohio and Mississippi Rivers and over the Natchez Trace.* Cleveland: Arthur H. Clark, 1923.

This is a 1971 reprint of the 1923 edition that documents Captain Samuel Mason, among others, who led pirates on the lower Ohio River, first from his home at Red Banks, now Henderson, Kentucky, then at Diamond Island, in the Ohio River approximately ten miles west of Henderson, and finally by 1797, from Cave-in-Rock, twelve miles east of Elizabethtown, Illinois. Also of particular note is the in-depth look at the lives of Micajah "Big" Harpe and Wiley "Little" Harpe, who were either brothers or first cousins. They rampaged across the frontier as America's first serial killers in 1798 and 1799. At one point they joined with the river pirates at Cave-in-Rock and killed at least three or four men while in Illinois. Overall, they are credited with at least forty murders.

## River Engineering

Bixby, William H. *Letter from the Acting Secretary of War, Transmitting, with a Letter from the Chief of Engineers, Report of Survey of Ohio River at Madison, Ind.* Washington, DC: United States War Department, 1900.

This is a letter from Maj. W. H. Bixby of the U.S. Army Corps of Engineers, who outlined the estimated cost of dredging the harbor of Madison to a depth of six feet up to the low-water front, pursuant to the instructions of the Secretary of War, April 10, 1899.

Campbell, Scott, and Bruce Goetzman. *Historic Structures Study of Ohio River Lock and Dam No. 35 Proposed for Thomas More College Biological Field Station, Campbell County, Kentucky.* Cincinnati: University of Cincinnati, [1990–94?].

This report was prepared by University of Cincinnati biology students under the supervision of Professor Goetzman. The students wrote a report on the history of Lock and Dam Number 35, took photographs to document their work, reported on the lock house and the lockkeeper's house, and provided three proposals for future work at the site.

Johnson, Leland R. *The Davis Island Lock and Dam, 1870–1922.* Pittsburgh: U.S. Army Corps of Engineers, Pittsburgh District, 1985.

This work chronicles the history of the Davis Island Lock and Dam, which was the first dam constructed on the Ohio River. It officially opened on October 7, 1885, with a large dedication ceremony. The Davis Island Dam was the first and largest Chanoine wicket dam built between 1878 and 1929 and one of the first concrete structures built by the U.S. Army Corps of Engineers. It was dismantled in 1922, when it was replaced by the Emsworth Locks and Dams less than a mile downstream of the original site.

Johnson, Leland R., and Charles E. Parrish. *Triumph at the Falls: The Louisville and Portland Canal.* Louisville: U.S. Army Corps of Engineers, Louisville District, 2007.

The authors trace the design and building of the two-mile Louisville and Portland Canal passage around the Falls of the Ohio. Examining the canal's history in fifty-year segments, beginning in the early nineteenth century, they examine how safe travel was achieved over the dangerous rapids and Falls that have challenged even today's improved inland river craft.

Lockwood, Daniel Wright. *Report of Examination of Ohio River with a View to Obtaining Channel Depths of 6 and 9 Feet, Respectively.* Washington, DC: Government Printing Office, 1908.

This volume begins with a letter from Secretary of War William H. Taft and includes an extensive report on creating channel depths of six and nine feet for vessels. The report is interspersed with maps and charts.

Merrill, William E. *The Davis Island Lock and Dam Portfolio.* Pittsburgh: U.S. Army Corps of Engineers, Pittsburgh District, 1985.

The plates are reproduced from original drawings submitted by Col. William E. Merrill to the Office of the Chief of Engineers in 1889 and originally published in 1892.

Newman, Clarence W. *Ohio River Navigation: Past, Present, Future*. Cincinnati: U.S. Army Corps of Engineers, Ohio River Division, 1979.

This booklet is designed to commemorate the fiftieth anniversary of the completion of a nine-foot navigable channel on the Ohio River, which was accomplished with the opening of Lock and Dams 52 and 53 in 1929. The arrangement of the booklet is topical rather than chronological.

Parrish, Charles E. *McAlpine Locks and Dam at the Falls of the Ohio*. Louisville: U.S. Army Corps of Engineers, Public Affairs Office, Ohio River Division, 2008.

This short historical treatment of the McAlpine Locks and Dam begins in 1825 with the construction of three lift locks, making it the first major engineering project on the Ohio River. The first official name of the system of canal locks was the Louisville and Portland Canal, completed in 1830, to allow shipping traffic to navigate through the Falls of the Ohio. The book is filled with wonderful photographs and diagrams.

Paskoff, Paul F. *Troubled Waters: Steamboat Disasters, River Improvements, and American Public Policy, 1821–1860*. Baton Rouge: Louisiana State University Press, 2007.

Given ice, snags, sandbars, and other riverbed hazards, "river improvement" has been important in the history of river navigation. In addition, it was and is highly political. This work traces the history of antebellum river engineering and argues that through river engineering, the federal government was more active than currently thought in promoting economic development in the young republic.

United States Army Corps of Engineers. *Hydraulic Gates and Dams in the Ohio River*. Washington, DC: Government Printing Office, 1875.

This volume begins with a letter from the secretary of war on the applicability of moveable hydraulic gates and dams to the improvement of the Ohio River, includes an extensive report on the hydraulic gates and dams in the Ohio River, and concludes with twenty plates, showing detailed illustrations of early hydraulic gates and dam technology.

## River People, Steamboats, and Rivers in the Arts

### Music, Theater, Art, and Photography

Carmer, Carl. *Songs of the Rivers of America*. New York: Farrar and Rinehart, 1942.

Edited by Carmer with music arranged by Albert Sirmay, this work weaves together song, folklore, and the history of American rivers. There are ten songs about the Ohio River alone, including "De Boatman's Dance" and "Eliza's Flight."

Gangewere, R. Jay. *Watercolor Paintings of the Ohio: Always a River*. New York: Scholastic, 1990.

Published in conjunction with *Always a River*, this booklet catalogs the winning paintings in the watercolor competition included in the *Always a River* barge exhibition with biographical material on the artists.

Hammerstein, Oscar. *Show Boat*. DVD. Burbank, CA: Turner Entertainment and Warner Home Video, 2000.

This DVD captures the 1951 film version of the novel by Edna Ferber (there were two other film versions in 1929 and 1936). The film featured Kathryn Grayson, Ava Gardner, and Howard Keel alongside a 170-foot paddle wheeler.

Miller, Roger, William Hauptman, and Mark Twain. *Big River: The Adventures of Huckleberry Finn—A Musical Play*. New York: Grove Press, 1986.

*Big River* was originally presented at the American Repertory Theatre in Cambridge, Massachusetts, under the artistic direction of Robert Brustein. It opened on February 22, 1984, with a cast that included Tony Shaloub. The play opened on Broadway at the Eugene O'Neill Theatre on April 25, 1985. In both instances, the designer's intent was to keep the look and feel of 1840s stagecraft with a backdrop of the Mississippi River.

———. *Big River: The Adventures of Huckleberry Finn: Original Broadway Cast Recording*. CD. Universal City, CA: MCA Records, 1985.

This recording from the original Broadway cast at Eugene O'Neill Theatre won seven Tony Awards in 1985, including Best Musical.

Reid, Robert L., and Dan Hughes Fuller. *Pilgrims on the Ohio: River Journey and Photographs of Reuben Gold Thwaites, 1894*. Indianapolis: Indiana Historical Society, 1997.

For six weeks in the spring and summer of 1894, noted historian and State Historical Society of Wisconsin director Reuben Gold Thwaites and his family traveled down the Monongahela and Ohio rivers. Thwaites's revealing photographs offer readers a unique opportunity to take a glimpse down the gateway into the nation's interior.

Simons, Richard S. *The Rivers of Indiana*. Bloomington: Indiana University Press, 1985.

Simons was an alumnus and professor of journalism at Indiana University. This volume contains many beautiful color photographs and includes eleven pages on the Ohio River under "Highways of Settlement."

Vandermyn, Armand. "Ohio River Song." Pittsburgh: A. J. P. Vandermyn, 1929.

Both the words and music of this song are by Armand J. P. Vandermyn. The arrangement is for ukulele. The cover of the sheet music features a photograph of the steamboat *Cincinnati* with a banner that reads, "1929 Ohio River Dedication Cruise, Pittsburgh to Cairo, Celebrating the Nine Foot Stage."

## Literature

Adams, John S., ed. *The Crystal Gem*. Boston: G. W. Cottrell, 1853.

This delightful miniature book incorporating a number of poems dealing with water includes the anonymous contribution "The River."

Berry, Wendell. *Sonata at Payne Hollow*. Monterey, KY: Larkspur Press, 2001.

Berry's play about Anna and Harlan Hubbard is set at their home on the Kentucky shore of the Ohio River at evening.

Dohan, Mary Helen. *Mr. Roosevelt's Steamboat: The First Steamboat to Travel the Mississippi*. New York: Dodd, Mead, and Co., 1981.

This is a fictionalized account of the voyage of the *New Orleans*, taking Lydia (Latrobe) Roosevelt as its protagonist. It was positively reviewed as an "engaging" historical novel, rather than a simple rehash of John H. B. Latrobe's *The First Steamboat on the Western Waters* (1871), by Leonard V. Huber of the Steamship Historical Society of America (1982).

Drago, Harry Sinclair. *The Steamboaters, from the Early Side-Wheelers to the Big Packets*. New York: Dodd, Mead, 1967.

Drago, an American novelist who averaged three books a year, turned his hand from historical fiction to nonfiction histories of the American West later in life. This work covers famous steamboats of the Ohio and Mississippi, such as the *Robert E. Lee*, as well as boats farther west.

Keyes, Frances Parkinson. *Steamboat Gothic*. New York: Julian Messner, 1953.

The title of Keyes's novel refers to a style of architecture that emerged along the banks of the Mississippi River, taking advantage of the abundance of timber in the region. Riverboat captains wanted the mansions along the river to resemble their elaborately decorated steamboats of the mid-1800s. The novel chronicles the life of a river man, Clyde Batchelor, and his family.

Lane, Carl D. *The Fire Raft*. Boston: Little, Brown, and Co., 1951.

This is a fictionalized account of the voyage of the *New Orleans*.

Simpson, Jack R. *If Ships Could Talk: Poems of the River and Sea*. Florissant, MO: Jack R. Simpson, 1982.

This volume contains almost fifty poems by Simpson dedicated to "the men and women of the river and the sea, both past and present, whose role in the commercial transportation of goods and services by water has for too long been taken too lightly." Also contains more than twenty poems by other poets.

Thom, James Alexander. *Follow the River*. New York: Ballantine Books, 1981.

Thom's novel recounts the captivity narrative of Mary Ingles, from the time of her capture by Shawnee Indians in Virginia in 1755 to her escape and odyssey that took place along much of the Ohio River.

Tourgée, Albion W. *The Mortgage on the Hip-Roof House*. Cincinnati: Jennings and Pye, 1896.

In a hip (or hipped) roof, all sides of the roof slope downward to the walls, usually with a fairly gentle slope. Thus, it is a house with no gables. Much of the narrative in Tourgée's book takes place on the steamboat *Queen of the West*.

Twain, Mark. *Adventures of Huckleberry Finn (Tom Sawyer's Comrade): Scene, the Mississippi Valley: Time, Forty to Fifty Years Ago*. New York: Charles L. Webster and Co., 1885.

Written over an eight-year period, Twain's dark, brilliant work endured attacks from the moment of publication due to its colorful descriptions of people and places along the Mississippi River.

———. *Life on the Mississippi*. London: Chatto and Windus, 1883. Repr., Boston: James R. Osgood and Co., 1883; New York: Harper and Brothers, 1903.

This classic of steamboating literature is a memoir by Twain, detailing his days as a steamboat pilot on the Mississippi River before and after the American Civil War.

## Juvenile Literature

Chambers, Catherine E. *Flatboats on the Ohio: Westward Bound*. Adventures in Frontier America. Mahwah, NJ: Troll Associates, 1984.

Set in 1836, this is a fictional account of the Sawyer family moving from Massachusetts to the Ohio River Valley frontier, eventually settling on the banks of the Wabash River. Along the way they meet a wide variety of people and experience danger and adventure.

Fichter, George S. *First Steamboat Down the Mississippi*. Gretna, LA: Pelican Publishing, 1989.

According to the Library of Congress, this book is "a fictional account of the eventful 1811 voyage down the Ohio and Mississippi Rivers on the steamboat 'New Orleans,' told through the eyes of a fourteen-year-old deckhand."

Hartford, John. *Steamboat in a Cornfield*. New York: Crown Publishers, 1986.

This is a retelling, in somewhat strained rhyming verse, of the 1910 grounding and subsequent "rescue" of the *Virginia*. Illustrated with wonderful reproductions of period images of the ship, steamboat crews and passengers, and a variety of documents, including maps, tickets, and newspapers.

Kroll, Steven. *Robert Fulton: From Submarine to Steamboat*. New York: Holiday House, 1999.

Illustrated by Bill Farnsworth, this children's book describes the life and work of the inventor who developed the steamboat and made it a commercial success.

Lloyd, Hugh. *Among the River Pirates*. New York: Grosset and Dunlap, 1934.

Hugh Lloyd was the pseudonym of Percy Keese Fitzhugh (1876–1950), best known for his multiple series of books dealing with Boy Scouting. Major prior characters include Tom Slade and Pee-wee Harris. The Skippy Dare series books were among his later works and were not as popular as his earlier scouting stories. This is a nice piece of period children's fiction dealing with river life and "adventure."

Newell, Gordon. *Paddlewheel Pirate: The Life and Adventures of Captain Ned Wakeman*. New York: E. P. Dutton and Co., 1959.

Based on the historic record, this fictionalized account of Captain Ned Wakeman deals with his "theft" of the impounded steamboat *New World*, which he subsequently piloted from New York around South America and to San Francisco. Wakeman was relatively well known in the 1870s, both as an adventurer in his own right and as the acquaintance of Mark Twain who was the inspiration for several characters in Twain's writings.

North, Sterling. *The First Steamboat on the Mississippi*. Boston: Houghton Mifflin, 1962.

Illustrated by Victor Mays, this historic novel covers the construction of the *New Orleans*, its historic voyage on the Mississippi River, and the life of inventor and engineer Nicholas Roosevelt who pioneered steam navigation.

Parks, Edd W. *Pioneer Pilot: A Boy's Story of the First Steamboat Voyage from Pittsburgh to New Orleans*. Whitefish, MT: Kessinger Publishing, 2008.

This fictionalized account of a young boy taken along with the *New Orleans* as part of her crew on her maiden voyage is a stellar example of a period piece with requisite brawling, Indians, and references to

Zadok Cramer, Pittsburgh bookbinder who published *The Navigator* series, helping early travelers navigate the western rivers of the United States.

Paxton, Mary. *River Gold*. Indianapolis: Bobbs-Merrill, 1928.

The dust jacket states, "Buried gold! River gold! Gam[blers'] gold! Pirates! Indians! Gather round, boys and girls, gather round. Take the Hangman's Oath, and you shall hear how . . . [three boys] hunted for gold—not on a far-off Treasure Island, but right here at home in the United States, in a river-bank of the Middle West." River piracy was a relatively common happenstance in presteamboat days, and consequently in river travel literature. The arrival of the steamboat, faster and with larger crews and numbers of passengers, effectively put an end to this piracy.

Rebman, Renée C. *Robert Fulton's Steamboat*. Minneapolis: Compass Point Books, 2007.

Author of several nonfiction books for children, Rebman writes about the life of artist and inventor Robert Fulton who is best known for his steamboat the *Clermont*.

St. George, Judith. *The Amazing Voyage of the* New Orleans. New York: G. P. Putnam, 1980.

Judith St. George has made a name for herself writing historical fiction and nonfiction for children and young adults. In 2000 her *So You Want to Be President?* was awarded the Caldecott Medal. This is her account of the 1811–12 voyage of the *New Orleans*.

*Douglas Denné is archivist and curator of Rare Books at Hanover College. Since 2009 he has also served as the Rivers Institute Collection librarian. Denné's research interests include nineteenth-century Presbyterian Church history, the history of the book, and descriptive bibliography.*

*Katherine McCardwell, former Rivers Institute Collection development librarian at Hanover College, is a graduate student in cultural anthropology at the University of Colorado at Boulder. Her primary research interests are the anthropology of museums, particularly as representing Native Alaskans, and the cultural construction of landscape and place.*

# Index

*Page numbers in italics indicate photographs or illustrations.*